Peter Norton's Advanced DOS 6,

2nd Edition

Peter Norton's
Advanced
DOS 6

2nd Edition

Peter Norton
Ruth Ashley
Judi Fernandez

////Brady

New York   London   Toronto   Sydney   Tokyo   Singapore

Acknowledgments

A project like this experiences myriad crises—some minor, a few major. We'd particularly like to thank Donna Tabler for helping out when the going got rough and Michael Sprague of Brady Books for always fielding the latest crisis with good humor.

Credits

Publisher
Michael Violano

Acquisitions Director
Jono Hardjowirogo

Managing Editor
Kelly D. Dobbs

Developmental Editor
Michael Sprague

Editorial Assistant
Lisa Rose

Book Designer
Michele Laseau

Cover Designer
HUB Graphics

Production Team
Jeff Baker
Claudia Bell
Jodie Cantwell
Brad Chinn
Mark Enochs
Brook Farling
Dennis Clay Hager
Joy Dean Lee
Roger S. Morgan
Linda Quigley
Michelle Self
John Sleeva
Greg Simsic

Overview

Contents

Introduction

If you're like most DOS users, you have already learned enough about the operating system to survive. You can boot and reboot, name and rename files, copy and delete files, format floppy disks, make and remove subdirectories, list directories, and change drives and directories. Maybe you've gone beyond these basic survival skills and learned to set the system date and time, view or print ASCII files, create a simple batch program, and so on.

> If you have not yet learned these basic skills, you first may want to look at *Peter Norton's DOS 6 Guide* (also published by Brady). Come back to this book when you feel at home with the basics.

You might suspect that you can do more with DOS, and you're right. Our intention in this book is to help you make better use of your system through DOS. By *better*, we mean faster, safer, easier, more efficient, and more effective. If you're responsible for other people's systems, you can set them up for better use, too. In particular, you can simplify tasks that confuse DOS beginners as well as automate their data protection systems to minimize the chance of data loss.

Even if you have a lot of DOS experience, including programming experience, you'll find a wealth of handy information in here, including undocumented commands and features, advanced techniques, warnings about pitfalls and how to circumvent them, and tips for making life easier for your work group.

Specifically, this book shows you how to:

- Set up a DOS system to simplify and speed everyday tasks through:

  Better use of DOS Shell features such as the program list and task switching

  More flexible and powerful batch programs

  Macros (using DOSKEY and ANSI.SYS)

  More powerful commands using features such as redirection

● Make all software run faster by making better use of resources through:

Optimum memory structuring

Reduced hard drive access times by reorganizing and caching the hard drive

RAM drives

● Save time, money, and stress by protecting your system's most valuable resource—your data—from all the nasties that go bump in the night (such as viruses and your own memory lapses) through:

A well designed and rigorously implemented backup system

Regular use of virus detection facilities

Protecting deleted data so that you can recover it easily

A wide range of data recovery techniques (from locating misplaced files to unformatting a floppy disk)

● Make it all more fun for yourself (and others) through:

More colorful command-prompt displays (including some elementary graphics)

More interesting messages

This book also is jam-packed with handy techniques for using the DOS filters (MORE, SORT, and FIND), capitalizing on the DOS environment, choosing the best copy command (DOS has four of them), configuring nonstandard I/O devices, setting up a system for foreign languages, modifying your boot process on-the-fly, and much more. (For BASIC programmers, Chapter 22 shows you how to upgrade to DOS's QBasic system.) We even explain what DOS doesn't do well and where you would be wise to seek a third-party program.

But what good are techniques if you don't understand the underlying concepts? You'll find clear-cut, comprehensive explanations of such system features as memory (including the difference between upper, extended, and expanded memory), the DOS environment, the File Allocation Table (FAT), how files get fragmented, those mysterious and frightening CHKDSK messages, and a lot more.

The DOS 6 Upgrade

This book assumes that you have successfully upgraded to DOS 6; we do not deal with earlier versions for the very good reason that the improvements in DOS 6 are important enough to be well worth the price of the upgrade package. If you haven't yet made the upgrade, our first few chapters will probably convince you to do so soon. This book is appropriate for readers who have just upgraded to DOS 6 (but know the basics of an earlier DOS version) as well as those who have been using DOS 6 for a while.

Conventions

We have used the following typographical conventions:

italics	Expressions in italics indicate variables to be replaced by specific values. For example, when we say that CHKDSK creates generic filenames in the form FILE*xxxx*.CHK, the *xxxx* indicates four characters that change from filename to filename. The actual filenames generated by CHKDSK are FILE0000.CHK, FILE0001.CHK, FILE0002.CHK, and so on. (Italics are also used for emphasis in some sentences.)
ALL CAPS	In regular text, commands, filenames, directory paths, drive names, and program names are shown in all caps simply to make them stand out from the context. For example, the expression "the copy program" refers to any program that makes a copy, but "the COPY program" refers specifically to the DOS program named COPY.

Commands are shown in all caps even though DOS usually ignores case. You can enter commands in any mixture of cases, and many users prefer to work with all lowercase characters. The few places where DOS is case-sensitive are pointed out in the appropriate chapters.

Command Formats

Many figures in this book provide complete reference information for DOS commands. (Figure 1.3 is a typical example.) These figures always include a format statement, such as the following totally hypothetical command:

CRUNCH *d*:[[=]*n*] ... [/C ¦ /D]

A legitimate CRUNCH command might be:

CRUNCH C:=5 D: E:15 /D

The conventions used in a command format are

[Square brackets]	In command formats, items enclosed in square brackets are optional. All other items are required. In the preceding example, the word CRUNCH and the drive name (represented by *d*:) are required, but the expression following the drive name and the /C and /D are optional.
	In addition, the expression that follows the drive name includes a nested option, which may be used only within the enclosing option. If you include the *n*, you can precede it with an equal sign, but you can't use the equal sign without the *n*.
ALL CAPS	All caps indicate words or expressions that must be included exactly as shown. (They need not be typed in all caps when you enter commands.) In the CRUNCH command, the word CRUNCH must be included as is; it cannot be abbreviated. The /C and /D switches are optional, but if used, they must be used as shown.
italics	Italics indicates items that must be replaced by a value when the command is entered. In the CRUNCH command, the *d* must be replaced by a drive name. In addition, the *n* must be replaced by a number if you choose to use that option.

Ellipsis...	Three dots indicate that the preceding expression can be repeated. In the CRUNCH command, you can repeat d:[[=]n] to crunch several drives.
|	A vertical bar indicates a mutually exclusive choice. In the CRUNCH command, you can include |C or |D, but not both.

Filespecs

We use the expression filespec in command formats and in regular text to indicate the conglomeration of elements that identifies a file or set of files. It can include a drive name, a path, and/or a filename (with or without wildcard characters). In many cases, a drive name alone is sufficient; all files in the current directory of that drive are implied. In other cases, you might find it necessary to include a path and/or a filename to identify the file(s) you want.

What's New in DOS 6?

1

Introduction

By the late 1980s, DOS 3.3 had become the standard version of DOS. DOS 4 introduced some new features, such as the DOS Shell, but they were not well received, and most users preferred to stay with DOS 3.3. DOS 5 was another story: the Shell was improved, utilities such as UNDELETE and DOSKEY were added, and most important of all,

several memory management facilities finally helped to free up some space in conventional memory—DOS's traditional Achilles's heel. DOS 5 was extremely successful and has become the new standard version. DOS 6 is essentially DOS 5 with a host of new utilities added; the basic system is mostly unchanged.

New DOS 6 Features

Briefly, the new utilities are as follows:

- **INTERLNK** lets you hook up two computers with a cable between their serial or parallel ports and access one computer from the other. It provides a way to transfer files between a laptop and a desktop computer without using floppies as a go-between. INTERLNK is explained in Chapter 8.

- **DoubleSpace** compresses disk data, letting you squeeze about twice as much data onto a drive. Chapter 12 explains DoubleSpace.

- **Backup** replaces DOS's traditional BACKUP and RESTORE with a graphical interface that makes it easy to set up and run a backup, to restore a few files or an entire disk, and even to compare backed-up files to their originals. DOS 6 includes both DOS and Windows versions of the new Backup. Chapter 13 explains how to use both versions.

- **Microsoft Anti-Virus** comprises several programs that detect viruses in your system, prevent them from functioning, and remove them if possible. Microsoft Anti-Virus includes a virus scanner for DOS, a virus scanner for Windows, and a virus monitor that works under both DOS and Windows. Microsoft Anti-Virus is explained in Chapter 15.

- **MEMMAKER** sets up your system to take full advantage of EMM386's upper memory support. MEMMAKER adapts your CONFIG.SYS and AUTOEXEC.BAT (and SYSTEM.INI if you use Windows) with the necessary commands to load your device drivers and TSRs into upper memory. It is explained in Chapter 10.

- DOS 5 introduced a new UNDELETE program; DOS 6 includes a significant improvement with **Delete Sentry**, which preserves deleted files in a hidden directory for a few days. DOS 6 also includes a Windows version of UNDELETE with a graphical interface and several features that the DOS version doesn't have, such as the capability to purge individual files. Chapter 16 explains both versions of UNDELETE.

- **DEFRAG** optimizes your hard drive by eliminating file fragmentation and moving all the free space to the end of the drive. Chapter 11 explains DEFRAG.

- **POWER** helps to conserve laptop batteries by reducing the power consumption when the computer is idle. Chapter 18 explains POWER.

- A new on-line **HELP** feature provides more thorough command documentation than DOS 5's version. Chapter 1 explains the new HELP system.

- **MSD** (which stands for Microsoft Diagnostics) lets you explore the technical details of your system, such as the exact location of programs in upper memory and your hard disk drive type (which is handy to know when your CMOS battery dies).

DOS 6 also makes available AccessDOS to assist users with disabilities. See your DOS User's Guide for details on ordering AccessDOS.

Additional DOS 6 Enhancements

DOS 6 has added some other welcome new features:

- You can now bypass individual commands in CONFIG.SYS and AUTOEXEC.BAT or even bypass the entire files when booting. This helps you get back up and running when you've introduced a flaw into your startup files and can't boot normally. The new boot procedures are explained in Chapter 5.

- You can set up alternative configurations for your system. Several new CONFIG.SYS commands let you display a menu, accept a choice from the keyboard, and select a configuration block based on the user's choice. Chapter 5 explains the new CONFIG.SYS commands.

- You can finally accept some keyboard input during a batch program and make decisions based on it. Only one character can be accepted, and you have to go through IF ERRORLEVEL to process it (sigh), but it's a start. The new CHOICE batch command is explained in Chapter 4.

Features Eliminated in DOS 6

You'll also find a number of old programs and files missing from DOS 6. Old utilities such as COMP and ASSIGN are no longer necessary, as they've been replaced by improvements such as FC and SUBST. RECOVER has been dropped for good reason: too many people managed to nuke their hard disk directory structure with it. Files such as the printer code page information (CPI) files are no longer needed with DOS 6.

The following files have been dropped from DOS 6. If you upgraded from an earlier version of DOS, you'll find that they're still in your DOS directory, and the programs still work. Those are your former files, which DOS 6's SETUP program did not eliminate. You can safely delete them unless you have batch programs that depend on them:

    4201.CPI

    4208.CPI

    5202.CPI

    ASSIGN.COM

    BACKUP.EXE

    COMP.EXE

    CV.COM

    EDLIN.EXE

    EXE2BIN.EXE

    GORILLA.BAS

    GRAFTABL.COM

    JOIN.EXE

    LCD.CPI

    MIRROR.COM

    MONEY.BAS

    MSHERC.COM

NIBBLES.BAS

PRINTER.SYS

PRINTFIX.COM

REMLINE.BAS

If you installed DOS 6 from scratch, you won't have these files. If you find that you need some of them, you can order them from Microsoft. See your DOS User's Guide for details.

Using SETVER

Now that you've installed DOS 6, you might find that some older applications won't start up because they check the DOS version number and are designed to work with a specific DOS version earlier than 6. In some cases, the application truly can't work with DOS 6, and you'll need to talk to the manufacturer about getting an updated version. (You might want to uninstall DOS 6 until you resolve the difficulty.) In most cases, all you have to do is fool the application into thinking that the correct DOS version is present, and it will function perfectly. The SETVER facility lets you lie to an application about the DOS version number.

Setting Up SETVER

SETVER uses a version table that must be loaded into memory via CONFIG.SYS during booting. DOS 6's SETUP automatically inserts the following command into your CONFIG.SYS file:

```
DEVICE=path\SETVER.EXE
```

If it's not there and you need to use SETVER, insert the command into CONFIG.SYS.

Some of your DOS utilities count on SETVER, so don't remove it from CONFIG.SYS without first examining the SETVER table to see whether you're using any of the programs that it communicates with.

If you need SETVER and your system is set up to take advantage of upper memory blocks, change DEVICE to DEVICEHIGH so that the version table will be loaded into upper memory. MEMMAKER will do this for you, as explained in Chapter 10.

Use the SETVER command without any parameters to list the current version table. You'll find that, in addition to your own entries, it contains quite a few entries inserted by Microsoft.

Setting a Version

The command to add or modify an entry to the SETVER table takes the following form:

```
SETVER [path] program-filename n.nn
```

The *path* tells SETVER where to find the SETVER program, not the program for which you're creating a new entry. You probably don't need it, but if you have other versions of SETVER.EXE on your drive (in OLD_DOS.1, for example), you want to be sure to reach the current version.

You can examine your DOS 5 SETVER table with the command SETVER C:\OLD_DOS.1. This could help remind you what entries you added in DOS 5 that you might need to add to the DOS 6 table.

The *program-filename* identifies the program to be lied to; include the filename and extension, but not a path, as in GAVOT.EXE. The *n.nn* identifies the DOS version number to report. For example, suppose that you have a program named COMSPIN that requires DOS 3.3. You could enter the following command to tell COMSPIN that DOS 3.3 is present:

```
SETVER COMSPIN.EXE 3.3
```

The SETVER command merely adds or changes an entry in the version table. You have to restart to load the changed table. Then you can try out the application in question. If it works, good. If not, you have to solve the problem some other way (such as upgrading the application software).

> Use extra caution when lying to an application with SETVER. The program could be fooled into accessing a disk incorrectly, and you could lose valuable data. For safety's sake, back up your hard disk drives every time you add or change an entry in the SETVER table.

SETVER Options

Use the /DELETE or /D switch to delete an entry from the version table. For example, to delete the COMSPIN entry, you would enter the following command:

```
SETVER COMSPIN.EXE /D
```

Add the /QUIET or /Q switch to suppress the confirmation message that is normally displayed when /D is used. (You can't suppress the long warning message that is displayed when you add or change an item in the table.)

Working with HELP

If you're teaching someone to use DOS 6 commands, show them the on-line HELP system early. You can see the table of contents (see fig. 1.1) by entering the word HELP with no parameters. Or, you can call up a specific topic with a HELP *topic*, as in HELP SETVER.

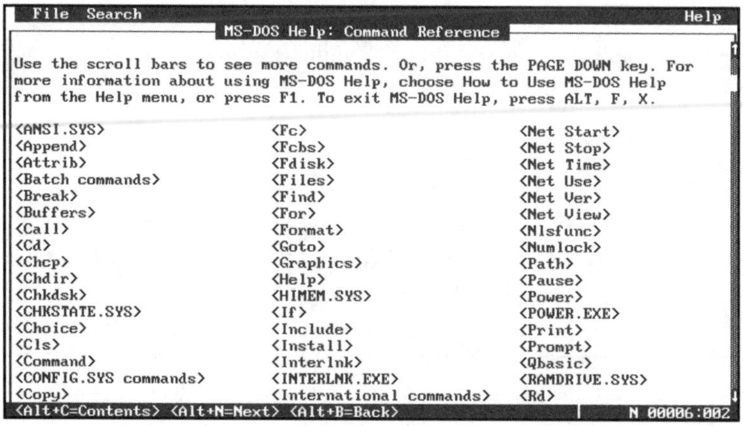

Figure 1.1.
HELP contents.

```
 File  Search                                                    Help
┌──────────────────── MS-DOS Help: Command Reference ────────────────────┐
Use the scroll bars to see more commands. Or, press the PAGE DOWN key. For
more information about using MS-DOS Help, choose How to Use MS-DOS Help
from the Help menu, or press F1. To exit MS-DOS Help, press ALT, F, X.

<ANSI.SYS>               <Fc>                    <Net Start>
<Append>                 <Fcbs>                  <Net Stop>
<Attrib>                 <Fdisk>                 <Net Time>
<Batch commands>         <Files>                 <Net Use>
<Break>                  <Find>                  <Net Ver>
<Buffers>                <For>                   <Net View>
<Call>                   <Format>                <Nlsfunc>
<Cd>                     <Goto>                  <Numlock>
<Chcp>                   <Graphics>              <Path>
<Chdir>                  <Help>                  <Pause>
<Chkdsk>                 <HIMEM.SYS>             <Power>
<CHKSTATE.SYS>           <If>                    <POWER.EXE>
<Choice>                 <Include>               <Print>
<Cls>                    <Install>               <Prompt>
<Command>                <Interlnk>              <Qbasic>
<CONFIG.SYS commands>    <INTERLNK.EXE>          <RAMDRIVE.SYS>
<Copy>                   <International commands> <Rd>
 <Alt+C=Contents> <Alt+N=Next> <Alt+B=Back>              N 00006:002
```

The File menu contains two commands: Print and Exit. The Print command prints either to a printer or a file. The Search menu includes the Find command to search the entire help system for a specified text string, such as "upper memory", and Repeat Last Find to continue the same search. You can also press F3 to repeat the last Find command.

Items in angle brackets are direct *jumps* to other areas of the HELP system. For example, selecting the <SETVER> jump displays the SETVER topic. On the bottom line, <Alt+C=Contents> displays the table of contents. <Alt+N=Next> jumps to the next topic in sequence; the entire HELP system has been sequenced so that you move from one topic to a related topic with this jump. <Alt+B=Back> returns to the topic viewed before this one; you can back up through your entire help session with Alt-B.

There are several ways to select a jump:

- Highlight it and press Enter.

- Click it.

- Press Alt-C, Alt-N, or Alt-B for the three jumps on the bottom line.

Figure 1.2 shows a typical HELP topic. When you first select a command topic, you see the syntax discussion. The two jumps at the beginning of the topic link to notes about the command and examples. When you're viewing one of those topics, there is a <Syntax> jump at the top so that you can return to the syntax discussion. Unfortunately, these links do not behave like menus. They disappear off the screen when you scroll down in the topic. You have to scroll back to the top to find and use them.

```
 File  Search                                              Help
                    MS-DOS Help: FORMAT
 ◄Notes►  ◄Examples►

                          FORMAT

 Formats a disk for use with MS-DOS.

 The FORMAT command creates a new root directory and file allocation table
 for the disk. It can also check for bad areas on the disk, and it can delete
 all data on the disk. In order for MS-DOS to be able to use a new disk, you
 must first use this command to format the disk.

 Syntax

     FORMAT drive: [/V[:label]] [/Q] [/U] [/F:size][/B!/S]

     FORMAT drive: [/V[:label]] [/Q] [/U] [/T:tracks /N:sectors] [/B!/S]

     FORMAT drive: [/V[:label]] [/Q] [/U] [/1] [/4] [/B!/S]

     FORMAT drive: [/Q] [/U] [/1] [/4] [/8] [/B!/S]

 <Alt+C=Contents>  <Alt+N=Next>  <Alt+B=Back>              N 00001:002
```

Figure 1.2.
A typical HELP
topic.

You can start HELP with the topic you want by entering a command in this
format: HELP *topic*. You can start directly with the notes or examples like
this: HELP *topic*--NOTES or HELP *topic*--EXAMPLES. (Yes, you must use
two hyphens.)

Brief Help

DOS 5's briefer help system, which concentrates on command syntax, is still available but under a different name, FASTHELP. When you enter the command
FASTHELP FORMAT, you see a display like the following:

```
Formats a disk for use with MS-DOS.

FORMAT drive: [/V[:label]] [/Q] [/U] [/F:size] [/B ¦ /S]
FORMAT drive: [/V[:label]] [/Q] [/U] [/T:tracks /N:sectors] [/B ¦ /S]
FORMAT drive: [/V[:label]] [/Q] [/U] [/1] [/4] [/B ¦ /S]
FORMAT drive: [/Q] [/U] [/1] [/4] [/8] [/B ¦ /S]
  /V[:label]  Specifies the volume label.
  /Q          Performs a quick format.
  /U          Performs an unconditional format.
  /F:size     Specifies the size of the floppy disk to format (such
              as 160, 180, 320, 360, 720, 1.2, 1.44, 2.88).
```

9

```
/B          Allocates space on the formatted disk for system files.
/S          Copies system files to the formatted disk.
/T:tracks   Specifies the number of tracks per disk side.
/N:sectors  Specifies the number of sectors per track.
/1          Formats a single side of a floppy disk.
/4          Formats a 5.25-inch 360K floppy disk in a high-density drive.
/8          Formats eight sectors per track.
```

FORMAT /? calls up the same display. The /? switch works with every DOS command and many third-party commands. If you write your own programs, you can make them available through the FASTHELP system by supporting the /? parameter.

FASTHELP with no parameters displays a complete list of DOS commands with a brief explanation of each. The list is automatically paged on a video screen, but it is printed without paging when redirected to a printer as follows:

```
FASTHELP > PRN
```

If you are responsible for helping a group of inexperienced people to use DOS, you might want to adapt the Help list to include your own notes, comments, and warnings; to document batch commands and macros that you have created; and most particularly, to modify the explanations of commands you have replaced with DOSKEY macros. You can modify the command list by editing the file named DOSHELP.HLP. The beginning of the file (see fig. 1.3) explains the proper way to edit the list.

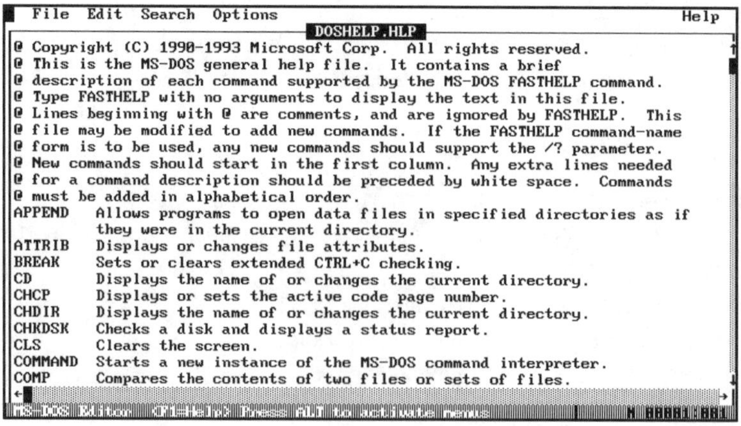

Figure 1.3.
Beginning of
DOSHELP.HLP
as viewed with
EDIT.

Some Shell Tricks

Don't be too quick to reject DOS Shell as child's play. It lets you do a number of things that the command prompt doesn't. For example, you can select any collection of files for processing by one command. Their names don't have to fit a global filespec; in fact, they don't even have to be in the same directory. Of course, task swapping lets you start up several programs at the same time and switch among them.

This chapter shows you some of the things you can do with the Shell's file management facilities. Chapter 2 describes how to start up and use programs in the Shell.

Startup Options

The DOSSHELL command includes switches to control text or graphics video mode; low, medium, or high resolution; and a black and white color scheme. But when you select these features from the Shell's Options menu instead of the command line, they are recorded in DOSSHELL.INI, and you don't have to select them again the next time. Unless you need one of the switches to make the screen readable in the first place, you're better off configuring the video from the Options menu.

> You can transfer your configuration to other computers by replacing their DOSSHELL.INI file with a copy of yours.

Drive List Tips

You can change drives without moving the cursor from your current position by pressing Ctrl-*drive*, as in Ctrl-D. This works from anywhere on the DOS Shell screen.

The first time you access a drive, DOS Shell reads the directory structure of that drive. From then on, it maintains the directory structure in memory so that it doesn't have to reread the drive. But if you update the structure from outside the Shell (with a File Run command, for example) or if you change floppies in a diskette drive, the directory list and file list will be out of sync with reality. You can force DOS to reread a drive by using any of the following techniques:

- Choose View Refresh or press F5 to refresh the current drive.

- Refresh a drive as you select it with the mouse by double-clicking it instead of single-clicking it.

- Refresh a drive as you select it from the keyboard by highlighting it and pressing Enter.

Directory Tree Tips

You can see more of a directory tree by choosing View Single File List, which eliminates the program list from the bottom of the screen and expands the file list and the directory tree. This option can make it easier to drag files from one directory to another.

When a large tree is expanded to show lower levels, the directory you want might not be showing in the window. A mouse user's natural instinct is to use the scroll bar to scroll to the right area. But it can be faster to type the first character of the directory name, which automatically scrolls the window so that the next directory starting with that character is selected.

When you're dragging files, you can scroll the directory tree by moving the pointer on top of the up arrow or down arrow in the directory tree's scroll bar.

File List Tips

The easiest way to copy and move files is to drag them from one location to another with the mouse. Dragging is pretty straightforward, but the following points aren't explained in the DOS documentation:

- The status of the Ctrl key determines the operation. If Ctrl is pressed, the selected files are copied; otherwise, they're moved. You can change operations in mid-drag by pressing or releasing the Ctrl key, because it's the status of the Ctrl key at the time that the mouse button is released which determines whether the files are moved or copied.

- In graphics mode, the shape of the mouse pointer indicates when it is over a valid or invalid destination. For valid areas, it indicates whether a single file or multiple files are being dragged. No matter what the video mode, the message line indicates when you are over a valid or invalid area and whether single or multiple files are being moved or copied.

- When dragging files to a directory on a different drive, use one of these techniques to reach the desired directory: (1) Make the desired destination directory the default directory on that drive and then drag the files to the drive icon in the drive list. (2) Choose View Dual File Lists and use the second directory tree to display the destination directory.

DOS Shell does not set the archive attribute of a new copy as DOS's copy commands do. If you're counting on archive attributes to select new or moved files for backup, you may have to set them yourself.

When Options Select Across Directories is selected, it's easy to drag more files than you meant to. The confirmation box doesn't list specific files' names, so you could end up moving or copying files unintentionally. For safety's sake, keep Options Select Across Directories off.

A safer way of selecting files from more than one directory is View All Files, which displays all the files in the directory in one file list.

The Shell offers two ways to locate a lost file when you know its name. One way is to choose View All Files and limit the display with a specific or generic filename filter (by using Options File Display Options). Or you can choose File Search, which opens a dialog box in which you can enter the specific or global filespec. You can choose to search the entire current drive or just the current directory. File Search produces a file list from which you can select and process files just as if it were the main file list.

Using EXPAND

If you did not install all of DOS 6 or if you deleted some files after installation, you might find yourself needing to copy some files from the installation disks to your hard drive. Most of the files are compressed on the disks, and you have to expand them before you can use them. Compressed files have an underscore as the last character of their extension. DOS 6 includes an EXPAND program to decompress them (see fig. 1.4). For example, to expand MSAV.EX_ from drive A to MSAV.EXE in C:\DOS, you could enter the following command:

```
EXPAND A:MSAV.EX_ C:\DOS\MSAV.EXE
```

You can specify more than one compressed filespec but not a global filespec. If you specify multiple filespecs, the destination must not include a filename. EXPAND will use the compressed filenames, including the underscores, and you will have to rename each one.

Figure 1.4.
EXPAND
command reference.

	EXPAND

Expands compressed file(s).

Format:

```
EXPAND [filespec ... [destination]]
```

Parameters:

none	Prompts for *filespec* and *destination*.
filespec	Identifies a compressed file that you want to expand.
destination	Specifies the location and/or name of the expanded file(s).

DOS at Your Command

2

Introduction

The better you understand DOS commands, the more effective your PC work will be, whether you spend most of your time working at the command prompt or in the Shell. Better commands are more powerful commands, which in turn provide more powerful batch programs as well as DOS

Shell program items and file associations, putting the full power of DOS at your command.

Redirecting Input and Output

Most of the DOS utilities read input (if any) from the keyboard and send their output in the form of messages to the monitor. The TIME command is a good example:

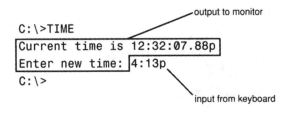

```
                                              output to monitor
C:\>TIME
Current time is 12:32:07.88p
Enter new time: 4:13p
C:\>
                                          input from keyboard
```

Standard Input and Output

To be more precise, many DOS utilities request standard I/O services from DOS. When standard I/O is requested, DOS reads from and writes to a device that it calls CON (for console), which is usually defined as the keyboard and monitor. But you can redirect standard input and/or output from CON to files or to other devices using the symbols shown in Table 2.1.

Table 2.1. Redirection Symbols

Symbol	Description
< source	Redirects input to come from a specified file or device
>destination	Redirects output to a specified file or device; an existing file is overwritten

Symbol	Description
>> destination	Redirects output to a specified file or device; an existing file is appended
*command1	command2*	The output from *command1* becomes the input to command2 (piping)

The symbols shown in table 2.1 are reserved by DOS and can't be used in any names you create, such as filenames or directory names.

Not all I/O can be redirected. Redirection works with any programs that request standard I/O services from DOS, which include many of the DOS utilities and perhaps some of your applications. However, many applications use their own I/O techniques, not DOS's standard ones, when communicating with the keyboard and monitor; they are not affected by redirection.

Furthermore, not all DOS utility input and output can be redirected. For example, the TYPE and COPY commands don't use standard input, but because they are designed to read from a file or device, input redirection is not necessary. Similarly, the PRINT command's print output can't be redirected to a file, because it does not use the standard I/O device. The only part of PRINT's output that can be redirected is the confirmation message that is normally displayed on the standard output device.

Standard Error Output

If a DOS utility encounters an error situation, such as a missing file, it sends the error message not to the standard output device but to a standard error output device, which DOS also displays on CON. Because redirection affects only standard output, not standard error output, error messages are not redirected. The total output from a command might include both types of output, as you can see here:

```
C:\>DIR BIMAX
   Volume in drive C is HARD DRIVE
   Volume Serial Number is 171D-78E4
   Directory of C:\
File not found
C:\>
```

} Standard output

} Error output

If you redirected the preceding command, the screen would still show the error message:

```
C:\>DIR BIMAX > BIMAX.DIR
File not found
C:\>
```

Meanwhile the redirected file (BIMAX.DIR) would contain only the standard messages:

```
Volume in drive C is HARD DRIVE
Volume Serial Number is 171D-78E4
Directory of C:\
```

You might not always find this feature desirable, but knowing that it exists lets you take occasional advantage of it. For example, you could write a DOSKEY macro to tell you whether or not a file exists:

```
DOSKEY ISFILE=DIR $1 $G NUL
```

This command defines a macro named ISFILE that looks for the filespec requested in replaceable parameter 1, redirecting the standard output to nowhere. Only the message File not found will be displayed.

You can redirect all keyboard input and monitor output by redefining CON using the CTTY command, a technique that's explained in Chapter 18.

Just to keep you on your toes, some programs use standard output to issue error messages (CHKDSK is one), and some programs use standard error output to issue standard messages (MORE is one). These aren't just flaky decisions by the program developers but are based on whether the messages in question are appropriately redirected when standard output is redirected. For example, if you redirect CHKDSK's output, the assumption is that you want to obtain a hard copy or a file copy for documentation purposes and that you want error messages included in the documentation.

Redirecting Output to a File

Perhaps the most common use of redirection is to store the standard output of a command in a file. For example, you could store the complete directory listing of drive C in a file called SAVECDIR with this command:

```
DIR C:\ /S /B > SAVECDIR
```

The C:\ parameter requests the root directory and the /S parameter causes all its descendants to be listed also. The /B parameter condenses the listing. SAVECDIR will be a plain-vanilla ASCII file that can be viewed by TYPE, edited by EDIT, printed by PRINT, and so forth.

Overwriting versus Appending

Both the > and >> symbols create a new file if the attached filespec is unique. The difference between these two symbols lies in what happens when the filespec identifies an existing file. With >, the existing file is replaced by the new output without warning, while >> causes the new output to be appended to the end of the existing file.

> The > redirection symbol will replace an existing file without warning. For safety's sake, use >> unless you're positive that you want an existing file replaced. Chapter 4 shows how to test for the existence of a file and issue commands accordingly.

Suppose that you want to write a batch job to create a file named SAVEDIRS containing the complete directories of drives C through E. Any previous version of SAVEDIRS should be replaced by the new file. The batch file could look like this:

```
DIR C:\ /S /B > SAVEDIRS
DIR D:\ /S /B >> SAVEDIRS
DIR E:\ /S /B >> SAVEDIRS
```

The first DIR command uses > to overwrite any previous SAVEDIRS. But the subsequent commands must use >> to append their outputs to the newly created file.

Redirecting I/O to Devices

You can also redirect standard I/O to devices using the names shown in Table 2.2. For example, the following command prints the complete directory of drive C:

```
DIR C:\ /S /B > PRN
```

Table 2.2. DOS Device Names

Name	Description
LPT1 through LPT3	Line (parallel) printers 1 through 3
PRN	The same as LPT1
COM1 through COM4	Communications (serial) ports 1 through 4
AUX	Auxiliary Post
CON	The user's console: the keyboard for input and the monitor for output (unless redirected via the CTTY command)
NUL	Nowhere (the data is simply dropped)

The device names shown in Table 2.2 are reserved by DOS and can't be used in names that you create.

LPT1 or PRN identifies the standard parallel printer, where DOS automatically directs all print output unless otherwise instructed. This is the default printer for the PRINT command and the PrintScreen key.

Chapter 20 explains how to redirect data intended for a parallel printer to another device using the MODE command.

Some Printer Incompatibilities

PostScript printers require special drivers, and DOS will not be able to print to them in their native modes. But most of these printers can be set to emulate a standard parallel printer (such as the Epson MX80) that DOS can handle, even if it can't take advantage of the printer's bells and whistles. Check your printer's documentation to find out how to make it emulate a standard parallel printer.

NUL: The Road to Nowhere

You might find the NUL device occasionally useful to suppress the standard output from a command, because output directed to NUL simply disappears. For example, the following command would display a message only if the file was not found:

```
DIR CASEY.TXT > NUL
```

Such techniques can sometimes be useful in a DOSKEY macro or batch file to suppress messages that an inexperienced person is not prepared to deal with.

Redirecting Input

The < symbol tells DOS to redirect standard input to the specified file or device. For example, to read standard input from COM1 instead of the keyboard, you could enter this command:

```
SORT < COM1
```

One purpose of redirecting standard input is to automate commands so that they require less user input. For example, if the file named C:\DOS\CR contains one blank line created by pressing the Enter key, the TIME command could be automated this way:

```
TIME < C:\DOS\CR
```

21

When DOS wants standard input, it reads from the CR file instead of the keyboard. After DOS displays the current time the single carriage return causes it to retain the current time, terminate TIME, and display the command prompt. You could use the CR file to automate DATE and PRINT in the same way. When used with PRINT, it causes the print function to be initialized to the default print device (PRN).

In a batch file, it's often important to specify a complete path name when redirecting input so the command will work no matter what drive or directory is current.

Automating a simple command such as TIME or DATE might seem on the surface like more bother than it's worth. But it helps to make batch files and DOSKEY macros run with less user interaction. If you're careful, you can automate more complex commands that require a series of keyboard inputs. For example, a standard FOR-MAT job requires three inputs (if you don't include the /V switch in the command), which are enclosed in square brackets in the following example:

```
C:\>FORMAT A:
Insert new diskette for drive A:
and press ENTER when ready...[Enter]
Checking existing disk format.
Saving UNFORMAT information.
Verifying 1.44M
Format complete.
Volume label (11 characters, ENTER for none)? [Enter]
    1457664 bytes total disk space
    1457664 bytes available on disk
        512 bytes in each allocation unit.
       2847 allocation units available on disk.
Volume Serial Number is 1035-0DE3
Format another (Y/N)?[N]
C:\>
```

You can automate the entire process by creating an input file containing two carriage returns and an N. If FMTIN contains the responses for the FORMAT command, you could execute the automated command like this:

```
FORMAT A: < C:\DOS\FMTIN
```

Each time DOS wants input from the keyboard, it reads the next line in the file.

Automating commands such as FORMAT bypasses normal safety checks. Use automation techniques with caution and don't put them in the hands of inexperienced people. Also, if an error situation arises requiring an unusual response, the program will probably hang up waiting for valid input from the disk file. Ctrl-Break will kill the hung-up program and restore the command prompt.

Piping

Piping passes data from one command to the next using a temporary file called a pipe. The standard output from the first command becomes the standard input to the second. Piping is most often used with the DOS filters, and you see many piping examples when the filters are explained in the next section.

Here's one quick trick you can do with piping. You have already seen how to automate a TIME or DATE command by redirecting the standard input to a file containing a carriage return. You can also pipe the carriage return to the TIME or DATE command. Here's one way to do it using the CR file that contains a single carriage return:

```
TYPE C:\DOS\CR ¦ TIME
```

The TYPE command sends the contents of the CR file to the pipe, and the TIME command reads it from the pipe. Thus, the carriage return contained in CR is passed to the TIME command.

As with other forms of redirection, piping affects standard I/O only.

Using ECHO To Automate Commands

A more convenient way to pipe a value to a command uses ECHO instead of TYPE. ECHO provides the value on the spot, so you don't need to have a response file made up in advance. For example, to pipe a Y to a DEL *.* command (to respond to Are you sure (Y/N)?), you could enter this command:

```
ECHO Y ¦ DEL *.*
```

ECHO followed by a period with no space generates a carriage return that can be used to automate commands such as TIME and DATE. Here's another way to automate the TIME command:

```
ECHO. ¦ TIME
```

This is the simplest way to automate commands that require single responses. It won't work with multiple response commands such as FORMAT, however, because ECHO can provide only one value.

The Temporary Pipe Files

To pipe, DOS must create two temporary files, generating filenames such as ABOABOBH and ABOABOBN. The temporary files are automatically deleted after the command is completed or interrupted with Ctrl-Break, but if you restart the computer or power it down during the command, the temporary files will be abandoned on the disk. You can safely delete them.

DOS writes temporary files in the current directory unless you have specified a standard temporary directory by entering a command like this (probably in AUTOEXEC.BAT):

```
SET TEMP=path
```

A piping command will fail if DOS can't write its temporary files because the drive is too full or the disk is write protected. (The SET command is explained in Chapter 9.)

The DOS Filters

DOS designates three of its utilities as filters—programs that read data from the standard input device, manipulate the data in some way, and write it to the standard output device. The three DOS filters are MORE, which breaks standard output into display pages; SORT, which puts lines in order; and FIND, which locates lines containing text strings.

What's My Line?

The three filters operate on lines of data, as delimited by carriage returns. In an ASCII file, such as a batch file or CONFIG.SYS, the lines are obvious. But many word processors store a carriage return in a file only when you press the Enter key to end a paragraph. Even though the word processor breaks paragraphs into several lines on the monitor and in print, DOS sees each paragraph as only one line. An exception to this rule is when the word processor saves a file in ASCII format instead of its native format. Then it might insert carriage returns in each paragraph to turn the displayed line breaks into real ones. So when applying any of the DOS filters to files created by word processors, the rule of thumb is: be sure you know in what format the file is stored.

MORE in a Minute

The MORE command in its simplest form contains just the word MORE, which causes DOS to read input from the keyboard and display it on the monitor, pausing at the end of each page until you press a key to continue. Because that is rarely a useful function, MORE is almost always used with redirection or piping. Before EDIT was included in DOS, MORE was often used to display files page by page, but because EDIT lets you scroll around in files, it's the better choice for examining files. If for some reason you want to view a file with MORE instead of EDIT, redirect the input to the file with a command in this format:

```
MORE < filespec
```

When working with a file containing lines longer than the screen width, MORE formats the lines so that all data can be seen.

You'll find MORE most useful to page through command output via piping. The following command lists all the directories and files on the current drive, one page at a time:

```
TREE \ /F ¦ MORE
```

It's Not My SORT

SORT's major reason for existence used to be to sort the output of the DIR command. But DIR's /O options now do a much better job of sorting directory information. SORT can still be useful on simple lists, such as an index with only one level of entries, but for any kind of complex job, you need a more sophisticated sort program.

Figure 2.1 shows the format of the SORT command. If you just enter the word SORT with no parameters or redirection, the utility reads from the standard input device, sorts the lines, and displays them on the standard output device. In case you ever find a need to do this, the sidebar explains how to enter data from the keyboard.

Entering Files from CON

Most DOS utilities that read input from CON look for an individual key press, such as Y or N, or for a single line terminated by the Enter key. But the three DOS filters actually look for a complete file to be entered from CON if you don't redirect the input to a stored file. In addition, you can use CON as the source for a COPY command, which also requires a file. A file is one or more lines terminated by an end-of-file marker (hex 1A, which is depicted on the screen as ^Z).

Before EDIT, most experienced DOS users knew how to enter a file via CON, as that was a quick-and-dirty way to create a short ASCII file such as a simple batch file. It was also a character-building experience, somewhat akin to boot camp or freshman hazing, for you could work on only one line at a time and could not go back to modify or correct lines that were already entered without restarting the entire file from the top.

Now that EDIT is available, you never have to enter files via CON, but if you haven't installed EDIT or prefer doing it the hard way, here are the instructions:

1. After you enter the MORE, SORT, FIND, or COPY command, DOS will put the cursor at the beginning of the next line and wait for you to start inputting data.

2. Type each line carefully. Inspect and correct it before pressing Enter. After you press Enter, there's no going back. (MORE and FIND will process the line immediately, then wait for the next line. The result is somewhat strange and probably not what you wanted or expected.)

3. When the last line has been entered, press F6 or type Ctrl-Z and press Enter to record the end-of-file mark. (FIND and SORT require the end-of-file mark to be appear at the beginning of a new line.) DOS will then process the file.

Figure 2.1.
SORT command reference.

SORT

Sorts ASCII data and displays results.

Format:

```
SORT [/R] [/+n] [< source] [> destination]
```

Parameters and Switches:

source	Identifies a file or device containing data you want to sort; the default is CON, which accepts input from the keyboard until you type Ctrl+Z.
destination	Identifies a file or device to which you want to send sorted data; default is CON, which displays sorted data on the screen.
/R	Reverses the sort order.
/+n	Starts sorting in column *n*; default is column 1.

Redirecting SORT I/O

Most of the time, you redirect SORT input to a file or receive the input from a previous command via piping. Output is frequently redirected to a file or piped to another command. For example, to sort the file called INDEX1 and display the output in pages, you could enter this command:

```
SORT < INDEX1 ¦ MORE
```

The DOS on-line documentation indicates that you can specify an input filename without using redirection, but that's not true. You must use the < symbol to read SORT data from an input file.

To save the same output in a file called INDEX2 instead of displaying it on screen, you could enter this command:

```
SORT < INDEX1 > INDEX2
```

SORT Collating Sequence

SORT's collating sequence is determined by the current code page (code pages are explained in Chapter 19). Table 2.3 shows the collating sequence for the keys found on a standard 101-key keyboard using the English code page. (Read down the first column, then read down the second column, and so on.) SORT ignores the difference between uppercase and lowercase letters.

Table 2.3. SORT Collating Sequence (Standard English Keys)

(space)	*	4	>	h	r	\
!	+	5	?	i	s	]
"	,	6	@	j	t	^
#	-	7	a	k	u	_

$	.	8	b	l	v	'
%	/	9	c	m	w	{
&	0	:	d	n	x		
'	1	;	e	o	y	}
(	2	<	f	p	z	~
)	3	=	g	q	[	

SORT Limitations

Unfortunately, SORT is severely limited in function:

- It does alphanumeric sorts only, which produces erroneous results when sorting numeric values.

- It locates the beginning of the data to be sorted strictly by position. It can't identify fields delimited by commas or tabs, the format used by many database and mail-merge files.

- Every line in the file is considered a separate record. There is no way to identify multiline records such as a name-and-address file might contain.

- It uses all the data from the beginning column through the end of the line as the sort key. You can't limit the length of the sort key, and you can't use primary and secondary sort keys.

Why You Can't Do a Two-Key Sort

This last point bears some extra discussion, because you might think you can accomplish a two-key sort by sorting first by the secondary key and then by the primary key. But a simple example shows why such a technique would work only by accident. Suppose that you have some name-and-address records that you want to sort by name, and for those records with identical names, by city. A sample set of records might look like this after sorting by city:

```
JONES       MARY        45 PINE ST          GRAND RAPIDS, MI
ADAMS       PETER       2314 FIR ST         LAS VEGAS, NV
JONES       MARY        316 LOCUST ST       PITTSBURGH, PA
ADAMS       PETER       16 FOREST RD        SILVER SPRING, MD
ADAMS       PETER       5064 ELM ST         TULSA, OK
```

Now, if you could sort by the name in columns 1 through 20 only, the result would be as desired. Whenever identical names were encountered, the records would retain their city order:

```
ADAMS       PETER       2314 FIR ST         LAS VEGAS, NV
ADAMS       PETER       16 FOREST RD        SILVER SPRING, MD
ADAMS       PETER       5064 ELM ST         TULSA, OK
JONES       MARY        45 PINE ST          GRAND RAPIDS, MI
JONES       MARY        316 LOCUST ST       PITTSBURGH, PA
```

But that's not what happens in fact, because SORT won't stop at column 20. It goes right on into column 21, 22, and so on to resolve identical records. The end result sorts the records by name, and for identical names, by street address, because that's the data that starts in column 21:

```
ADAMS       PETER       16 FOREST RD        SILVER SPRING, MD
ADAMS       PETER       2314 FIR ST         LAS VEGAS, NV
ADAMS       PETER       5064 ELM ST         TULSA, OK
JONES       MARY        316 LOCUST ST       PITTSBURGH, PA
JONES       MARY        45 PINE ST          GRAND RAPIDS, MI
```

There is no way to use SORT to order these records by name first and city second.

Using Other Sort Programs

As we said at the outset, SORT will do for small, simple jobs, but for anything complex, you need another sort program. You might already have a sort utility that will better meet your needs. All the major word processors include sort facilities, with WordPerfect's being especially full of features. Most word-processor sorters can be used on any file that is in the word processor's native format or in ASCII format. All database managers are capable of sorting their own databases, while spreadsheet programs can sort their own worksheets. However, the database and spreadsheet sorters probably can't be used on independent (that is, "not invented here") files.

What a FIND

The FIND command, shown in Figure 2.2, can help you locate individual lines from a file or from command output. When combined with the DIR command, it can even help you locate lost files that don't match a global filename.

Figure 2.2.
FIND command reference.

FIND

Searches for a specific string of text in a file or files.

Format:

```
FIND [/V] [/C] [/N] [/I] "string" [filespec ...]
```

Parameters and Switches:

"string"	Specifies the group of characters you want to search for. The quotation marks are required.
filespec	Identifies a file to be searched.
/V	Displays all the lines not containing the specified string.
/C	Displays only a count of all the lines that contain the specified string.
/N	Includes line numbers in the display.
/I	Ignores case.

Notes:

If you omit *filespec*, FIND takes input from the DOS standard input source, usually the keyboard or a pipe.

Locating Lines

Suppose that you can't remember the name of the file containing a letter about a defective compact disc. The current directory has three files that might be right: DISCLET, CDRETURN, and CDCOMP. You could find out which one includes the expression "compact disc" and the context of the expression with a command like this:

```
C:\>FIND "compact disc" /I DISCLET CDRET CDCOMP
---------- C:\DISCLET
---------- C:\CDRET
I have just received the enclosed compact disc, opened
it, and listened to it only once. Unfortunately, it
skips in several places. I am returning it to take
advantage of your "Full Replacement" guarantee. Over
the last few years, I have purchased more than 100
compact discs from your service and this is the first
problem I have ever encountered.
---------- C:\CDCOMP
It will be some time before I can afford to add a CD
ROM drive. At the present, I have two high-density
diskette drives (one of each) and a 40M hard disk. By
the time I can afford a compact disc-style drive,
maybe they'll be able to write as well as read.
Wouldn't that be great!
```

Although it looks like FIND displayed lines that don't contain "compact disc," remember that in text documents such as these, each paragraph is one line, so each paragraph that contains "compact disc" is displayed in its entirety. FIND wrapped the long paragraphs into shorter lines on the screen. You can see in this example that DISCLET does not mention "compact disc." The other two files do mention it, and it's clear which one is the desired letter. When doing a search like this, it's a good idea to include the /I switch (ignore case) so that you'll match references to "Compact disc" and "Compact Disc" as well as "compact disc."

Searching All Files for a Text String

Unfortunately, FIND does not let you use a global filespec, so it's difficult to search all the files in a directory for a particular text string. It's even difficult to search all DOC or TXT (or whatever) files. You probably can't list all the filespecs in one command because you'll exceed the 127-character command limit. But take heart. Chapter 4 shows you how to accomplish it by combining FIND with the FOR command.

Locating Lines in Command Output

One common use of FIND is to select particular lines from command output. For example, suppose that you want to display the current time or date without seeing the rest of the output from an automated TIME or DATE command. You could do it like this:

```
C:\>ECHO. ¦ TIME ¦ FIND "Current"
Current time is  7:31:30.18a
C:\>C:\>ECHO. ¦ DATE ¦ FIND "Current"
Current date is Tue 10-01-1991
C:\>
```

There are many other applications of this particular technique. To see how much space is left on a disk:

```
C:\>DIR ¦ FIND "free"
                16189440 bytes free
C:\>
```

To see disk capacity:

```
C:\>CHKDSK ¦ FIND "disk space"
  21387264 bytes total disk space
C:\>
```

To see how the TEMP variable is currently set:

```
C:\>SET ¦ FIND "TEMP"
TEMP=C:\DOS
C:\>
```

Locating Files in a Directory Listing

The DIR command will display files that match a global filename or that have certain attributes. But how can you find all files created on April 1, or all files containing "RA" anywhere in their names (not just the first two letters)? Piping DIR output to FIND can help you with these types of tasks. The following command lists all the files in the current directory that contain "RA" anywhere in their filenames:

```
C:\>DIR ¦ FIND "RA"
COLDNEWS XRA      9103 08-30-91  11:52a
PIRATES  PCX     39625 08-30-91  11:52a
PRACTICE HSG     36478 08-30-91   3:15p
C:\>
```

Because FIND is normally case-sensitive, it's important to use all capitals inside the quotes when searching DIR output unless you use /L (for lowercase) with DIR or /I (to ignore case) with FIND.

Expanding this command to cover an entire branch or drive creates problems because of the way that DIR usually lists its output, with the directory name on a separate line from the filename. FIND would list only the file entries and you would have no idea what directories they belong to. When /S is used with /B, the complete path is included with each filespec. Using /B and /S, you can find all the files in a complete branch whose names contain a particular text string:

```
C:\>DIR \ /S /B ¦ FIND "RA"
C:\VENTURA
C:\DOS\RAMDRIVE.SYS
C:\DOS\GRAFTABL.COM
C:\DOS\GRAPHICS.COM
C:\DOS\GRAPHICS.PRO
C:\HSG\GRAB.EXE
C:\>
```

You can't see the size, time, and date information, but at least you can see where to find each file.

More Shell Tricks

You can run a program from the Shell by selecting it from the program list, choosing the File Run command and entering a command in the resulting dialog box, opening its program file in the file list, or opening a data file that's associated with it.

Defining Program Items

Your personalized program list can make a big difference in the effectiveness of the Shell. By adding to it the items you use often, especially those that are candidates for task swapping, you'll create a convenient, flexible, and fast way to start up programs. Program items can be particularly helpful for inexperienced DOS users, as they are one of the easiest ways to start up a program, and you can make them quite flexible.

Figure 2.3 shows the two dialog boxes that you use to define a program item; the second box appears when you press the Advanced button. The Program Title and Commands are required, but everything else is optional.

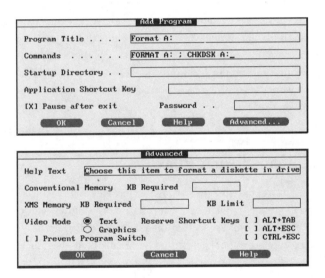

Figure 2.3.
Defining a
program item.

The example in the figure shows how you can combine two or more commands in the Commands field. Separate them by semicolons surrounded by spaces. In the example, the program item would execute first the FORMAT command and then the CHKDSK command. Replaceable parameters (%1 through %9) are permitted, along with any other parameters and switches that are appropriate for the command. Each individual command can have up to 127 characters, and the entire Commands field is limited to 255 characters.

Calling Batch Programs

Executing a batch file from a program item might require using the CALL command. When you reference a batch file without CALL, DOS links to the batch file and never returns to the program item. There's no problem if the batch file is the only command in the Commands field or if it's the last one. But if it's not the last one, you need to use CALL so that DOS will return to the list of commands when the batch program terminates. Chapter 4 explains CALL in more detail.

Weak Password Protection

Don't expect a lot of protection from the password facility in the program list. When a password exists, DOS Shell requires the password to be entered in order to open or edit the item. But you can delete a group or item without knowing the password. Furthermore, as you'll see under "A Trip through DOSSHELL.INI" later in this chapter, anyone can find out passwords by viewing the DOSSHELL.INI file. So passwords prevent access only by people who don't know very much about DOS (and obviously haven't read this book).

Application Shortcut Keys

You might want to define an Application Shortcut Key for programs with task swapping potential—that is, programs that run continuously until you intentionally exit them, such as editors, word processors, and database managers, as opposed to programs that execute a specific function and terminate themselves, such as FORMAT and ATTRIB. The shortcut key acts as a hotkey to switch to a task after the program item has been started up and appears on the active task list.

To define a shortcut key, place the cursor in the Application Shortcut Key field and press any combination of Ctrl, Shift, and/or Alt plus a keyboard character. Any combination is acceptable except those listed in Table 2.4.

Table 2.4. Reserved Application Shortcut Keys

Key combinations	Reserved functions
Ctrl-C and Shift-Ctrl-C	Emulate the Break key
Ctrl-H and Shift-Ctrl-H	Emulate the Backspace key
Ctrl-I and Shift-Ctrl-I	Emulate the Tab key
Ctrl-M and Shift-Ctrl-M	Emulate the Enter key
Ctrl-[and Shift-Ctrl-[	Emulate the Esc key

You may find situations in which two or more items on the active task list have the same hotkey. Pressing the key combination switches to the next task in the list having that hotkey; you repeatedly press the hotkey until you reach the task you want.

Memory Requirements

The Advanced dialog box includes several items that specify memory requirements for the program item when task swapping is in effect. These items are used only with task swapping.

Conventional Memory KB Required specifies the minimum amount of memory that must be present for the program to be loaded; the default is 128K. Entering a figure here does not affect how much memory is allocated to the program when it's loaded; DOS always gives it all available memory. But it does affect how much memory is saved on disk when you switch to another task; that can be a key factor in how many tasks you can start up under the task swapper as well as the amount of time it takes to swap a task out or in. If you know that a program requires only 7K to run, by all means enter a 7 under Conventional Memory KB Required so the task swapper doesn't save the default 128K for this program.

When you start up DOS Shell, it requests all available extended memory from HIMEM.SYS and does its own management of the extended memory facility. The two extended memory fields, XMS Memory KB Required and XMS Memory KB Limit, identify the minimum and maximum amounts of extended memory that should be allocated to a program during task swapping. The defaults are 0 and 384K, respectively. When a task is swapped out, its extended memory is held for it (unlike conventional memory, which is swapped out to disk); no other task can access that area of extended memory. So the amount of extended memory that is set aside for one task influences whether or not another task can be loaded. For this reason, do try to fill in these two XMS fields for all programs that require extended memory, if you can determine what their requirements are.

Video Mode affects how much memory is assigned to the video buffer. It should always be Text (even if the program uses graphics mode) unless you are using a CGA monitor and are having trouble switching to a program. The Graphics setting allocates more memory for the video buffer, which some CGA monitors need in some situations.

Task Switching Limitations

Some programs are not fully compatible with task swapping, and you can establish limitations in the Advanced dialog box. Check Prevent Program Switch to eliminate task swapping altogether for this program item. Once such an item is started, the user must exit it to return to the Shell screen or any other task. If you just need to inhibit one or more task swapping hotkeys because the program uses them for other functions, all you have to do is check the pertinent keys under Reserve Shortcut Keys.

Replaceable Parameter Dialog Box

Whenever you include a replaceable parameter in the Commands field of the Add Program dialog box, DOS opens the dialog box shown in Figure 2.4. Here you define a dialog box to be displayed whenever the program item is opened so that the user can enter a value for the replaceable parameter.

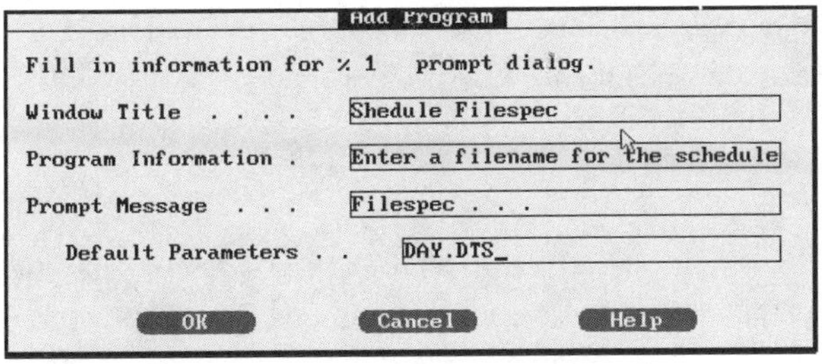

Figure 2.4.
Defining a dialog box for a program item.

The first three fields determine the text to be placed in the dialog box. The last field sets a default value for the replaceable parameter. In addition to a fixed default value, such as the one shown in the figure, two special parameters are available: %F and %L. %F fills in as a default value the filename that is selected in the file list when the program item is opened. %L fills in the value that was used the last time the item was executed. In any case, the user can overtype the default value when executing the program item.

Associating File Extensions with Programs

It's fairly easy to set up file associations. Figure 2.5 shows how to associate the DOC extension with Microsoft Word by highlighting any DOC file in the file list, selecting File Associate, and filling in the command that starts up the program.

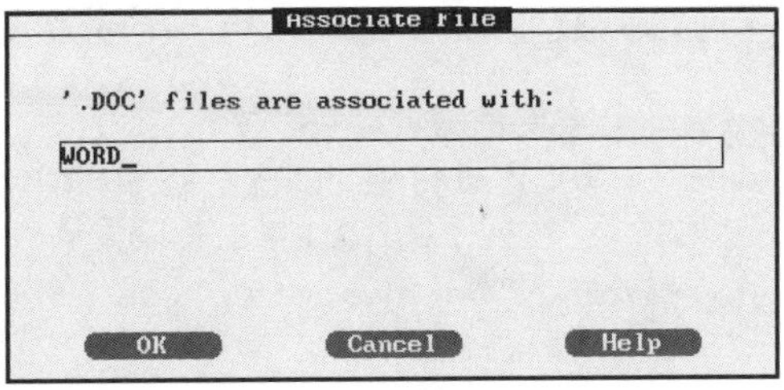

Figure 2.5.
Associate File dialog box.

When filling in the Associate File dialog box, keep in mind how DOS will use the command-text you place there. When you open an associated file, DOS creates a command like this:

```
command-text filespec
```

You can include in the box whatever *command-text* is appropriate when starting up the desired program from the command prompt, such as a path, some switches, and other parameters. You can even combine commands with semicolons (surrounded by spaces) and include replaceable parameters (%1 through %9). DOS will display a dialog box for each replaceable parameter when you open an associated file, but each dialog box is blank—that is, it has no prompts to remind you what type of information is needed, which may not be desirable.

You can also create file associations from the program's perspective: highlight the program file, select File Associate, and fill in the name(s) of associated extension(s). When you do that, you have no opportunity to include parameters or switches in the command-text.

A program can be associated with many extensions, but an extension can be associated with just one program. If you accidentally associate an extension with a second program, the first association is replaced by the second.

A Trip through DOSSHELL.INI

DOSSHELL.INI is the key to the Shell setup. This very important setup file is designed to be edited by an ASCII editor such as DOS's EDIT. Figure 2.6 shows the beginning of the file (EGA/VGA version), which contains a significant warning: don't let your editor shorten the long lines or the file will no longer be valid. Here are a few more warnings for you:

● Make a backup copy before viewing or modifying the file, just in case the editor damages it.

● If you view or modify it with a word processor, be very careful that it gets saved in ASCII mode and does not get formatted in any way.

● Don't modify any punctuation marks, especially brackets ([]) and braces
({}) unless you know exactly what you're doing. They're crucial to the
structure of the file.

```
┌ File  Edit  Search  Options                              Help ┐
│              ┌─────── DOSSHELL.INI ───────┐                    │
│EGA.INI/VGA.INI                                                 ▓
│*************** WARNING ***********************                 │
│This file may contain lines with more than 256                 │
│characters. Some editors will truncate or split                │
│these lines. If you are not sure whether your                  │
│editor can handle long lines, exit now without                 │
│saving the file.                                                │
│                                                                │
│Note: The editor which is invoked by the                       │
│      MS-DOS 5.0 EDIT command can be used                       │
│      to edit this file.                                        │
│*************** NOTE ****************************                │
│Everything up to the first left square bracket                 │
│character is considered a comment.                              │
│****************************************************            │
│[savestate]                                                     │
│screenmode = graphics                                           │
│resolution = low                                                │
│startup = filemanager                                           │
│filemanagermode = shared                                        │
│sortkey = name                                                  ▓
│◄                                                             ►  │
│MS-DOS Editor  <F1=Help> Press ALT to activate menus   CN 00001:001│
└────────────────────────────────────────────────────────────────┘
```

Figure 2.6.
Beginning of
DOSSHELL.INI.

Savestate Section

The savestate section (see fig. 2.7) shows the status of various Shell parameters. You
can see the direct relationship between parameters like *screenmode* and display
hiddenfiles and menu-controllable features such as the display mode
(Options Display) and the file display options (Display Hidden/System Files).

```
┌ File  Edit  Search  Options                              Help ┐
│              ┌─────── DOSSHELL.INI ───────┐                    │
│[savestate]                                                     │
│screenmode = graphics                                           │
│resolution = low                                                │
│startup = filemanager                                           │
│filemanagermode = shared                                        │
│sortkey = name                                                  │
│pause = disabled                                                │
│explicitselection = disabled                                    │
│swapmouse = disabled                                            │
│tasklist = enabled                                              │
│switching = enabled                                             │
│mouseinfo = 6.02,ignore                                         │
│sortorder = ascending                                           │
│displayhiddenfiles = enabled                                    │
│replaceconfirm = enabled                                        │
│deleteconfirm = enabled                                         │
│mouseconfirm = enabled                                          │
│crossdirselection = disabled                                    │
│                                                                │
│                                                                │
│◄                                                             ►  │
│MS-DOS Editor  <F1=Help> Press ALT to activate menus   CN 00005:001│
└────────────────────────────────────────────────────────────────┘
```

Figure 2.7.
DOS Shell
parameter Status.

Programstarter Section: Program List Definitions

The programstarter section contains the definitions of the items on the program list. In Figure 2.8, you can see the definition of a program group titled Manage Daily Schedule, which has the Ctrl-D hotkey and executes this command:

```
SCHEDULE %1
```

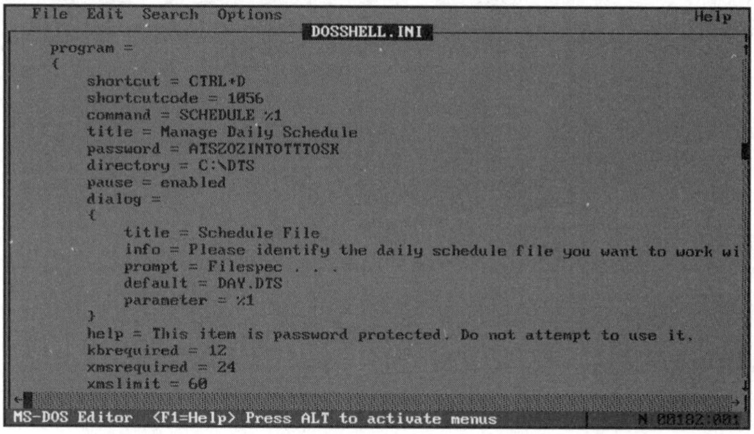

```
File  Edit  Search  Options                                        Help
                         DOSSHELL.INI
   program =
   {
       shortcut = CTRL+D
       shortcutcode = 1056
       command = SCHEDULE %1
       title = Manage Daily Schedule
       password = ATSZOZINTOTTTOSK
       directory = C:\DTS
       pause = enabled
       dialog =
       {
           title = Schedule File
           info = Please identify the daily schedule file you want to work wi
           prompt = Filespec . . .
           default = DAY.DTS
           parameter = %1
       }
       help = This item is password protected. Do not attempt to use it.
       kbrequired = 12
       xmsrequired = 24
       xmslimit = 60
MS-DOS Editor  <F1=Help> Press ALT to activate menus        N 00182:001
```

Figure 2.8. *Program group and item definitions.*

Program Passwords in DOSSHELL.INI

This item's password was originally defined as "A Stitch in Time." DOSSHELL.INI has slightly encrypted it by moving all lowercase letters up six letters in the alphabet and converting them to uppercase so that "a" becomes "G." (Uppercase letters are unchanged.) This is not enough encryption to fool anyone who really wants to access the password. Not only that, but the encrypted version will also work as the password to access the program item. You can see why the password protection offered by DOS Shell won't fool too many people.

Color Schemes

At the end of the programstarter section, each of the color schemes is defined (see fig. 2.9). You can edit this section to alter the predefined color schemes or add new ones. It doesn't take too much effort to figure out what each field represents on the screen and the correct format to define a new color scheme. It usually takes a bit of trial and error to put colors together that are effective under all circumstances.

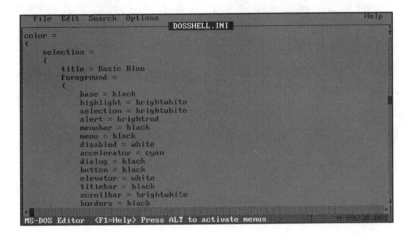

Figure 2.9.
Screen color definitions.

The 16 available colors are white, red, brown, green, blue, cyan, magenta, black, and bright versions of each of these (brightwhite, brightred, etc.). Brightblack appears as gray on most screens, and brightbrown appears as yellow. White is grayish, while brightwhite is white.

File Associations

The final section of DOSSHELL.INI, which shows the file associations, comes in handy for discovering file associations that you weren't aware of. When you first install DOS, you can see the associations predefined by Microsoft (see fig. 2.10). Later on, you might want to review this section to see what associations are currently in effect.

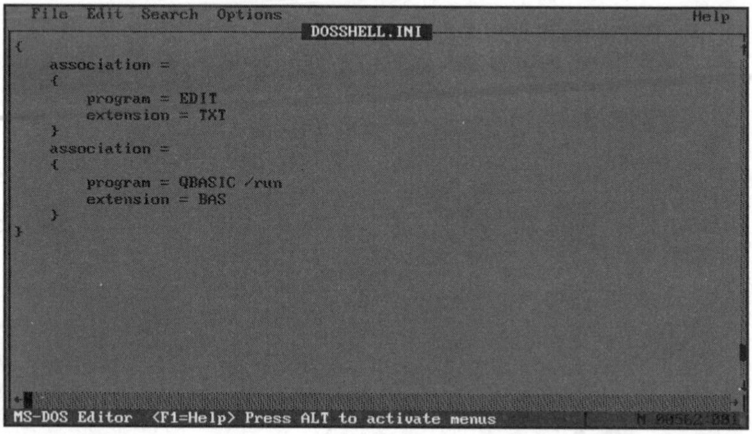

Figure 2.10.
File association
definitions.

```
  File  Edit  Search  Options                                    Help
┌───────────────────────────┤ DOSSHELL.INI ├────────────────────────────┐
{
    association =
    {
        program = EDIT
        extension = TXT
    }
    association =
    {
        program = QBASIC /run
        extension = BAS
    }
}
```

MS-DOS Editor   <F1=Help> Press ALT to activate menus

Basically Better Batches

3

Introduction

DOS's batch program facility lets you create your own programs out of the commands you use every day plus a special set of batch commands.

A relatively simple batch program lists one or more commands to be executed in sequence, serving the primary purpose of conserving keystrokes (and potential errors). For example, you might create a batch program called W that switches to a particular drive and directory and starts up Microsoft Word. The W batch program contains the following lines:

```
E:
CD \WORDDOCS
WORD
```

Such programs can bypass problems in typing (or even remembering) unfriendly commands. When Ventura Publisher installs itself, the program installs a batch file called VP that starts up the desktop publisher with the following commands:

```
C:
CD \VENTURA\DICT
EDCODICT
DRTLCFG -M6 -B2 -E3 -AA -PC:\VENTURA\DICT\
DLOAD ENGLISH<C2>CD \VENTURA
DRVRMRGR VPPROF %1 /S=SDFVGAH5.VGA/M=32
```

Imagine having to type these commands from scratch.

Although a straight command sequence can be useful, the true power of batches becomes evident when you generalize them to handle a variety of situations and to process repetitive sets of data. This chapter and Chapter 4 explore advanced batch features.

A Quick Review of Batch Basics

A batch program must be stored in ASCII (unformatted) form and named in the following manner:

filename.BAT

Use EDIT or any ASCII text editor to create batch files.

You can create a batch file containing DOSKEY's current command history by entering a command in this format:

```
DOSKEY /H > filename.BAT
```

To execute a batch program, enter the filename as a command. DOS will open the batch file and read and execute each command in turn. To interrupt processing and kill the batch job, press Ctrl-C or Ctrl-Break (they are equivalent). DOS asks the following:

```
Terminate batch job (Y/N)?
```

If you press Y, the entire batch job is terminated. If you enter N, only the current command is terminated, and DOS goes on to the next command in the batch file.

If you merely want to pause the batch job without terminating the current command, press the Pause key instead of Ctrl-Break. Pause suspends processing of a program (batch or not) until you press a key other than Pause.

You can't use redirection in a command that executes a batch file. If you try, the redirection is ignored. However, you can use redirection as usual in commands contained within a batch file.

Chapter 9 describes a trick that lets you redirect the output of a batch job using the COMMAND command.

Batch File Content

Any commands that can be entered at the DOS prompt can be included in a batch file, except for DOSKEY macros. In addition, the commands shown in Table 3.1 have been specifically designed for use in batch files.

Table 3.1. Overview of Batch Commands

Command	Description
CALL	Executes another batch program and returns to the current batch program
CHOICE	Reads input from the keyboard
ECHO	Controls command echoing and displays messages
FOR	Repeats a command for a set of variables
GOTO	Transfers to another line in the batch file
IF	Tests whether a condition is true or false
PAUSE	Suspends execution until the user presses a key
REM	Inserts comments in the batch file
SHIFT	Permits processing of multiple command-line parameters

What's in a Name?

In selecting a name for your batch file, it helps to understand how DOS searches for a program in response to a command. Suppose that you want to execute the ROSE batch program:

1. If you enter ROSE as a command without the BAT extension, DOS searches for the program in the following order:

   a. If DOSKEY is enabled, it looks for a DOSKEY macro named ROSE. (If the command name is preceded by one or more spaces, this step is bypassed.)

   b. Next, DOS looks for an internal command named ROSE.

   c. Next, DOS looks in the current directory for a file named ROSE.COM, ROSE.EXE, or ROSE.BAT, in that order. (If all three files exist, DOS finds and loads ROSE.COM and never notices the other two.)

d. Next, DOS looks in the first directory of the search path for ROSE.COM, ROSE.EXE, or ROSE.BAT, in that order.

e. DOS continues to search each directory in the search path, in the order they are specified in the PATH command, until a program file is found.

2. To bypass DOSKEY macros and COM and EXE files (but not internal commands), to search the current directory first, and then to search each directory of the search path for ROSE.BAT, include the BAT extension in the command, as in the following:

```
C:\>ROSE.BAT
```

Because BAT programs have the lowest priority, you should make their names unique unless you intend to take advantage of the program pecking order to achieve a special effect.

Bypassing COM and EXE Files

Notice that DOSKEY macros take precedence over any other kind of program, including internal commands. You can use this feature to override a DOS program with a DOSKEY macro. For example, suppose that you want the people in your workgroup to always use XCOPY instead of COPY. You can create a COPY macro that intercepts all COPY commands and turns them into XCOPY commands:

```
DOSKEY COPY=XCOPY $*
```

DOSKEY replaces the $* parameter with all the parameters from the invoking command line. So whatever filespecs and switches were entered with the COPY command are passed on to the XCOPY command.

Sometimes, you just want to disable a command so that inexperienced people can't use it. You could replace it with a message like the following:

```
DOSKEY FDISK=ECHO Please don't use this command; call J. North on
extension 457.
```

These macros don't completely disable the commands they supersede. You can still execute COPY and FDISK commands by preceding them with spaces. DOSKEY ignores commands that start with spaces.

DOSKEY macros are not as flexible as batch files, so you might want to override a command with a batch file instead of a DOSKEY macro. But how can you do that when batch files have lower priority than internal commands, COM, and EXE files? You can use DOSKEY to capture the command and call the batch file. For example, suppose that you want to redirect FORMAT commands to a batch file that guides an inexperienced user through the formatting process. The following command creates a DOSKEY macro that will do the trick:

```
DOSKEY FORMAT=FORMHELP.BAT
```

Floppy Batches

DOS reads and executes one batch command at a time. When execution of one command is finished, DOS returns to the batch file to read the next command. This practice can cause some complications when you are executing a batch program from a floppy disk. If you change disks during the execution of a command, DOS must ask for the disk containing the batch file in order to continue the job. You see the following message:

```
Insert disk with batch file
Press any key to continue . . .
```

This message appears even if no more commands are in the batch file, because DOS doesn't know the batch file is empty until it tries to read a command and discovers the end-of-file mark.

If you remove the floppy disk containing the batch file without inserting another disk, you see the following message, which always appears when DOS tries to read an empty drive:

```
Not ready reading drive A
Abort, Retry, Fail?
```

When this message appears, insert the batch file disk in the drive and press R for "Retry."

Clobbering the Batch File

If you know, or even suspect, that a batch program will be executed from a floppy disk, watch out for commands that might process that same disk. Some commands, such as FORMAT, routinely give you the chance to change the floppy disk before starting to work, as long as the commands aren't automated. The REPLACE and XCOPY commands wait for you to change the disk only if you include a /W switch (for Wait) in the command. Most of the commands that can affect a floppy disk or its files, including such commands as DEL *.* and RENAME, offer no opportunity to switch to another floppy disk. If such commands appear in a batch file on a floppy disk and refer to the same floppy drive, the commands might destroy the batch file, which is probably not what was intended.

If you suspect that a batch program may be run from a disk and has the potential for clobbering the batch file, be sure to include a warning message in the program and give the user a chance to change disks or cancel the program. The next section explains how to do this.

Message Control

You can do a lot more to control displayed messages from within a batch program than you can from the command prompt or a DOSKEY macro. In addition to redirecting standard output (which is explained in Chapter 2), you can suppress command echoing, display your own messages, and pause until the user responds by pressing a key.

The CLS command, which has no parameters or switches, is a good way to clear the screen of old commands and messages at the beginning of a batch program and perhaps at appropriate points during the program.

Command-Line Echoing

If left to its own devices, DOS displays each command line preceded by a blank line when processing a batch file. Suppose that a batch file named DT.BAT contains the following commands:

```
ECHO. | DATE | FIND "Current"
ECHO. | TIME | FIND "Current"
```

Executing DT looks something like this:

```
C:\>DT
C:\>ECHO. ¦ DATE ¦ FIND "Current"
Current date is Tue 10-22-1991
C:\>ECHO. ¦ TIME ¦ FIND "Current"
Current time is 6:47:23.76a
C:\>
C:\>
```

The first line shows the DT command being entered. The second line (not counting blank lines) echoes the first command from DT, and the third line shows its standard output. The fourth line echoes the next command from DT, and the fifth line shows its standard output. The two blank command prompts appear at the end of every batch job when command-line echoing is not suppressed. The first one shows up when DOS tries to read another command from the batch file and discovers the end-of-file mark, signaling that the batch program is done. The second is the normal command prompt, which returns so that you can enter your next command.

> When creating a batch file, if you type a carriage return at the end of the last command (which most people do) three (3!) blank command prompts are displayed at the end of the batch job.

This job would take slightly less time, take up less screen space, and make a lot more sense to an inexperienced user if you could suppress the echoed command lines so that the entire job appears as follows:

```
C:\>DT
Current date is Tue 10-22-1991
Current time is 6:47:23.76a
C:\>
```

You can suppress the echoing of any individual command (as well as the blank line preceding it) by prefixing the command with @, as in the following:

```
@ECHO. ¦ DATE ¦ FIND "Current"
@ECHO. ¦ TIME ¦ FIND "Current"
```

This revised version of the program still produces the extra command prompt at the end of the job, because you can't suppress the end-of-file mark with @:

```
C:\>DT
Current date is Tue 10-22-1993
Current time is 6:47:23.76a
C:\>
C:\>
```

The ECHO OFF command (see Figure 3.1 for the ECHO command format) turns off all future command echoing, including the blank line that precedes each command line, until an ECHO ON command is encountered or the batch file ends. Use @ to suppress the ECHO OFF command itself.

The following batch file has the desired effect of suppressing all command lines, all blank lines, and the extra command prompt(s) at the end of the job. In other words, only the command output is displayed.

```
@ECHO OFF
ECHO. ¦ DATE ¦ FIND "Current"
ECHO. ¦ TIME ¦ FIND "Current"
```

ECHO

Turns command echoing features on or off or displays a message.

Format:

```
ECHO [message ¦ ON ¦ OFF]
```

Parameters and Switches:

none	Displays the current setting of ECHO.
ON I OFF	Turns command echoing on or off.
message	Displays *message* on the screen.
ECHO.	This special ECHO command displays a carriage return (a blank line). Be sure that no space appears between ECHO and the period.

Figure 3.1.
ECHO command reference.

This method is the most common way of suppressing command echoing in batch jobs. @ECHO OFF is the first command in nearly every batch file.

You might occasionally want to echo a command, which you can do by turning ECHO ON for that command and then turning it OFF again.

ECHO Messages

You also can display your own messages during a batch file with commands in the following format:

ECHO *message*

Use a command in the following format to display a blank line between messages (no space should appear between ECHO and the period):

ECHO.

Earlier examples in this chapter used ECHO to generate a carriage return to pipe to the DATE and TIME command; but when the output isn't redirected, it causes the carriage return (a blank line) to be displayed on the monitor.

ECHO messages look strange when command echoing is on because you see the message in the ECHO command and then as output on the next line:

```
C:\>ECHO Let's format the diskette in drive A:
Let's format the diskette in drive A:

C:\>ECHO.

C:\>ECHO Insert the correct diskette in the drive.
Insert the correct diskette in the drive.
```

The messages look just right when command echoing is turned off:

```
Let's format the diskette in drive A:
Insert the correct diskette in the drive.
```

You might think that ECHO followed by a space would display a blank line, but that causes DOS to display ECHO IS ON or ECHO IS OFF. ECHO followed by a space and then a period causes DOS to display a line containing a period. To generate a blank line, you have to use ECHO. with no space preceding the period.

Using ECHO in Batch Programs

When you're preparing a batch job for a user, make liberal use of ECHO messages to keep the user informed of what is going on. For example, suppose that you are creating a batch program named VAULT to move a branch from the hard disk to floppy disk. You might do it as follows:

```
@ECHO OFF
CLS
ECHO **********************************************
ECHO *                                            *
ECHO *  This program moves all the DOC files      *
ECHO *  from the DOCS branch to the diskette in   *
ECHO *  drive A:.                                  *
ECHO *                                            *
ECHO **********************************************

ECHO First copy the files to drive A:
XCOPY C:\DOCS\*.DOC /S A:

ECHO Then delete the branch from C:
DELTREE /YC:\DOCS

CLS
ECHO **********************************************
ECHO *                                            *
ECHO *              All done!                     *
ECHO *                                            *
ECHO **********************************************
```

When ECHO is ON, the REM command also can be used to display messages in a batch program. However, when ECHO is OFF, REM commands produce no output and serve only to document the batch file itself.

Pausing

When you have automated the commands in a batch file and added your own messages, output lines might scroll off the screen before a user gets the chance to examine them. You can use the PAUSE command to suspend processing until a key is pressed (see fig. 3.2).

Figure 3.2.
PAUSE batch
command reference.

PAUSE

Temporarily suspends processing of a batch program and prompts the user to press any key to continue.

Format:

PAUSE

Notes:

The user's response to Pause is not meaningful unless it is one of the break keys (Ctrl-C or Ctrl-Break). Any other response continues the batch program. See CHOICE for a command that lets users enter a meaningful response.

In the preceding batch program, you may want the program to pause after the first message to give yourself or another the chance to change floppy disks, as follows:

```
@ECHO OFF
CLS
ECHO ********************************************
ECHO *                                          *
ECHO *   This program moves all the DOC files    *
ECHO *   from the DOCS branch to the diskette in   *
ECHO *   drive A:.                               *
ECHO *                                          *
ECHO *   Make sure the correct diskette is in    *
ECHO *   drive A: before continuing.            *
ECHO *                                          *
ECHO ********************************************
PAUSE
```

```
ECHO First copy the files to drive A:
XCOPY C:\DOCS\*.DOC/S A:

REM Then delete the branch from C:
DELTREE /Y C:\DOCS

CLS
ECHO ********************************************
ECHO *                                          *
ECHO *               All done!                  *
ECHO *                                          *
ECHO ********************************************
```

The pause also gives someone the chance to cancel the program using Ctrl-Break after reading the preceding message.

Replaceable Parameters

A batch program becomes more generally useful if you set it up so that command specifics (such as filespecs) can be entered when the program is executed. You use the replaceable parameters (%0 through %9) for this purpose. The following SPACE.BAT program has limited usefulness because it displays the amount of space occupied by BAK files (a specific) on the current drive (another specific):

```
@ECHO OFF
ECHO The space occupied by *.BAK files on the current drive is:
DIR \*.BAK /S ¦ FIND "file(s)"
```

The program becomes more generalized if you use %1 to represent the filespec and %2 to represent the drive name:

```
@ECHO OFF
ECHO The space occupied by %1 files on the %2 drive is:
DIR %2\%1 /S ¦ FIND "file(s)"
```

Now you can include a filespec and drive name when you execute the batch program, if you enter the following command:

```
SPACE *.DOC D:
```

DOS substitutes `*.DOC` for %1 and `D:` for %2 everywhere in the batch file. The commands that are processed follow:

```
@ECHO OFF
ECHO The space occupied by *.DOC files on the D: drive is:
DIR D:\*.DOC ¦ FIND "file(s)"
```

A Simple Application of Replaceable Parameters

The following two programs, named START.BAT and STOP.BAT, may be used to track project work time. When you start working on a project, enter **START** *project* at the command prompt. The date and time are recorded in the TIMETRAK file. When you stop working on the project, enter **STOP** *project*. TIMETRAK will be an ASCII file that you can edit, print, and delete as needed.

```
@ECHO OFF
REM START.BAT
ECHO Started working on %1 >> C:\TIMETRAK
ECHO. ¦ DATE ¦ FIND "Current" >> C:\TIMETRAK
ECHO. ¦ TIME ¦ FIND "Current" >> C:\TIMETRAK
ECHO. >> C:\TIMETRAK

@ECHO OFF
REM STOP.BAT
ECHO Stopped working on %1 >> C:\TIMETRAK
ECHO. ¦ DATE ¦ FIND "Current" >> C:\TIMETRAK
ECHO. ¦ TIME ¦ FIND "Current" >> C:\TIMETRAK
ECHO. >> C:\TIMETRAK
```

How Replaceable Parameters Work

DOS identifies the words on a command line by the spaces that separate them. The first word is always the command itself, which must be the name of a DOSKEY macro, an internal command, an executable program (COM or EXE), or a batch program (BAT). All subsequent words on the line are parameters. (A switch is a type of parameter.) After loading the requested program, DOS passes all the parameters to it.

However, when executing a batch file, DOS processes all replaceable parameters before executing a command. %0 is always replaced by the first word on the command line—the command that executed the batch file. You sometimes see %0 used in ECHO messages.

The symbol %1 is replaced by the first parameter on the command line, %2 by the second parameter, and so on up to %9, which is replaced by the ninth parameter. To allow for more than nine parameters, you have to use the SHIFT command, which is explained later in this chapter.

Null Parameters

A missing parameter is replaced by a null value. In the SPACE batch file, if you omit the drive-name parameter, %2 is replaced by a null value, resulting in the following batch job, which accesses the current drive because no drive is specified:

```
@ECHO OFF
ECHO The space occupied by *.DOC files on the  drive is:
DIR \*.DOC /S ¦ FIND "file(s)"
```

(Notice how carefully the message is worded so that it reads all right when the drive name is null.) If you omit the filespec parameter too, %1 also is replaced by a null value, resulting in the following batch job, which reports on all files on the current drive:

```
@ECHO OFF
ECHO The space occupied by  files on the  drive is:
DIR \ /S ¦ FIND "file(s)"
```

Because DOS identifies parameters by position, you can omit parameters at the end of the command line only. In the SPACE example, you have no way to omit the filespec but include the drive name, as the first parameter on the command line will always be substituted for %1, whether it makes sense or not.

Keep this fact in mind when deciding which parameter in a batch job should be %1, which should be %2, and so on. The parameters most likely to be omitted should come last. In the SPACE example, there's a natural inclination to make the drive name %1 and the filespec %2, because that's the order in which they appear in the DIR command. However, because people frequently want to specify a filespec and omit the drive name, the two replaceable parameters have been reversed.

Also pay some attention to how a command will function with null values for the replaceable parameters. The SPACE program provides a good example. Suppose that you decide to include the colon from the drive name in the fixed text of the DIR command and replace %2 with the drive letter only. The batch file would appear as follows:

```
@ECHO OFF
ECHO The space occupied by %1 files on the %2: drive is:
DIR %2:\%1 /S ¦ FIND "file(s)"
```

To execute it for the TXT files on drive D:, you enter the following:

```
SPACE *.TXT D
```

Both occurrences of %2 are replaced by the letter D, and the batch job works perfectly. However, what if you omit the second parameter, trying to access the current drive? The commands to be processed after substitution are as follows:

```
@ECHO OFF
ECHO The space occupied by *.TXT files on the : drive is:
DIR :\*.TXT /S ¦ FIND "file(s)"
```

The filespec :*.TXT is unacceptable to DOS and causes the DIR command to fail. To avoid this failure, leave the colon out of the fixed text and enter it with the drive name.

It's not always possible to make every parameter replaceable by a null. When a batch job has required parameters, they should be the first parameters on the command line, and you should let people know which parameters are required and which are optional.

SHIFT

Nine replaceable parameters are more than enough for most batch files, but should you want more than that, the SHIFT command can be used to process an unlimited number of parameters. SHIFT, which has no parameters of its own, causes all the command-line parameters to be shifted down one position so that the value that was formerly substituted for %1 is now substituted for %0; the value that was %2 is now %1; and so on. At the other end of the command line, the tenth parameter is now substituted for %9, which makes that parameter available for the first time.

Suppose that you want to write a multiple-delete command called DELS.BAT that can accept up to 12 filespecs. One way to do it is as follows:

```
@ECHO OFF
ECHO Deleting %1
DEL %1
ECHO Deleting %2
DEL %2
ECHO Deleting %3
DEL %3
ECHO Deleting %4
DEL %4
ECHO Deleting %5
DEL %5
ECHO Deleting %6
DEL %6
ECHO Deleting %7
DEL %7
ECHO Deleting %8
DEL %8
ECHO Deleting %9
DEL %9

SHIFT
REM The 10th parameter is now %9
ECHO Deleting %9
DEL %9

SHIFT
REM The 11th parameter is now %9
ECHO Deleting %9
DEL %9

SHIFT
REM The 12th parameter is now %9
ECHO Deleting %9
DEL %9
```

Another way to accomplish the same result is as follows:

```
@ECHO OFF
ECHO Deleting %1
DEL %1
    .

    .

    .
ECHO Deleting %9
DEL %9

SHIFT
SHIFT
SHIFT

ECHO Deleting %7
DEL %7
ECHO Deleting %8
DEL %8
ECHO Deleting %9
DEL %9
```

Unfortunately, if a user enters fewer than 12 parameters, the final DEL commands will be executed with no filespec, causing error messages to be displayed. Chapter 4 includes a better solution to this problem.

Dumb Replacement

DOS applies no intelligence whatsoever to the parameter replacement process. DOS simply does a character-by-character substitution of %n with the characters in the parameter. No surrounding spaces are added. If the result doesn't make sense, DOS won't know it until it tries to execute the command. Suppose that the final command in DREK.BAT appears as follows:

```
%3%1 %2
```

What if you invoke DREK with the following command line?

```
DREK R *.COM DI
```

After substitution, the final command in DREK.BAT appears as follows:

```
DIR *.COM
```

This example shows how you can apply a little creativity to make dumb replacement work for you, if necessary.

Escaping Replacement

Because of the way DOS handles the symbol % in a batch file, DOS ends up deleting every single occurrence of this symbol, even if it isn't attached to a digit to represent a replaceable parameter. You occasionally may need to use the % symbol in a batch file without having it deleted. For example, you may need to reference a file named TEN%ERS. Double the % symbol to keep it from being deleted. To print the file named TEN%ERS from within a batch file, use the following command:

```
PRINT TEN%%ERS
```

DOS will replace the %% with % before processing the command.

Batch Logic

Introduction

A batch program can include commands to link to other batch programs, read keyboard input, make decisions, and create loops for repetitive processing. For experienced programmers, the commands available in DOS will be familiar, if somewhat awkward when compared to the facilities available in BASIC or C. This chapter introduces a touch of programming logic concepts (just the basics) for readers who have never programmed before.

Linking Batch Files

As batch programs get more complex, it's often convenient for one batch file to link to another. For example, suppose that you have a program named FMT.BAT that formats a floppy disk and handles all possible errors that can occur; it's more than a hundred lines long. Now, you're creating a batch program that sets up floppy disks with a new application; it must format several disks before copying files to them. You could copy the formatting routine into the new batch file, or you could link to FMT.BAT to do the formatting.

Linking offers some very real advantages:

- You save disk space by not copying the hundred plus lines into another file.

- If you improve FMT.BAT, the improvements carry through to all programs that link to it.

The major disadvantages are that the link itself takes time, which slows down the program making the link; future modifications to FMT.BAT could make it inappropriate to some programs that link to it; and if you move, rename, or delete FMT.BAT, the link will no longer be valid.

Chaining versus Calling

You can link to another batch program in two ways, as shown in Figure 4.1. When you *chain* to another program, you transfer completely to that program, causing the first batch program to be terminated. When the chained program ends (without chaining to another program), the batch job terminates, and DOS resumes control. However, when you *call* another batch program, you transfer to it temporarily; when it's finished, you return to the original batch program, picking up with the instruction after the one that did the calling.

Calling

To call another batch file, use a command in the following format:

```
CALL batch-command
```

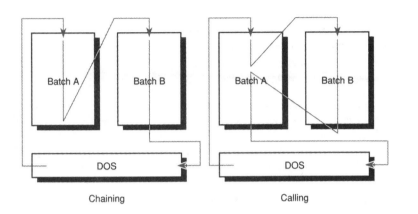

Figure 4.1.
Calling and chaining to other batch files.

For example, the following command calls FMT.BAT:

```
CALL FMT
```

When the FMT program ends, DOS returns to the command following this CALL command.

Include whatever parameters on the CALL command that you would use when executing the program from the command prompt. For example, if FMT accepts an optional drive name and volume label as replaceable parameters, you could use the following command:

```
CALL FMT A: TOTMASTER
```

Redirection is ignored in a CALL command, as it is in any command that executes a batch program.

Chaining

When you execute a batch file without the CALL command, DOS chains to it. For example, the following command chains to FMT.BAT:

```
FMT A: TOTMASTER
```

Any time you include a command in one batch program that executes another batch program without using CALL, a chain takes place, and the first batch program is *automatically terminated*. In the following batch file, the COPY command will never be executed because the FMT command chains to another batch program:

```
@ECHO OFF
ECHO Put the master diskette in drive B:
PAUSE
FMT B:
COPY C:\TOTDIR\*.* B:
```

You can correct the problem by inserting CALL in front of the FMT command.

> A batch program executes other types of programs, such as COM and EXE programs, without chaining. In the preceding batch program, ECHO, PAUSE, and COPY cause programs to be executed without chaining. Only links to other batch programs cause chaining to take place.

Passing Replaceable Parameters

You can use replaceable parameters in a linking command; DOS replaces them before executing the link. For example, the following command passes two parameters from the calling program to FMT.BAT:

```
CALL FMT %3 TOTMASTER
```

As usual, the %3 will be replaced by the third parameter from the command line that executed the calling program; if that parameter is A:, the CALL command as executed becomes:

```
CALL FMT.BAT A: TOTMASTER
```

The called batch program, FMT.BAT, treats the A: as %1 and TOTMASTER as %2. It has no awareness that the A: was originally %3 to the calling program.

Replaceable parameters are not automatically passed from the linking program to the linked program. You must include in the linking command any parameters to be passed to the linked program, and they must be in the correct order and format for the linked program, just as if you executed the same program from the command prompt.

Multiple Links

When you link to a second batch program, it may link to another. There is no limit to the number of links you can make in a batch job. Program A may chain to Program B, which calls Program C, which chains to Program D, and so on. Your batch jobs will be easier to manage, revise, and debug if you limit them to a few links, however.

Recursion

A batch file can link to itself, creating a situation called *recursion*. The batch job will repeat endlessly until something interrupts it, such as a condition becoming true or someone pressing Ctrl-Break.

Killing a Batch Job with Links

If you press Ctrl-Break (or Ctrl-C) during a batch job involving links, DOS displays its usual message:

```
Terminate batch job (Y/N)?
```

If you enter Y, the entire batch job (including all linked programs) is killed. If you enter N, only the current command is killed.

Branching

DOS includes some commands that let you decide what to do next in a batch program based on a specific condition. Some typical conditions are as follows:

- Does the C:\ AUTOEXEC.BAT file exist?

- Did the preceding command succeed?

- Did the user enter Y or N?

- Does %1 equal "/S"?

Types of Branches

Branches can range from extremely simple to fairly complex (although not as complex as you can achieve in true programming languages such as BASIC or C).

Bypass Branches

Figure 4.2 illustrates the simplest kind of branch, in which you execute a routine if the condition is true but bypass it if the condition is false, or vice versa. This branch is called a *bypass branch* because only one path (the true path or the false one) causes a routine to be executed. The other branch bypasses that and goes on to the next step. Notice that both branches end up at the same place eventually.

Figure 4.2.
Bypass decision logic.

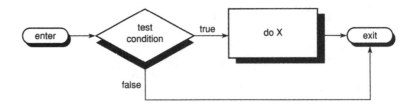

Some typical bypass decisions are as follows:

- If C:\ AUTOEXEC.BAT exists, rename it as C:\ AUTOEXEC.OLD.

- If the preceding command failed, issue a warning message.

- If the user entered a Y, format the floppy disk in drive A.

- If %1 equals "SORT", sort the source file.

Alternative Branches

Another common type of branch has two paths, as illustrated in Figure 4.3. One routine is executed if the condition is true, and another routine is executed if it's false. Typical alternative branches are as follows:

● If C:\AUTOEXEC.BAT exists, copy it to A:; otherwise, create a new A:\AUTOEXEC.BAT.

● If the preceding copy command succeeded, delete the source files; otherwise, display an error message and terminate.

● If the user entered a 1, display AUTOEXEC.BAT; otherwise, display CONFIG.SYS.

● If %3 equals "/P", print the target file; otherwise, display it on the monitor.

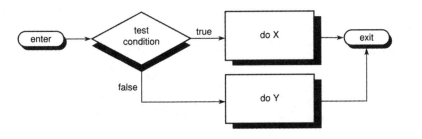

Figure 4.3.
Alternative decision logic.

The IF Command

Figure 4.4 shows the IF command, which is used for decision-making in batch programs.

Exit Codes

Many programs set an exit code when they terminate. The exit code is a number between 0 and 255 that indicates whether the program achieved its function or what type of error occurred. No set meanings for exit codes exist; each program defines the exit codes it issues, although a 0 generally means that the program was completely successful. The FORMAT program provides a typical example of exit codes:

0   The disk was successfully formatted (no errors)

3   The user interrupted with Ctrl-C or Ctrl-Break

4   Some (unspecified) type of error occurred, and the disk was not successfully formatted

5   A problem was identified and reported to the user, who chose to cancel the format job

Figure 4.4.
IF command reference.

IF

Executes a command if (and only if) a condition is true

Format:

IF [NOT] *condition command*

Parameters:

condition   The condition to be tested, which must be one of the following:

ERRORLEVEL *n*   The condition is true if the preceding program's exit code equals or exceeds *n*.

EXIST *filespec*   The condition is true if the specified file exists.

string1==string2   The condition is true if the two text strings are equal.

command   The command to be executed if the condition is true.

Note:

NOT negates the result of the condition so that the command is executed if the condition is false.

Unfortunately, not all of the DOS programs set exit codes, so it's not always possible to test for successful completion of an individual command in a batch file. Appendix A lists the exit codes set by the DOS utilities. If a DOS command isn't in the list, it doesn't set an exit code.

Your application programs and third-party utilities also may set exit codes. Check their documentation to find out.

The ERRORLEVEL Condition

The ERRORLEVEL condition tests the exit code of the preceding program. You specify a number, as in **IF ERRORLEVEL 3**, and the condition is true if the exit code equals or exceeds that number. The following commands format the disk in drive A and, if that fails for any reason, display the message `Try again with another diskette`.

```
FORMAT A:
IF ERRORLEVEL 1 ECHO Try again with another diskette
```

> Because FORMAT doesn't use exit codes 1 and 2, you could just as easily say IF ERRORLEVEL 3. But it's common usage to say IF ERRORLEVEL 1 to discriminate between 0 (complete success) and all other exit codes.

You can include NOT in an IF command to negate the result of the condition; that is, the condition is true only if the exit code is less than the specified number. The following routine displays a message only if the format is successful:

```
FORMAT A:
IF NOT ERRORLEVEL 1 ECHO Remove the diskette from drive A:
```

It's easy to get tangled up in IF ERRORLEVEL logic, especially when you reverse it with NOT. A logic chart like the ones in Figure 4.5 can help you analyze a command, determine when it will be true and when false, and decide what's going to happen in each case.

The Short Life of the Exit Code

The exit code lasts only until another program changes it. Even if the next program doesn't set specific exit codes, the exit code may be reset to 0. Commands such as CALL and ECHO don't reset the exit code, but other commands (especially nonbatch commands) may. Therefore, if you're going to process an exit code, do it immediately.

Figure 4.5.
Sample IF logic
charts.

condition	IF ERRORLEVEL 3	
exit codes	0, 1, 2	3, 4, ...
result	false	true
action	continue	kill program

condition	IF NOT ERRORLEVEL 2	
exit codes	0, 1	2, 3, ...
result	true	false
action	delete files	display message

The IF command does not reset the exit code. You can use several IF commands in a row to process various exit code possibilities after a command like FORMAT or XCOPY.

IF and Bypass Branches

The IF command is perfectly set up for a simple bypass branch. If the condition is true, it executes a single command and goes on to the next line. If the condition is false, it goes on to the next line. To execute more than one command when the condition is true, which is often the case, you can use CALL to execute another batch program, as in the following:

```
IF ERRORLEVEL 1 CALL BADFORM
```

All the examples you have seen so far are bypass branches. To accomplish alternative branches, you need to use the GOTO command, which is explained next.

Telling DOS Where To Go

Suppose that you're trying to accomplish an alternate decision like this: If the last command was successful, call GOODFORM; otherwise, call BADFORM.

The following program will not work:

```
IF NOT ERRORLEVEL 1 CALL GOODFORM
CALL BADFORM
```

It doesn't work because the CALL BADFORM command is executed in both cases.

The GOTO command is used to branch away from the current sequence of commands to another point in the program (see fig. 4.6). To accomplish an alternative branch, you jump to another section of the program for the true path. Only the false path goes on to the next line after the IF statement:

```
IF NOT ERRORLEVEL 1 GOTO GOODFORM
REM If DOS reaches the next line, the FORMAT command
failed for some reason.
...
...   (commands to handle FORMAT error)
...
GOTO NEXTSTEP

:GOODFORM
...
...   (commands to handle a successful format)
...

:NEXTSTEP
...
...
...
```

In the preceding routine, if the condition is true, indicating that the exit code is 0, you branch to the GOODFORM label in the same program. Several commands may be in the GOODFORM section. At the end, you fall into NEXTSTEP, which continues the batch processing. If the condition is false, the GOTO command is not executed, and you fall through into the commands that process an exit code greater than 0. At the end of that false branch is an extremely important command: GOTO NEXTSTEP. This command branches around the GOODFORM routine. Without it, you would fall into GOODFORM after the false branch was completed, which is not desired when you're trying to create an alternate branch.

DOS ignores all but the first eight characters of a line beginning with a colon, so you can add explanatory comments to label lines to document your program logic.

Figure 4.6.
GOTO *batch*
command reference.

GOTO

When used in a batch program, sends DOS to a line with the specified label.

Format:

GOTO *label*

Parameter:

label   Identifies the line to go to.

GOTO is also essential in creating multiple alternatives. For example, the following routine tries to display the exit code resulting from the FORMAT command:

```
FORMAT A:
IF ERRORLEVEL 5 ECHO Exit code is 5
IF ERRORLEVEL 4 ECHO Exit code is 4
IF ERRORLEVEL 3 ECHO Exit code is 3
IF ERRORLEVEL 0 ECHO Exit code is 0
```

However, the following is what the output looks like when the exit code is 4:

```
Exit code is 4
Exit code is 3
Exit code is 0
```

Because these IF commands come one after the other, DOS executes each one in turn, regardless of the outcome of the preceding one. IF ERRORLEVEL 5 is false, so that message is not displayed. IF ERRORLEVEL 4 is true, so its message is displayed. IF ERRORLEVEL 3 and IF ERRORLEVEL 0 also are true, and their messages are displayed as well. The result is not what you wanted.

The following routine completely processes the exit codes from the FORMAT command:

```
:FORMATSTEP
FORMAT A:
IF ERRORLEVEL 5 GOTO HANDLE5
IF ERRORLEVEL 4 GOTO HANDLE4
IF ERRORLEVEL 3 GOTO HANDLE3
```

```
REM If DOS reaches this line, the exit code must be 0
ECHO Exit code is 0
GOTO NEXTSTEP

:HANDLE3 This routine handles an exit code of 3
ECHO Exit code is 3
GOTO NEXTSTEP

:HANDLE4 This routine handles an exit code of 4
ECHO Exit code is 4
GOTO NEXTSTEP

:HANDLE5 This routine handles an exit code of 5
ECHO Exit code is 5

:NEXTSTEP The program continues on from here
```

It's important to test from the highest exit code to the lowest so that the first true condition encountered is the one that equals the exit code.

Testing for Files

Sometimes it's handy to test for the presence or absence of a file before deciding what to do next. IF [NOT] EXIST is used for this purpose. The classic example prevents the COPY command from overwriting an existing file by testing the target filename first. The program named PCOPY.BAT (for Protected COPY) may look something like the following file. %1 is the source filespec, and %2 is the target.

```
@ECHO OFF
IF EXIST %2 GOTO NOCOPY
COPY %1 %2
GOTO ENDING

:NOCOPY
ECHO The %2 file already exists. Please move, delete,
ECHO or rename it before trying this command again.

:ENDING
```

This routine fails if you omit the filespec for %2. This routine also produces an un-desired result if you specify a drive and/or path for %2 but omit the filename, because the IF EXIST condition turns out to be false, and the copy is made, even if the target directory does contain a file of the same name.

IF [NOT] EXIST also can be used in bypass decisions. The following command copies A:\AUTOEXEC.BAT to C:\ only if it doesn't already exist on C:\:

```
IF NOT EXIST C:\AUTOEXEC.BAT COPY A:\AUTOEXEC.BAT C:\
```

The following command renames C:\ AUTOEXEC.BAT if it exists:

```
IF EXIST C:\AUTOEXEC.BAT REN C:\AUTOEXEC.BAT AUTOEXEC.OLD
```

Testing for a Directory

Suppose that you want to find out whether the current directory has a subdirectory named TEMP. IF EXIST TEMP will not work because EXIST doesn't identify subdirectories. However, the special filename NUL is valid for every existing directory, so use the following command to see whether TEMP exists:

```
IF EXIST TEMP\NUL command
```

Comparing Text Strings

At first glance, comparing two text strings may seem totally useless: IF APPLES==APPLES is obviously true, and IF APPLES==ORANGES is just as obviously false. However, one or both of those text strings can be a replaceable parameter, giving you the power to check out the parameters entered on the command line.

The following batch program tests to see whether the first parameter is /F; if so, the batch program reformats the disk in drive A before copying files to it. If the first parameter is anything but /F, the disk is not formatted.

```
@ECHO OFF
IF %1==/F FORMAT A:
COPY C:\MYAPP\*.* A:
```

Testing for Null Values

Sometimes, you need to put quotes around *string1* and *string2*. In the preceding example, if someone omitted the parameter when running the batch program, the IF command would look like the following:

```
IF ==/F FORMAT A:
```

The condition ==/F is not acceptable and would cause a syntax error that would make the rest of the program fail. Putting quotes around *string1* and *string2* avoids this problem. With quotes, a null parameter yields this command, which is perfectly acceptable:

```
IF ""=="/F" FORMAT A:
```

Because a null does not equal /F, the FORMAT A: command would not be executed.

> If you use quotes, both parameters must be quoted.

You also can use quotes to test for a null parameter. To find out whether %3 is null, use a command like the following:

```
IF "%3"=="" GOTO CONTINUE
```

When the user omits the third parameter, DOS interprets the command as follows:

```
IF ""=="" GOTO CONTINUE
```

Because a null does, in fact, equal a null, the GOTO CONTINUE command is executed.

Nested IFs

You can nest an IF command inside another IF command. The inner IF command is executed when the outer IF command is true. The following GOTO command is executed if the current exit code is equal to or greater than 4 but less than 5; in other words, if it is 4:

```
IF ERRORLEVEL 4 IF NOT ERRORLEVEL 5 GOTO CODE4
```

The IF ERRORLEVEL 5 command is executed only if the IF ERRORLEVEL 4 command is true, and the GOTO command is executed only if both IF commands are true. The following GOTO command is executed if %1 is neither Y nor N:

```
IF NOT %1==Y IF NOT %1==N GOTO BADINPUT
```

Case is important in string comparisons. In the preceding command, a lowercase y or n would not be considered the same as Y or N, and the GOTO instruction would be executed. You could adjust the command to permit users to enter either uppercase or lowercase letters as follows:

```
IF NOT %1==Y IF NOT %1==y IF NOT %1==N IF NOT %1==n
GOTO BADINPUT
```

If there's any possibility that a user will omit the value, use quotes around the strings to avoid killing the program with a syntax error.

Loops

A loop is a routine that can be executed more than once. Two types of loops are possible—open and closed. An open loop tests a condition and terminates itself when the condition becomes true. A closed loop repeats and repeats with no way out until someone interrupts it from outside, usually by pressing Ctrl-Break or by rebooting. Most closed loops are mistakes, but you may find occasion to use one on purpose.

Figure 4.7 diagrams the logic of an open loop. You perform an action (such as a FORMAT command) and then test a condition (such as whether the exit code is 0). If the condition is false, you repeat the loop. When it's true, you exit the loop and go on with the program. The loop is executed until the condition becomes true. An open loop affects the condition in some way so that it may be true the next time it's tested.

In some routines, it makes more sense to test the condition at the beginning of the loop instead of at the end. This test allows for the possibility that the condition is true from the start, and the routine should never be executed.

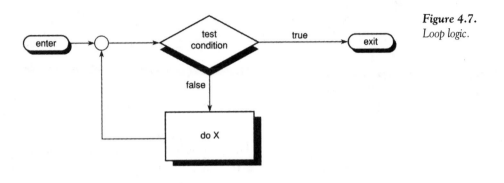

Figure 4.7.
Loop logic.

Sample Loop

Suppose that you want to execute FORMAT until it is successful. This type of loop is usually completed the first time, but if the first disk is bad or some other problem occurs, the loop will be repeated:

```
:FORMATLOOP
FORMAT A:
IF NOT ERRORLEVEL 1 GOTO ENDING

REM If DOS reaches this line, FORMAT was not successful

ECHO FORMAT failed for some reason. To try again
ECHO with another diskette, insert the diskette
ECHO and press any key except Ctrl+C or Ctrl+Break.
ECHO To quit now, press Ctrl+Break and enter Y
ECHO when you see "Terminate batch job (Y/N)?"
PAUSE
GOTO FORMATLOOP

:ENDING
```

Loops Involving SHIFT

In Chapter 3, you saw a program to delete up to 12 filespecs. This program can be set up as a loop to delete *any number* of filespecs. The loop ends when no more parameters are left to process:

```
:DELLOOP Deletes any number of files
IF "%1"=="" GOTO ENDING
DEL %1
SHIFT
GOTO DELLOOP
:ENDING
```

Each loop starts by checking for a null value in the first parameter. If it's null, the program jumps to ENDING and terminates. If it's not null, a DEL command is issued for that parameter. Then all the parameters are shifted down, so the next one becomes %1, and the program returns to the beginning of the loop.

Using FOR To Create Loops

Another looping technique uses the FOR command (see fig. 4.8) instead of IF. When you get used to its ugly-duckling format, you will discover that there is a swan in there somewhere. One big advantage of FOR is that it can be used at the command prompt; it's the only way to create repetitive processing at the command prompt.

FOR repeats a specified command for a set of items. You could process 12 filespecs as follows:

```
FOR %%F IN (%1 %2 %3 %4 %5 %6 %7 %8 %9) DO DEL %%F
SHIFT
SHIFT
SHIFT
FOR %%F IN (%7 %8 %9) DO DEL %%F
```

The first FOR command in the preceding causes nine filespces to be processed. If none of the filespecs are global, nine DEL commands are issued as follows:

```
DEL %1
DEL %2
  .
  .
  .
DEL %9
```

Figure 4.8.
FOR command reference.

FOR

Repeats a command for each item in a set.

Format:

FOR %*x* ¦ %%*x* IN (*set*) DO *command*

Parameters:

%*x* | %%*x*   Identifies a replaceable variable that can be used in *command*; it may be any non-numeric character. Use %*x* at the command prompt and %%*x* in a batch program.

(*set*)   Identifies a set of variables to replace %*x* or %%*x*. The parentheses are required.

command   Specifies the command to repeat, including its parameters and switches.

Notes:

Separate items in *set* by spaces.

Command cannot be another FOR command.

You can redirect *command*'s output using > or >>, but you can't use ¦ to pipe its output.

When FOR is used at the command prompt instead of in a batch file, the second word takes the form of %*x*. When FOR is used in a batch program, you must double the percent sign—%%*x* instead of %*x*—so that DOS will not delete the % from the command.

Global Filespecs in the Item Set

When a global filespec appears in the item set, DOS issues a separate command for each matching filename. If 100 filenames match the global filespec, 100 separate commands are generated. Suppose that you want to delete all the files in three different directories. You could do it as follows:

```
C:\>FOR %X IN (C:\MYAPP\*.* C:\MYAPP\DATA\*.*
C:\MYAPP\PROGRAMS\*.*) DO DEL %X
```

This command could generate hundreds of DEL commands. It may not be the most efficient way to get the job done.

> Remember that any individual command line can have up to 127 characters.

FOR and FIND

Do you find it frustrating that FIND will not accept a global filespec? How can you search all the files in the current directory or all the DOC and TXT files, when you can't use a global filespec in the command? The answer lies in combining FIND with FOR. FOR will turn the global filespecs in the item set into specific filenames and generate a separate FIND command for each one. The following command searches all the files in the current directory for the string "JNF":

```
FOR %%F IN (*.*) DO FIND "JNF" %%F
```

When you issue a command like this, be prepared to press Pause (or Ctrl-S) to page the output. Piping it to MORE doesn't help; piping has no effect with the FOR command.

To check only the DOC, TXT, and BAK files, use a command such as the following:

```
FOR %%F IN (*.DOC *.TXT *.BAK) DO FIND "JNF" %%F
```

Using FOR with CALL

You can use CALL in a FOR command (even at the command prompt) to apply a whole program to the item set. For example, the following command invokes the batch program named RESTAMP for every file in the current directory:

```
FOR %F IN (*.*) DO CALL RESTAMP %F
```

In each generated RESTAMP command, the individual filename is passed as the first parameter. (RESTAMP should use %1 to access this parameter.)

> If you reference a batch file without using CALL, the job will be terminated after the first execution of the batch file, defeating the purpose of the FOR command.

Using FOR with IF

FOR provides a simple way to test a variety of different cases with the IF command. The following command jumps to GOODINPUT if %1 is Y, y, N, or n:

```
FOR %%X IN (Y y N n) DO IF "%1"=="%%X" GOTO GOODINPUT
```

The CHOICE Command

At long last DOS includes a command to read user input from the keyboard and make decisions based on it. The CHOICE command is pretty limited, as input commands go, but it's better than nothing. Figure 4.9 shows the format of this new command.

CHOICE displays a message and a prompt on the monitor screen, reads a single character from the keyboard, and sets the exit code to indicate what character was entered. For example, suppose that this command appeared in a batch program:

```
CHOICE Do you want to prepare another disk
```

The message on the screen appears as follows:

```
Do you want to prepare another disk [Y,N]?
```

If the user enters Y or y, CHOICE sets the exit code to 1; if N or n, 2. If the user presses Ctrl-Break or Ctrl-C, CHOICE sets the exit code to 0. Any other input causes a beep, and CHOICE keeps waiting for an acceptable response.

Figure 4.9.
CHOICE
command reference.

CHOICE

Lets a user choose between options during a batch program.

Format:

CHOICE [/C:*list*] [/N] [/S] [/T:*char,sec*] [*text*]

Parameters and Switches:

/C:*list*   Defines a *list* of characters that the user can type to select choices. The colon is optional.

/N   Causes CHOICE not to display any prompt.

/S   Causes CHOICE to distinguish between uppercase and lowercase; otherwise case is ignored.

/T:*char,sec* Causes CHOICE to pause for *sec* seconds before defaulting to *char*. The colon is optional. *Char* must be a character from *list*. *Sec* must be between 0 and 99. Don't include any spaces in this parameter.

text   Specifies *text* to be displayed before the prompt.

Notes:

CHOICE prompts for input by displaying *list* enclosed in brackets with the characters separated by commas and followed by a question mark If you use /C:AB, it appears as "[A,B]?" Without /S, the list appears in uppercase.

If you omit /C, CHOICE uses YN as a default list.

If you use /N, CHOICE displays *text* with no prompt.

You must enclose *text* in quotation marks if it includes a slash (/).

With /T, CHOICE defaults to *char* after *sec* seconds. Otherwise, it waits for the user to type a character from *list* (or Ctrl-C or Ctrl-Break). If the user enters any other response, CHOICE beeps and continues to wait.

CHOICE sets the ERRORLEVEL parameter according the user's response: 1 for the first character in *list*, 2 for the second character, and so on. If the user chooses Ctrl-C or Ctrl-Break, CHOICE sets ERRORLEVEL to 0. If an error occurs, such as a bad parameter in /T, CHOICE sets ERRORLEVEL to 255.

Suppose that you're writing a batch program to format a floppy disk and copy the entire DELIVERY branch to it. You may have to do this a dozen times in a row, so you want to be able to repeat the program. You could set it up in the following way:

```
@ECHO OFF
:START Prepare a delivery disk
FORMAT %1 /U /V:"SETUP DISK" < FMTIN
XCOPY C:\DELIVERY /S /V %1
CHOICE Do you want to prepare another disk
IF ERRORLEVEL 2 GOTO ENDING
IF ERRORLEVEL 1 GOTO START
:ENDING (the end)
```

This little program formats a disk, copies the desired branch to it, and asks whether you want to prepare another one. If you enter N, the exit code is 2, and it jumps to the end. However, if you enter Y, the exit code is 1, and it loops back to the beginning. If you should press Ctrl-Break but respond N to the question `Terminate batch job [Y/N]?`, the exit code is set to 0, which winds up at the :ENDING label by default.

CHOICE Variations

Include the /C:*list* parameter to define a list of choices instead of the default Y and N. For example, if you want the user to enter A, B, or C in response to a menu (displayed by ECHO commands), you would specify /C:ABC. If for some reason you don't want to permit lowercase a, b, and c as acceptable alternatives, include the /S (for "sensitive") switch. CHOICE displays the prompt `[A,B,C]?` and sets the exit code to 1 if the user enters an A, 2 for a B, and 3 for a C.

If you leave out the *text* parameter, no message is displayed with the prompt. You may want to do this if you have already used ECHO commands to display a menu. In fact, you can suppress the prompt itself with the /N switch.

Use the /T parameter to set up a default choice to be taken if the user doesn't type anything within a specific time limit. For example, to choose option A after 10 seconds, include /T:A,10 in the CHOICE command.

Starting Up DOS

5

Introduction

DOS 6 has introduced a variety of new features for the startup files. If there's a problem in CONFIG.SYS or AUTOEXEC.BAT, you can now bypass both files or bypass individual lines and complete the booting process without having to resort to a floppy disk. Also, you can now set up alternate configurations in CONFIG.SYS so that you can select the configuration that you want to use each time you boot.

Bypassing the Startup Files

When you boot DOS 6, the message `Starting MS-DOS...` appears on the screen for a few seconds. To bypass both CONFIG.SYS and AUTOEXEC.BAT, press and release F5 or hold down a Shift key. You see the following message:

`MS-DOS is bypassing your CONFIG.SYS and AUTOEXEC.BAT files.`

When you do this, DOS may not be able to find COMMAND.COM; if so, it asks you where to find the command processor. Type the full filespec, including the drive name and path, as in C:\DOS\COMMAND.COM.

When the system is successfully booted, you see the default command prompt, which is just the current drive name (no path) followed by >. There will be no program search path. Devices that need installable device drivers, such as your mouse, will not work. Programs can't use extended or expanded memory because there are no memory managers. You can fix some of these problems from the command prompt—for example, you can enter a PATH command to set the program search path—but you can't load memory managers or device drivers. As soon as you identify and fix the problem in the startup files, you should reboot to restore your normal system.

To eliminate the two-second delay when the `Starting MS-DOS...` message is displayed, insert a SWITCHES /F command in CONFIG.SYS.

Bypassing Individual CONFIG.SYS Commands

Instead of bypassing the startup files in their entirety, you can bypass individual lines in CONFIG.SYS and specify whether or not AUTOEXEC.BAT should be executed. To do this, press F8 when you see the `Starting MS-DOS...` message. DOS displays each line from CONFIG.SYS followed by `[Y,N]?` Enter Y to execute the line or N to bypass it. When CONFIG.SYS is finished, DOS displays the following question:

`Process AUTOEXEC.BAT [Y,N]?`

Press Y to execute AUTOEXEC.BAT or N to bypass it.

Inhibiting Bypasses

To prevent people from bypassing the startup files, include the command SWITCHES /N in CONFIG.SYS.

Prompting for CONFIG.SYS Commands

You can set up individual CONFIG.SYS commands so that DOS will prompt you for confirmation every time you boot. Insert a question mark (?) before the equal sign (=) to do this. For example, you could set up a RAM drive to be installed only when you say so. Insert the following command in CONFIG.SYS:

```
DEVICE?=C:\DOS\RAMDRIVE.SYS
```

If MEMMAKER has adapted the command with /L and /S switches, remember that the question mark goes with the equal sign, as follows:

```
DEVICEHIGH /L:1,8902 /S ?=C:\DOS\RAMDRIVE.SYS
```

Using Configuration Blocks

DOS 6 includes a set of new commands for CONFIG.SYS that let you display a menu, input a choice from the keyboard, and execute a block of commands according to which menu item was chosen. The following sample CONFIG.SYS file shows how these commands are used:

```
[MENU]
MENUITEM=EXPAND, Set up expanded memory
MENUITEM=NO-EXPAND, Don't set up expanded memory
MENUCOLOR=15,1
MENUDEFAULT=NO-EXPAND, 10

[COMMON]
DEVICE=C:\DOS\HIMEM.SYS
DOS=HIGH
```

```
BUFFERS=15
FILES=40

[EXPAND]
DEVICE=C:\DOS\EMM386.EXE RAM
DOS=UMB

[NO-EXPAND]
DEVICE=C:\DOS\EMM386.EXE NOEMS
DOS=UMB
```

The first block of commands defines a menu that will appear on the command prompt screen as follows:

```
MS-DOS 6 Startup Menu

--------------------

    1.  Set up expanded memory
    2.  Don't set up expanded memory

Enter a choice: 2    Time remaining: 10
```

The menu appears in bright white letters on a blue background. If the user doesn't enter a choice, the time remaining counts down to zero; then the default choice (2) is taken.

The block of commands labeled [COMMON] is executed no matter which choice is taken. The block labeled [EXPAND] is executed only if the first choice is selected. The block labeled [NO-EXPAND] is executed only if the second choice is selected.

Defining a Menu

To define a menu, create a block labeled [MENU]. For each item in the menu, insert a command in the following format:

```
MENUITEM=blockname[,menu-text]
```

The *blockname* identifies the block of commands to be executed if this item is chosen. *Blockname* can be up to 70 characters long and contain any printable characters except spaces, commas, \, /, ;, =, [, and].

Menu-text identifies the text to be displayed in the menu. *Menu-text* can be up to 70 characters long. If you don't define any menu text, the block name is displayed.

The MENUCOLOR command defines the colors for the menu screen:

```
MENUCOLOR=text[,background]
```

The codes used to define the colors are shown in Table 5.1.

Table 5.1. Color Codes

Code	Color	Code	Color
1	Black	9	Gray
2	Blue	10	Bright blue
3	Green	11	Bright green
4	Cyan	12	Bright cyan
5	Red	13	Bright red
6	Magenta	14	Bright magenta
7	Brown	15	Yellow
8	White	16	Bright white

The default background color is black.

The MENUDEFAULT command established a default if the user doesn't make a choice within so many seconds. The command format is as follows:

```
MENUDEFAULT=blockname[,timeout]
```

Blockname identifies the configuration block to be executed by default. *Timeout* establishes the number of seconds to wait before taking the default, from 0 to 90 seconds. If you omit *timeout*, DOS waits forever. The default is taken when the user presses the Enter key without typing a menu choice.

Submenus

You also can define submenu items; a submenu is displayed if the associated menu item is selected. The following example uses a submenu for the first menu item:

```
[MENU]
SUBMENU=EXPAND, Set up expanded memory
MENUITEM=NO-EXPAND, Don't set up expanded memory
MENUCOLOR=15,1
MENUDEFAULT=NO-EXPAND, 10

[COMMON]
DEVICE=C:\DOS\HIMEM.SYS
DOS=HIGH
BUFFERS=15
FILES=40

[EXPAND]
MENUITEM=SMALL, 2M minimum
MENUITEM=BIG, 4M minimum
MENUDEFAULT=SMALL, 10

[SMALL]
DEVICE=C:\DOS\EMM386.EXE RAM 2048
DOS=UMB

[BIG]
DEVICE=C:\DOS\EMM386.EXE RAM 4096
DOS=UMB

[NO-EXPAND]
DEVICE=C:\DOS\EMM386.EXE NOEMS
DOS=UMB
```

The initial menu looks the same as before. However, if the user chooses item number 1, the following submenu appears:

```
1.  2M minimum
2.  4M minimum
```

```
Enter choice: 1    Time remaining: 10
```

To define a submenu, insert a command in the main menu in this format:

```
SUBMENU=blockname[,text]
```

The *blockname* should refer to a block that defines menu items for the submenu.

Common Blocks

A block labeled [COMMON] is executed no matter which menu choice is taken. Place in this block all the commands that should be executed regardless of the menu choice. In the preceding example, the common block is positioned so that it is executed before the alternate blocks so that HIMEM.SYS is loaded before EMM386.EXE.

You can have more than one common block. You could rewrite the preceding example so that the DOS=UMB command appears in a second common block that comes after the alternative blocks that load EMM386.EXE. The revised CONFIG.SYS would appear as follows:

```
[MENU]
SUBMENU=EXPAND, Set up expanded memory
MENUITEM=NO-EXPAND, Don't set up expanded memory
MENUCOLOR=15,1
MENUDEFAULT=NO-EXPAND, 10

[COMMON]
DEVICE=C:\DOS\HIMEM.SYS
DOS=HIGH
BUFFERS=15
FILES=40

[EXPAND]
MENUITEM=SMALL, 2M minimum
MENUITEM=BIG, 4M minimum
MENUDEFAULT=SMALL, 10

[SMALL]
DEVICE=C:\DOS\EMM386.EXE RAM 2048

[BIG]
DEVICE=C:\DOS\EMM386.EXE RAM 4096

[NO-EXPAND]
DEVICE=C:\DOS\EMM386.EXE NOEMS

[COMMON]
DOS=UMB
```

It's a good idea to insert at the end of CONFIG.SYS a [COMMON] block, even if it's empty. This way, when you install new applications that add commands to CONFIG.SYS, the new commands go into a common block instead of your last alternate configuration block.

Including Blocks

The INCLUDE command lets you include one configuration block in another. Suppose that you have a situation in which a set of commands appears in three out of five of the alternative configurations, as follows:

```
[MENU]
...

[COMMON]
...

[JUDI]
DEVICE=C:\DOS\EMM386.EXE NOEMS
DOS=HIGH
DEVICEHIGH=C:\DOS\ANSI.SYS /K
FCBS=20

[PETER]
DEVICE=C:\DOS\EMM386.EXE NOEMS
DOS=HIGH
DEVICEHIGH=C:\DOS\ANSI.SYS /K
FCBS=20
...

[RUTH]
...

[MIKE]
DEVICE=C:\DOS\EMM386.EXE NOEMS
DOS=HIGH
DEVICEHIGH=C:\DOS\ANSI.SYS /K
FCBS=20
...
```

```
[SCOTT]
...

[COMMON]
```

The commands in the [JUDI] block are repeated in the [PETER] and [MIKE] blocks. Furthermore, [JUDI] doesn't contain any other commands that don't belong in the [PETER] and [MIKE] blocks. In this situation, you could use the INCLUDE command to avoid repeating the commands in question, as follows:

```
[MENU]
...

[COMMON]
...

[JUDI]
DEVICE=C:\DOS\EMM386.EXE NOEMS
DOS=HIGH
DEVICEHIGH=C:\DOS\ANSI.SYS /K
FCBS=20

[PETER]
INCLUDE=JUDI
...

[RUTH]
...

[MIKE]
INCLUDE=JUDI
...

[SCOTT]
...

[COMMON]
```

The INCLUDE commands cause all the commands in the [JUDI] block to be executed. Not only does this save you some time and space, it makes it easier to modify those particular commands for all the configuration blocks that use them.

Chapter 9 shows you how to deal with alternate configurations in
AUTOEXEC.BAT.

Directory Management

Introduction

DOS 6 includes two new directory management commands that DOS users have been wanting for a long time: DELTREE deletes an entire branch without making you empty each directory first, and MOVE renames a directory.

This chapter also describes some ways that you can manipulate your directory structure when you have to deal with less-than-perfect programs.

MOVE

The MOVE command has two basic functions: to move files from one directory to another and to rename directories. Figure 6.1 shows the MOVE command format for renaming directories. You cannot rename the current directory, and both the old name and the new name must have the same path. If ACTIVE is a child of the current directory, the following command renames it as INACTIVE:

```
MOVE ACTIVE INACTIVE
```

Figure 6.1.
MOVE command reference (to rename directories).

MOVE

Renames a file or directory.

Format:

```
MOVE oldname   newname
```

Parameters:

oldname   Identifies the directory to be renamed.

newname   Specifies the new name for the directory.

DELTREE

You used to have to delete a branch one directory at a time, making sure that each directory was empty first. The process was awkward and sometimes frustrating, especially if some of the directories contained hidden, system, or read-only files. It was nearly impossible to delete a branch in a batch program unless you knew the name of every directory in the branch.

Now you can accomplish the entire task with one DELTREE command (see fig. 6.2). DELTREE deletes all the files in the specified directory, regardless of attributes, along with all its descendants and their files. To delete the branch headed by \ACTIVE93, enter the following command:

```
DELTREE \ACTIVE93
```

When you enter this command, DELTREE asks you to confirm the deletion. You can bypass the confirmation step by including the /Y switch in the command, but it must come before the path name or DELTREE ignores it. The /Y switch is particularly useful when you want to delete a temporary branch that you created in a batch program; with /Y, DOS doesn't ask users to confirm a DELTREE command for a branch they have never heard of.

> DELTREE comes in handy even when a directory has no subdirectories. It deletes the directory without making you empty it first.

If you try to delete the current directory, DELTREE deletes all its files and its descendants, but it doesn't delete the directory itself. If you try to delete the branch headed by the root directory, DELTREE deletes all the files in the root directory along with the rest of the directory structure, but it doesn't delete the root directory. If you don't specify the /Y switch, it asks you to confirm every file in the root directory.

If the current directory is contained in the branch to be deleted, DELTREE deletes the files throughout the branch, and it deletes whatever directories it can, but it retains the current directory and its ancestors.

> DELTREE is a good way to delete all the files in the current directory regardless of attributes. However, keep in mind that DELTREE also will delete all the directory's descendants, if it has any.

You can use wildcards in the name of the directory to be deleted. DELTREE will delete all directories *and files* that match the global name. For example, suppose that the current directory contains subdirectories named BUDGET93 and BUDGET94. In addition, it contains a file named BUDGETS. The command DELTREE BUDGET* would delete the file as well as the two branches. For safety's sake, omit the /Y switch when you use a global name. Suppose that you want to delete all BAK files on drive C. The following command accomplishes the task:

```
DELTREE C:\*.BAK
```

Figure 6.2.
DELTREE
command reference.

DELTREE

Deletes a directory and all its files and subdirectories; deletes files in a directory.

Format:

```
DELTREE [/Y] path ¦ filespec
```

Parameters and Switches:

/Y   Carries out DELTREE without first prompting you for confirmation.

path   Specifies the directory at the top of the branch that you want to delete.

filespec   Specifies file(s) and/or directories that you want to delete.

Notes:

You can't use DELTREE to delete the current directory. You can, however, delete files and children of the current directory.

You can use wildcards. DELTREE deletes every file and subdirectory (with all its contents) whose name matches the global name.

DELTREE always prompts you for confirmation before deleting a file or a branch.

When DELTREE is successful, it returns an exit code of 0.

PATH

It's inconvenient to have to change drives and directories or to specify a path for programs that you use frequently. The PATH command (see fig. 6.3) sets up a program search path—a list of directories that DOS will search when trying to find a program that has no path specified and isn't in the current directory. The following PATH command identifies three directories to be searched:

```
PATH C:\DOS;C:\WORD;C:\123
```

Figure 6.3.
PATH command reference.

PATH

Defines a search path for external executable files (including batch files).

Format:

```
PATH-[path [;path]...]
```

```
PATH ;
```
Parameters:

none   Displays the current search path.

path   Identifies a directory to search for program files.

;   When used as the only parameter, clears the search path.

You probably have a PATH command in your AUTOEXEC.BAT file; it sets your search path while booting. Any major application that includes its own installation program probably adds its directory to your PATH command in AUTOEXEC.BAT automatically—maybe even putting itself first in the path. Review and adjust your PATH command periodically to make sure that it still reflects the way you work on your computer.

PATH Recommendations

Be sure to use absolute filespecs in the PATH command so that DOS can find the directories no matter what drive or directory is current. For the fastest search times, the directories should be listed in order from the most frequently used to the least frequently used. That way, most searches will be resolved in the first few directories of the search path, and only occasionally will DOS reach the end of the search path.

Also, keep the search path as short as possible so that DOS doesn't have to search a long time to decide that a program file cannot be found.

Invalid Directory Message

If the PATH command references a path that doesn't exist, DOS will not notice or issue a warning until it is actually searching for a program and tries to access the missing directory. Then DOS displays the following message and goes on to the next directory in the search path:

```
Invalid Directory
```

When you see this message, review your PATH command and fix it if necessary. You also may get this message if your hard drive is starting to develop problems and DOS encounters difficulty finding a directory. Run CHKDSK to see whether it can find and fix any problems.

You also will run into problems if you have included a floppy disk drive in the path. You will get an error message if DOS finds the drive empty while traveling the search path.

Managing the Search Path

Enter PATH with a semicolon (as in PATH;) to cancel the current path. Enter the following command to see your current PATH:

```
C:\>PATH
PATH=C:\DOS;C:\WORD;C:\123
C:\>
```

Notice that the message assumes the form of a legitimate PATH command. You can take advantage of that to preserve and restore the current path in a batch program that changes the path temporarily. In the following example, the current path is saved in a file called SETPATH.BAT and then restored by executing that batch file:

```
REM Save the current path in a batch file:
PATH > C:\SETPATH.BAT
   .
   .
   .
```

```
REM Restore the former path:
CALL C:\SETPATH
DEL C:\SETPATH.BAT
```

Recommendations for Directory Structure

You can do a number of things to optimize your directory structure for ease of use and fast file access.

To keep paths short, avoid creating more than three or four levels of subdirectories. The longer the path, the more chance of making a typing error. Also, DOS commands are limited to 127 characters, and you would run out of command space when trying to copy the following:

```
C:\JNFILES\WP\DOCS\DOSBOOK\FIGURES\FIG3-1.PCX
```

to

```
D:\STORAGE\BACKUPS\JNF\DOCS\DOSBOOK\FIGURES\SAVE3-1.PCX
```

The time to access a file on your hard disk will be shortest if all your directories are located near the beginning of the disk (with the ones in the search path being the first ones), with the files you use most often (such as the DOS program files) coming immediately after. This means that the read-write heads don't have to move very far to find a directory and then a desired file. However, it's difficult to arrange your hard disk that way using only DOS commands. If you notice your disk access time slowing down as you add more directories and files to your hard disk, you may consider getting one of the third-party utilities that reorganizes a disk for faster access.

> Another major factor in disk access speed is file fragmentation, which is discussed in Chapter 11.

Restructuring a Directory Tree

You may occasionally have to deal with some older software that recognizes drives A and B only or doesn't accept path names. The SUBST command can help you out until you upgrade or replace the out-of-date software.

You also may sometimes find it convenient to create a search path for data files much as the PATH command does for program files. The APPEND command makes a directory available no matter what directory is current.

This discussion groups these commands together because they all mask the true directory structure and must be approached with a great deal of caution—they can fool your software into accessing the wrong directory or files. Use them only when necessary and no longer than necessary. APPEND is never necessary, and most experts recommend that you never use it.

Many commands that work on drives and directories should not be applied to masked ones. They could end up producing erroneous (or even disastrous) results. Restricted commands are listed in the command reference figures and in your DOS documentation. Any time you use SUBST or APPEND, keep a red flag at the back of your mind that commands such as FORMAT and CHKDSK are dangerous.

SUBST

Suppose that you're working with an early version of a program called LOCKOUT that expects its program files to be on drive A and its data files to be on drive B. You don't even have a separate drive B. However, you have created two RAM drives, D and E, and copied the necessary files to them. The following batch program uses the SUBST command to reassign the drive names. Figure 6.4 describes the SUBST command.

```
@ECHO OFF
REM Reassign drives A and B:
C:
SUBST A: D:\
SUBST B: E:\
```

```
REM Run LOCKOUT:
A:
LOCKOUT

REM Restore the rightful drive names:
C:
SUBST A: /D
SUBST B: /D
```

Figure 6.4.
SUBST command
reference.

SUBST

Reassigns a drive name to refer to a path.

Format:

SUBST [*drive: path*] ¦ [*drive:* /D]

Parameters and Switches:

none   Displays substitutions currently in force.

drive   Identifies drive name to be reassigned.

path   Specifies path to be referred to by *drive*.

/D   Deletes the indicated substitution.

Notes:

Path must refer to a path on an existing drive. *Path* may include a drive name; if it does not, DOS assumes that *path* is on the drive current at the time SUBST is executed.

After a substitution is made, any reference to *drive* is redirected to *path*. If *drive* actually exists, you will not be able to access it until you cancel the substitution. (If *drive* contains your DOS commands, you will not be able to use any external DOS commands, including SUBST.)

Do not use the following commands on a substituted drive name: ASSIGN, MSBACKUP, CHKDSK, DISKCOMP, DISKCOPY, FDISK, FORMAT, LABEL, MIRROR, RECOVER, RESTORE, SYS.

Start by switching to drive C to make sure that neither drive A nor B is current, because the current drive can't be redirected via a SUBST command. After the substitutions are made, any reference to drive A actually accesses D:\, and any reference to drive B: actually references E:\. The last two commands in the batch clear the substitutions so that A and B are normal again. It's necessary to switch to another drive before clearing them because you can't clear the substitution for the current drive.

SUBST also solves problems with programs that don't recognize paths. (For example, early versions of WordStar didn't.) Suppose that you have a program named PLUS4 that recognizes only drive names, not paths. You want to use PLUS4 with the C:\TODAY directory. You can assign it a fake drive name, called a *virtual* drive name, as in this batch program:

```
@ECHO OFF
SUBST F: C:\TODAY
PLUS4
C:
SUBST F: /D
```

When PLUS4 asks for a drive name, entering F: causes it to access the C:\PLUS4 directory.

Choosing a Drive Name for SUBST

In the PLUS4 example, there is no real drive F. We could have used a real drive such as A or B, but that would have made the real drive unavailable as long as the substitution was in effect. We didn't use a RAM drive name for the same reason.

Whatever drive name you choose must be available. Although DOS offers the potential of 26 drive names (A through Z), it doesn't automatically make all of them available. By default, DOS permits either five drive names (A through E) or the number of drive names that you actually have drives for (including RAM drives), whichever is larger. You must use the LASTDRIVE command in CONFIG.SYS (see fig. 6.5) to make more drive names available.

Suppose that you have a common setup—two floppy disk drives (A and B) and one hard drive. The names D and E are available for SUBST and ASSIGN commands. What if you have four hard disk drives (C through F)? By default, no virtual drive names are available for SUBST and ASSIGN commands. You can make two virtual drive names available (G and H) by inserting the following command in C:\CONFIG.SYS:

```
LASTDRIVE=H
```

Figure 6.5.
LASTDRIVE
CONFIG.SYS
command reference.

LASTDRIVE

Specifies the highest drive letter, and therefore, the maximum number of drives that your system can access.

Format:

```
LASTDRIVE=x
```

Parameter:

x   Specifies a drive letter, A through Z. The minimum value is the highest drive letter in use by your system.

DOS maintains a drive name table in memory, with each entry taking nearly 100 bytes. You can conserve valuable memory space by requesting only as many drive names as you actually need. If you make all possible drive names available by inserting LASTDRIVE=Z in CONFIG.SYS when in fact you need only four drive names, you're wasting a couple of kilobytes of memory space.

Switching Disk Drives with SUBST

SUBST also can help you solve a problem that crops up occasionally. Suppose that you want to install an application from 3 1/2-inch disks, which fit only in your B drive, but the application must be installed from the A drive. You can make the installation work by substituting B:\ for A: before starting up the installation program:

```
C:\>SUBST A: B:\
C:\>A:
A:\>INSTALL
```

After the installation program is finished, use the following:

```
A:\>C:
C:\>SUBST A:  /D
```

If you need to boot from a disk that fits only in your B drive, more drastic measures are called for. You have to switch the cables to your A and B drives and, for 286 or higher machines, run the SETUP program to redefine the drives. (See your hardware manual or your dealer for instructions on how to access and use SETUP for your machine.)

TRUENAME

When you have masked the true directory structure with SUBST or ASSIGN, you may be confused about what the current directory is or in what directory a file resides. DOS includes an undocumented command called TRUENAME (see fig. 6.6) that shows the true path of a directory or file.

Figure 6.6.
TRUENAME
command reference.

<u>**TRUENAME**</u>

Identifies the true location of a directory or file.

Format:

TRUENAME [*drive* ¦ *path* ¦ *filespec*]

Parameters:

none	Displays the true name of the current drive and directory.
drive	Displays the true name of *drive*.
path	Displays the true name of the indicated directory.
filespec	Displays the true filespec of the indicated file.

To find out the true name of the current directory, enter TRUENAME with no parameters. The result appears as follows:

```
A:\>TRUENAME
C:\LOCKOUT\
A:\>
```

To find out the true location of a file, enter the filespec as a parameter:

```
A:\>TRUENAME LOCKOUT.DAT
C:\LOCKOUT\LOCKOUT.DAT
A:\>
```

This message would be displayed even if the current directory does not contain a file named LOCKOUT.DAT. All TRUENAME does is fill in the true path; it doesn't check to see whether the file exists.

APPEND for Your Thoughts

APPEND looks great on the surface—it makes the files in a specified list of directories available no matter what directory is current. APPEND resembles the PATH command but applies to data files. However, the fly lands in the ointment when you're modifying a file from an appended directory, as illustrated in Figure 6.7.

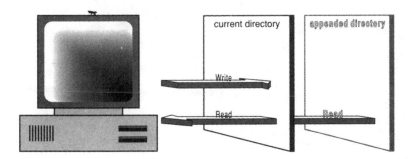

Figure 6.7.
Directory mix-ups
with APPEND.

The problem occurs when an application updates a file by saving a new copy instead of rewriting the existing copy. To the application, the file appears to be in the current directory; only DOS knows about the appended directory. Therefore, the application saves the updated version in the current directory, and DOS doesn't reroute it to the appended directory. The overall result is that the new version is in the wrong directory, and the original version, in the right directory, has not been updated. This can happen not only to the data files you work on but also the support files that are essential to an application's functions (such as DOSSHELL.INI).

In case you think this is a rare problem, you should understand that most applications update files this way—all the major word processors, desktop publishers, graphics developers, text editors, spreadsheet programs, and so on. The most common exceptions are database managers, which tend to update files in place rather than save new copies.

The slight convenience that APPEND offers is not worth the dangers.

Copying Files

7

Introduction

DOS's copying commands have evolved from COPY, which has many limitations, to the much more sophisticated XCOPY, MOVE, and REPLACE. You also may need to use DOS backup programs to make copies in certain cases.

Comparing COPY and XCOPY

Table 7.1 compares advantages and disadvantages of the two main copying commands, COPY and XCOPY.

Table 7.1. Comparing COPY and XCOPY

Command	Advantages	Disadvantages
COPY	Can concatenate files	Slower than XCOPY
	Can change the date/time stamp on a file	Selects files by name only
	Can copy to and from nondisk devices	Handles only one directory at a time
		Doesn't set exit code
		Terminates when target disk is full
		Can't handle large files
		Has no prompt facility
		Replaces files of the same name on a target disk without warning
XCOPY	Faster than COPY	Terminates when target disk is full
	Will copy branch structure (including empty subdirectories, if requested)	Can't concatenate files
	Can create destination directories	Can't change date/time stamp

Command	Advantages	Disadvantages
	Selects files by name, date, and/or archive attribute	Can't copy to/from nondisk devices
	Will turn off archive attributes of copied files, if requested	Can't handle large files
	Sets exit code	Replaces files of the same name on a target disk without warning
	Will prompt you with names of files selected for copying, if requested	Sometimes has to ask whether the target is a file or a directory

COPY and XCOPY are the two commands that do garden-variety copies, and XCOPY is the command of choice for a number of reasons.

- When copying multiple files, COPY reads and then writes one file at a time; whereas XCOPY reads as much data as memory will hold and then writes that much data, a much faster method.

- COPY can select files by name only, but XCOPY also can select files by their archive attribute and date/time stamp. This feature lets you use XCOPY to back up your hard disk if you don't care for the new Backup programs.

- COPY can select files from one directory only; whereas XCOPY can copy an entire branch, creating subdirectories under the destination directory as needed to duplicate the source branch.

- XCOPY will create the destination directory if it doesn't already exist.

- Sometimes, empty files are created by an application. An empty file has a directory entry, including a name, but contains no data. COPY will not copy an empty file, but XCOPY will. Which is better? That depends on what you want.

- Unlike COPY, XCOPY sets an exit code (see Appendix A). This is an advantage when copying files in batch programs, especially if you plan to erase the source files after copying them.

COPY can do a few things that XCOPY can't: COPY can concatenate (combine) files, change the date/time stamp for a file, and copy to and from nondisk devices. Generally, you should use COPY for these functions and XCOPY for everything else.

XCOPY and the Backup Programs

Neither COPY nor XCOPY can handle a file larger than the size of the target disk. If you need to copy a very large file, you'll need to use one of the backup programs, which can compress data on the target disk as well as span a file over two or more diskettes, if necessary. The backup programs are explained in Chapter 13.

If you have installed DBLSPACE, you can squeeze a lot more data on a target disk. Chapter 12 explains DBLSPACE.

XCOPY can be used to copy a large set of files that will require several target disks, but the procedure is awkward. You have to clear the archive attributes of all the source files in the process, which could interfere with your normal backup routine. Here again, one of the backup programs is probably the better choice.

The backup programs have a third major advantage in making copies: they have the best verification facility of any of the copy programs. They reread the destination file, compare it to the source file, and correct the destination file if necessary.

However, the backup programs don't produce usable copies; you have to run them again to restore the backed up files to their original form. Therefore, if you want to use a backup program to transfer a very large file or a large set of files to another computer, the target computer also must be using DOS 6 and have the backup programs available. You couldn't use a backup program to create distribution disks for customers, for example, unless you know that they have DOS 6.

INTERLNK provides another means of transferring large files and large sets of files between computers without having to use disks in the middle. Chapter 8 explains INTERLNK.

XCOPY versus DISKCOPY

You often may need to copy an entire disk. The DISKCOPY command makes a track-by-track copy of one floppy disk to another disk of exactly the same size. XCOPY also can be used to copy whole diskettes, which it does on a file-by-file basis, with the following advantages:

- You don't need to use the same size source and target disks. You could copy a 1.2M disk to a 1.44M disk, for example.

- XCOPY doesn't copy the source disk's formatting, which may not be accurate for the target disk. For example, DISKCOPY copies bad sector markings from the source to the target, blocking out sectors on the target diskette that aren't really bad.

- DISKCOPY fails if there are bad sectors on the target disk; XCOPY doesn't.

- DISKCOPY destroys any existing files on the target disk; XCOPY doesn't.

- With DISKCOPY, if files are fragmented (split into separate parts) on the source, they have the same fragmentation on the target. XCOPY actually defragments files as it copies them, as long as the target disk was empty to start with.

The XCOPY Command

Figure 7.1 shows the format of the XCOPY command (which some people call "ex-copy;" some call "cross-copy;" and some call "extended copy"). In its simplest form, it copies a file or set of files from one place to another. The following command copies all the DOC files from the current directory to the default directory on drive A, where they will receive the same names they have in the current directory:

```
C:\PLAYS>XCOPY *.DOC A:
Reading source file(s)...
VOLUMES.DOC
ENCOUNTR.DOC
        2 File(s) copied
```

Figure 7.1.
XCOPY command
reference.

XCOPY

Copies files and subdirectories.

Format:

```
XCOPY source [destination] [/A ¦ /M] [/D:date] [/P]
[/S [/E]] [/V] [/W]
```

Parameters and Switches:

source	Identifies the file(s) you want to copy.
destination	Specifies the location where the copy should be written; the default is the current directory.
/A	Copies only source files with positive archive attributes; does not change the archive attributes.
/M	Copies only source files with positive archive attributes; turns off the archive attributes.
/D:*date*	Copies only source files created or modified on or after *date*.
/P	Prompts you for permission to copy each selected file.
/S	Extends copying to the entire branch headed by the source directory.
/E	Copies empty subdirectories when copying to the entire branch. You must use /S if you use /E.
/V	Verifies each copy.
/W	Displays a message and waits for you to press a key before beginning to copy files.

Notes:

XCOPY turns on the archive attribute of each copy but copies the source files' date/time stamps.

When *source* includes a filename, *destination* can include a filename, and the two files can be in the same directory. When the *source* filespec includes wildcards, and *destination* is a directory, XCOPY selects each file matching the specification.

If both *source* and *destination* include global filespecs, XCOPY looks for and replaces destination files with the same wildcard characters in their filenames, creating new files as necessary. For example, in XCOPY CHAP*.DOC A:CHAP*.BAK, XCOPY copies CHAP1.DOC to A:CHAP1.BAK, creating A:CHAP1.BAK if necessary.

If *source* is global and *destination* is a single file, XCOPY copies each file in turn to the same *destination* file; *destination* ends up as the last *source* file copied.

If *destination* does not identify an existing directory and does not end with \, XCOPY asks you whether *destination* is a directory or a file. (If it ends with \, XCOPY knows that the destination is a directory.)

If you use XCOPY in a batch file or DOSKEY macro to copy files to or from a floppy disk, you can use /W to provide time for someone to insert a disk in the drive before XCOPY starts processing files.

You can create a backup system using XCOPY. Use XCOPY without the /A, /M, or /D switches to do a full backup. Use XCOPY with /M for incremental backups or /A for differential backups. /D with an appropriate date also can be used for an in-between backup; use the date of the last full backup for a differential backup or the date of the last incremental backup for another incremental backup.

If *date* is the day of the previous backup, you may end up with duplicate copies of files created on *date* before you backed up: one in the previous backup and one in this backup. If *date* is the day after the previous backup, you may miss files created on the day of the previous backup but after you backed up.

Copying Branches

One of XCOPY's strengths is copying complete branches. Suppose that you want to copy a branch from drive C to drive D. You don't even have to create the target directory first; XCOPY will do it for you. After turning off all hidden and system attributes (because XCOPY will not copy hidden or system files), use a command such as the following:

```
XCOPY C:\JNFSET D:\JNFSET /S /E
```

If the D:\JNFSET directory does not exist, XCOPY starts by asking the following question:

```
Does D:\JNFSET specify a file name
or directory name on the target
(F = file, D = directory)?
```

In this case, you need to answer D for directory. XCOPY creates the directory and copies all files and subdirectories to it so that it ends up being a duplicate of the JNFSET branch on the C drive.

> You can avoid the `file or directory` question by putting a backslash after the destination path so that it cannot be mistaken for a filename:
>
> ```
> XCOPY C:\JNFSET D:\JNFSET\ /S /E
> ```

If D:\JNFSET already exists, XCOPY uses the existing branch, creating subdirectories only if they're missing from the target branch.

If you include a filespec with XCOPY and /S, only the specified files are copied to the destination. Without /E, directories that will not receive any files or subdirectories aren't created. With /E, all target subdirectories are created, whether they are empty or not.

Copying a File to the Same Directory

XCOPY can copy a single file to the same directory as long as you assign it a new name. In this case, XCOPY always asks the `file or directory` question, to which you answer F for file. (If you answer D, XCOPY creates a directory as a child of the current directory and copies the file to the new directory using its old filename.)

Avoiding Disk Full Termination

One disadvantage that both COPY and XCOPY share is the irksome habit of terminating themselves when the target disk is full. Suppose that you have indicated that all *.DOC files should be copied to drive A, and COPY or XCOPY copies about half of them before the disk is full. Then it quits, returning you to the DOS prompt. Now what do you do? If you insert another disk in the A drive and reenter the same COPY or XCOPY command, the same files will be selected and copied a second time because the program has no way of knowing that some of the files are not wanted. Your only recourse is to figure out which files have not yet been copied and copy them one by one.

You can avoid this problem in several ways. One way is to use DOS Shell, which enables you to continue a copy operation after changing the target disk. Another solution uses the backup programs, which are discussed in Chapter 13. A third solution uses the archive attributes with XCOPY. The drawback to this solution is that it alters the archive attributes of the source files, which can affect your backup system later on. Nevertheless, it may be the best solution for the problem. The XCOPY procedure works as follows:

1. Turn on the archive attribute of every file you want to copy. (Also, turn off hidden and system attributes if you want to copy those files.)

2. Start XCOPY for those files using the /M switch to turn off the archive attribute of each successfully copied file.

3. When the current disk is full, insert a new disk and repeat step 2. The files that have already been copied will not be recopied because their archive attributes are now off.

A batch file for this procedure may look something like the one that follows. %1 is the filespec of the files to be copied. This procedure prints out the original attributes of the source files so that they can be restored later if necessary.

```
@ECHO OFF
REM Record the current attributes in case we want to
REM restore them when the job is done.
ECHO Current attributes for the %1 files: > PRN
```

```
ECHO. > PRN
ATTRIB %1 /S > PRN

REM Turn on the archive attributes for all %1 files.
REM Also, turn off their hidden and system attributes.
ATTRIB %1 /S +A -H -S

:COPYLOOP
REM Copy all the %1 files that have positive archive
REM attributes. Turn off attributes as you copy:
ECHO Insert the next target diskette in drive A:
PAUSE
XCOPY %1 A: /S /M

REM Repeat loop if XCOPY terminated unsuccessfully
REM for any reason.
IF ERRORLEVEL 1 GOTO COPYLOOP

:ENDING
ECHO ****************************************************
ECHO *                                                  *
ECHO *  The archive, hidden, and system attributes      *
ECHO *  have been removed from the source files.        *
ECHO *  Check the printout and restore attributes as    *
ECHO *  needed.                                         *
ECHO *                                                  *
ECHO ****************************************************
```

You could make this job more useful by adding the following features:

- Accept the target drive name or path as %2.

- Accept Y or N as %3 to indicate whether or not hidden and system files should be copied or accept the Y or N from the keyboard with the CHOICE command.

Pruning and Grafting

The tree surgeon's terms, *pruning* and *grafting*, are used in PCs to describe the movement of a directory or branch from one parent to another. If you don't have a third-party utility to prune and graft, you can do it using XCOPY and DELTREE. In the following list of steps, *path1* identifies the directory or branch to be moved, and *path2* identifies the new parent.

1. Document hidden, system, and read-only attributes so that they can be restored later if necessary:

   ```
   ATTRIB path1\*.* /S > PRN:
   ```

2. Remove the following attributes:

   ```
   ATTRIB path1\*.* /S -H -S
   ```

3. Copy the entire branch to the new parent directory (which XCOPY will create if it doesn't already exist):

   ```
   XCOPY path1 path2 /S /E /V
   ```

4. After making sure that the branch was copied correctly, remove the source branch:

   ```
   DELTREE /Y path1
   ```

5. Using the printout from step 1, restore the hidden, system, and read-only attributes to each file as necessary:

   ```
   ATTRIB filespec attribute(s)
   ```

It's possible to make a batch file out of steps 1 through 4, but the last step can't be done in a batch program because you will not know the filespecs and attributes in advance.

Verification

Mistakes can occur during a copy operation as a result of hardware failure, disk media failure, or power fluctuations. Mistakes are rare as long as your drive is healthy, but they do happen sometimes. By default, DOS does not verify copies. The /V switch forces each copy to be verified, which slows down the copy process. You should be aware that this is not a 100-percent verification. It will catch most, but not all, errors. Verification methods, including a foolproof one, are discussed in Chapter 14.

Clobbering Files with XCOPY and COPY

Both COPY and XCOPY have one problem in common. They both clobber an existing file without warning. For example, if you copy A:\MEMBERS.DB to C:\SFGROUP\MEMBERS.DB, but SFGROUP already contains a file named MEMBERS.DB, COPY and XCOPY replace the existing file with the copy, and you will not see any message that the replacement was made. You will not be able to recover the clobbered file with DOS's UNDELETE, either.

Recovering a Clobbered File

If you do accidentally replace a file during a copy, all is not necessarily lost. COPY and XCOPY replace the file entry in the directory and mark the old file's space for reuse, but they don't actually overlay the data on the disk. A third-party recovery program that can access unallocated disk space, such as the Norton Utilities' UnErase, can recover the data.

However, you must recover the clobbered data immediately, as it's highly vulnerable sitting in reusable disk space. The next data you add to the disk may go into that space. In fact, if you start up an application such as a word processor, it may open a temporary file for itself during its startup routine and use the space you want to rescue. Therefore, when you realize that you have clobbered a file and that you need to recover it, don't do *anything* until you have recovered it.

But, go ahead and try recovering even if you have added data to the disk. You may get lucky and be able to rescue all or at least part of the data.

Difficulties in Avoiding Clobbering

You may think that you can write a batch program using IF EXIST to identify an existing file with the same name in the destination directory, but a total solution is not really possible because of the variety of ways that the source and destination can be expressed in an XCOPY command. The following routine works if the source (%1) is a single or global filespec referring only to the current directory (with no path specified); the target (%2) is the path of another directory; and no XCOPY switches (such as /S) are specified.

```
REM Warn user about files that won't be copied:
FOR %%F IN (%1) DO IF EXIST %2\%%F ECHO %%F won't be
copied because a target version already exists

REM Copy files that won't clobber existing copies:
FOR %%F IN (%1) DO IF NOT EXIST %2\%%F XCOPY %%F %2
```

Burying the XCOPY command in the FOR command slows the copy procedure tremendously, but you need to check only one file at a time with IF [NOT] EXIST, or the results could be wrong.

You could create a batch program using FOR, CHOICE, IF, and CALL that gives the user the option of copying a file when a target version exists, but that makes a complex job out of a function that is already available with the REPLACE command, as you see at the end of this chapter.

Moving Files

Until DOS 6, if you wanted to move files by using commands instead of DOS Shell, you had to copy them to the destination and delete the source files. This procedure always was risky because it was difficult to verify that the copies were successful before deleting the originals. Now DOS 6 includes a MOVE command (see fig. 7.2) that removes the risk. If you have batch files that use the old copy and delete method, you should update them with MOVE.

The COPY Command

The COPY command has some features you can't find anywhere else in DOS:

- COPY can concatenate files; it combines two or more files into one.
- COPY can update the date/time stamp on a file.
- COPY can copy to and from devices.

Figure 7.3 shows the format of COPY for concatenating files only.

Figure 7.2.
MOVE command
reference.

> ### MOVE
>
> Moves one or more files to another location.
>
> **Format:**
>
> MOVE *filespec* [...] *destination*
>
> **Parameters:**
>
> | | |
> |---|---|
> | *filespec* | Identifies the file(s) you want to move or rename. |
> | *destination* | Identifies the file or directory to which you want to move file(s) or the new name for the file. |

MOVE assumes that the last entry on the command line is *destination*. Any other entries on the line are *filespecs*. *Filespec* may include wildcards. You can move all the DOC files to drive A with this command:

```
MOVE *.DOC A:
```

If you move more than one file, *destination* must be a directory, not a filename.

If you move only one file, *destination* can be (or include) a new filename; in that case, the file is moved and/or renamed. If the *destination* file already exists, MOVE overwrites it without warning you. (Notice the difference from RENAME, which will not give a file a name already in the directory and will not move a file to a new directory.)

Concatenating Files

Suppose that you want to combine three ASCII files named PART1, PART2, and PART3 into a new file named REPORT. The following command will do it:

```
C:\DOCS>COPY PART1 + PART2 + PART3 REPORT
PART1
PART2
PART3
     1 File(s) copied

>C:\DOCS>
```

Figure 7.3.
COPY *command reference (for concatenation).*

COPY (for concatenation)

Combines two or more files into one.

Format:

```
COPY [switches] source [+...] [destination] [switches]
```

Parameters and Switches:

source   Identifies the file(s) to be copied.

destination Identifies the new file to be created.

/A   Uses ASCII mode for the copy.

/B   Uses binary mode for the copy.

Notes:

For the full COPY format, see your DOS reference manual.

The /A or /B switch affects the filespec preceding it and all subsequent filespecs until it reaches a filespec that is followed by another /A or /B switch.

The message says `1 File(s) copied` because only one file was created (or replaced). The following command may or may not have the same effect:

```
C:\DOCS>COPY PART? REPORT
```

Because a global source filespec is used with a single target filespec, the plus sign is not necessary. COPY will concatenate all matching source files into the one target file. This match may include more files than you intended. Furthermore, the order of the files will be as they appear in the directory. If PART2 appears first, it will be the first file copied to REPORT.

When creating a file, DOS places it in the first available directory entry, which may be the former entry of a deleted file. For this reason, the order of entries in a busy directory seems arbitrary. Even if you write PART1 first, PART2 next, and PART3 last, these three files could appear in any order in the directory.

127

Appending Files

Sometimes, you want to concatenate files by appending them to an existing file. For example, suppose that you want to append PART2 and PART3 to PART1 instead of creating a new file. All you have to do is omit the target filespec from the command, as in the following:

```
COPY PART1 + PART2 + PART3
```

In this case, if COPY can't find PART1, it will concatenate PART3 into PART2 (if PART2 exists). When a target file is not specifically identified, COPY uses the first file from the left end of the command that it finds.

The following command is legitimate but may not have the same result, because a different set of files may be identified, and they may appear in a different order. The target file will be the first file in the directory that matches the PART? filespec:

```
C:\DOCS>COPY PART?
```

A variation on this command controls the target file by specifically identifying it:

```
C:\DOCS>COPY PART? PART1
```

This command could create a strange problem. Because PART1 is specified as the target file, COPY opens it and begins appending each source file to it. After the first file is appended, PART1 is irrevocably changed. If COPY then finds the PART1 entry in the directory and realizes that it matches the filespec for a source file, it also realizes that it can't append PART1 to itself. The following message is displayed:

```
Content of destination lost before copy
```

This message looks devastating, but in fact it's perfectly normal. It means that, because the target file has already been changed, it can't be used as a source file. In fact, things are progressing just as they should. You can safely ignore this message.

The Effect of Concatenation on Certain File Types

If PART1, PART2, and PART3 are ASCII (unformatted) text files, they concatenate with no problems. Other types of files are not so easy.

Data Files

Suppose that PART1, PART2, and PART3 were created by a word processor and stored in its native format. They probably have header and trailer information surrounding the text itself. When you concatenate them, all three sets of headers and trailers are included in the file, creating a hybrid that can no longer be processed by the original word processor. The same problem exists with files created by most of today's applications: desktop publishers, spreadsheets, databases, and so on.

To concatenate such files to be usable, don't use COPY; concatenate the files from within the application so that it can create and remove headers and trailers as appropriate.

Binary Files

As with application data files, you do not produce a usable product by concatenating binary files such as executable program modules. Concatenating two program modules not only will produce an invalid program module, it may create a program that could damage your data. Here again, if you want to combine files, use the proper tools. For example, use a linkage editor to combine two executable program modules.

Updating Date/Time Stamps

When DOS copies a file, it doesn't update the file's date/time stamp because the time and date identify the file's version. When you concatenate files, however, the current time and date are assigned to the newly created file because it is a new version.

You can trick DOS into assigning the current time and date to a file by pretending to concatenate it with a command in the following format:

```
COPY source-filespec+,, [destination]
```

Be sure to use a single source filespec, because a global one would cause a real concatenation to take place. Therefore, if you want to update the date/time stamp on all your *.TXT files, do them one at a time; you can use the FOR command to get it all done with one command. The two commas after the plus force DOS to stop concatenating. If the destination is included, the copy is made and only the target file receives the new date/time stamp. If there is no destination, the source file receives the new date/time stamp.

The following batch program changes the date/time stamp to any value you want on a group of files, where %1 is the new time; %2 is the new date; and %3 through %9 are optional filespecs, which can be global. (The /B in the COPY command is explained shortly.)

```
@ECHO OFF
TIME %1 > NUL
DATE %2 > NUL
FOR %%F IN (%3 %4 %5 %6 %7 %8 %9) DO COPY /B %%F+,,
ECHO The system time and date have been changed.
ECHO Please reset the correct time:
TIME
ECHO Please reset the correct date:
DATE
```

Matched Concatenations

COPY permits a special technique in which it will concatenate files with matching filenames but different extensions. An example should make this clear:

```
COPY *.TXT + *.ADD *.NEW
```

This command causes COPY to concatenate FORM.TXT with FORM.ADD to create FORM.NEW, TEACH.TXT with TEACH.ADD to create TEACH.NEW, and so on. If the directory contains TEACH.ADD but not TEACH.TXT or vice versa, an error message is displayed, and TEACH.NEW is not created.

The following are some variations on matched concatenations:

- You can specify more than two source files:

```
COPY *.1 + *.2 + *.3 + *.4  *.ALL
```

- You can omit the target filespec to concatenate into the first filespec:

```
COPY *.TXT + *.ADD
```

Copying to and from Devices

COPY lets you copy files to and from devices, using the device names shown in table 4.2. The following is a quick-and-dirty way to print a file without using DOS's PRINT (which loads a TSR into memory and formats the printout):

```
COPY filespec PRN
```

You can copy files to and from serial ports, but the result is unlikely to be satisfactory without a communications program acting as an intermediary.

You can concatenate files while copying to a device. The following command concatenates all TXT files and prints the results:

```
COPY *.TXT PRN
```

The ABCs of /A and /B

The /A and /B switches can be important in copying and concatenating files, but in order to use them properly, you have to understand a bit about DOS file storage.

Clusters and Slack

DOS stores files in disk storage blocks called clusters or allocation units. Every disk has a fixed cluster size, which depends on the size of the disk and the program that formatted it. For example, a small-capacity (360K) floppy disk has 512-byte clusters, but a large-capacity disk, such as a 80M hard disk, may have 2048-byte clusters (or larger). The cluster size is set during formatting.

DOS allocates disk space to files in whole clusters. If a file doesn't use a complete cluster, the leftover space at the end of the cluster is called *slack*. On a disk with 2048-byte clusters, a one-byte file will occupy one whole cluster with 2047 bytes of slack. A 15K file will occupy eight clusters with 1K of slack at the end of the last cluster. Slack space is wasted space; it can't be allocated to any other file. It may contain leftover data from a previous file (or files) that occupied more of the cluster.

Avoiding Slack When Accessing Files

When DOS reads a file for copying, printing, concatenation, or some other operation, it wants to read only the valid file data and ignore the slack. DOS has two methods of identifying the end of legitimate data in a cluster:

- The ASCII method depends on an end-of-file (EOF) mark—which is ^Z or hex 1A—appearing as the last character in the file. When using the ASCII method, DOS scans the data it reads and stops when it encounters hex 1A. (If a file has no EOF mark, DOS uses the file's size to decide when to stop reading.)

- The binary method uses the file's size as recorded in its directory entry. If the directory entry says that the file is 3267 bytes, DOS will read exactly 3267 bytes from the disk. Any hex 1A characters in the data are read just like other data.

The problem with the ASCII method is that it works only with files that do not contain inadvertent EOF marks as part of their data, as may happen with binary files, worksheets, graphics files, and other application files. The only files that work reliably with the ASCII method are true ASCII files—files containing only ASCII character data and no formatting information. The binary method, however, always works.

DOS also has ASCII and binary methods of writing files. With the ASCII method, DOS adds the EOF mark to the end of the file. With the binary method, it doesn't.

Some DOS utilities (especially the older and more elementary ones) use the ASCII method, and others use the binary method. Utilities designed to work with ASCII format files, such as TYPE and PRINT, use the ASCII method. Utilities that should work with any type of file, such as XCOPY and MOVE, use the binary method.

COPY Methods

COPY sometimes uses one method and sometimes the other. It uses the binary method for most copy processes. For processes that make sense only with ASCII files, such as concatenation and copying to CON or PRN, it uses the ASCII method. You can force it to use the other method with the /A and /B switches.

You can force COPY to use the ASCII method to read a source file by including the /A switch before or after the source filespec. You can force COPY to use the ASCII method of writing a file, which adds an EOF mark to the end of the copy, by including the /A switch after the target filespec. The EOF mark is never essential to DOS programs, but you may have some other software that requires it. (Most modern programs don't.)

You can force COPY to use the binary method to read a source file by including the /B switch before or after the source filespec. If you have a reason to concatenate binary files, you have to use the /B switch to force COPY to read the source files in binary mode, because COPY concatenates in ASCII mode by default.

You can force COPY to write a file in binary mode, which omits the EOF mark, by placing a /B after the target filespec. You need this switch when concatenating binary files if you don't want DOS to add an EOF mark to the end of the new file.

Date Stamping Non-ASCII Files

You need the /B switch when updating the date/time stamp on a non-ASCII file. If you don't use /B, the concatenation process will truncate the file at the first byte containing hex 1A. Without /B, DOS also adds an EOF mark to the end of the file. Specify a /B before the filespec to make sure that the whole file is copied with the new date/time and that no EOF mark is added. The following example updates the date/time stamp on the file named DEFRAG.COM:

```
COPY /B DEFRAG.COM+,,
```

Copying Files to a Device

Be sure to use /B when copying a non-ASCII file to a device, as COPY uses ASCII mode with many devices, and any non-ASCII values in the file may not be handled correctly.

The REPLACE Command

REPLACE has two special functions, both based on its capability to select files by comparing the contents of the source and target directories. Figure 7.4 shows the format of the REPLACE command.

- It will replace files that are present in the source directory but are missing in the target directory (*replace* is used here in the sense of restoring something that has been lost).

- It will replace files that exist in both the source and target directories (*replace* here has the sense of substituting one item for another).

Replacing Missing Files

Suppose that you deleted several files from C:\PROPS, and you have changed your mind. It's too late to undelete them, but you have copies on another computer. (If the copies were made with a backup program, this won't work.) The REPLACE command may be the easiest way to restore them. The following command will select all files that exist on A but do not exist on C:\PROPS:

```
REPLACE A: C:\PROPS /A /P
```

Because you used the /P switch, REPLACE will display each filespec and let you decide whether or not to copy it. This helps us avoid unwanted replacements.

Replacing Existing Files

Suppose that you have installed an application several places on your hard disk. Now you receive an update. The following command seeks out and replaces all the files on the hard disk that have the same name as the files on the disk in drive A:

```
REPLACE A: C:\ /R /S
```

REPLACE's /U (update) switch causes a file to be replaced only if its date/time stamp indicates that it is an older version than the matching source file.

REPLACE

Replaces or adds files from one directory to another.

Format:

REPLACE *filespec path* [/P] [/R] [/W] [/S] [/U] [/A]

Overwrites files in the target directory with matching files from the source directory.

Parameters and Switches:

filespec Identifies the source file(s).

path Identifies the target directory.

/P Prompts for confirmation before replacing a file.

/R Replaces files that are read-only in the target directory as well as nonread-only files.

/W Waits for you to press a key before beginning to search for source files.

/S Searches all subdirectories of *path* to find files to be replaced.

/U Examines the date/time stamps of source and target files and replaces (updates) files in the target directory only if they are older than the source files that replace them.

/A Replaces missing files on the target directory. Don't use with /R, /S, or /U.

Figure 7.4.
REPLACE
command reference.

Using REPLACE with /P To Avoid Clobbering Existing Files

REPLACE with the /P switch can be used to copy files without overwriting existing files. The following batch file uses REPLACE twice—first to replace existing files with permission and then to add missing files (no permission needed). The overall effect is to copy all files identified by %1 to the destination. (To avoid early termination of the first command, even read-only files are replaced in the destination.)

```
@ECHO OFF
REPLACE %1 %2 /P /R
REPLACE %1 %2 /A
```

This batch program can handle only one subdirectory at a time, so it lacks a lot of XCOPY's punch, and it's extremely slow when compared to XCOPY, but it is a safe way to copy files from one directory to another.

INTERLNK

8

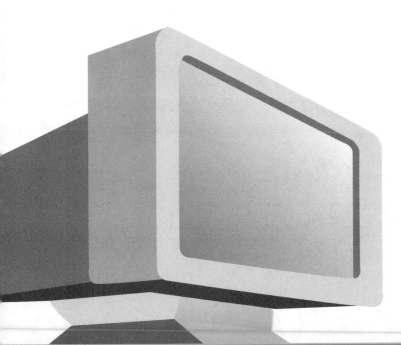

Introduction

DOS 6's new INTERLNK feature lets you hook up two computers and access one from the other. You can, for example, copy and move files from one to the other, run programs that are installed on only one of them, and use the one computer's printer from the other.

INTERLNK was designed to let you access a desktop computer from your laptop so that you can transfer and print the files that you have developed on the road. But it comes in handy anytime you have two computers close to each other that aren't networked.

When you connect two computers with INTERLNK, one is the *server* and one is the *client* (see fig. 8.1). The server can do nothing on its own while the connection is in force. The only thing you can enter from its keyboard is the command to break the connection. The client does all the work. It can access the server's drives and parallel ports as if they were part of its own configuration. INTERLNK assigns drive names and port names so that it can do this. For example, suppose the client normally had one hard drive, drive C. INTERLNK would assign the drive name D to the server's drive C. The client can copy files from its hard drive to the server's hard drive by copying them from drive C to drive D.

Figure 8.1.
The client-server connection.

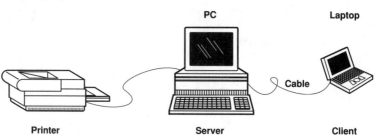

Client drives and ports
A:
B:
C:
D: = Server drive C:
E: = Server drive D:
LPTI: = Server port LPTI

Overview of the INTERLNK Procedure

To connect two computers with INTERLNK, you follow this procedure:

1. Cable the two computers together.

2. Run the INTERSRV program on the server. This sets up the computer in server mode.

3. Load the INTERLNK.EXE driver on the client via CONFIG.SYS. This completes the connection.

If you leave the INTERLNK.EXE driver in CONFIG.SYS all the time, it does not try to make a connection when the client is not cabled to another computer or when the other computer is not yet in server mode. In that case, you need to take one more step to complete the connection. You enter the INTERLNK command on the client when you're ready to go.

Cabling the Two Computers

You can cable the computers together through either their serial ports or their parallel ports. You must use the same type of port on each one, of course, but they don't have to have the same port number. You could, for example, cable LPT1 on the client to LPT3 on the server.

Use one of these types of cable:

- 3-wire serial cable

- 7-wire null-modem cable

- Bidirectional parallel cable

Setting Up the Server

Figure 8.2 shows the INTERSVR command, which you use to place a computer in server mode. If you want to use all the default settings, just enter the word INTERSVR. All the server's drives and ports are made available for redirection when you don't specify otherwise. To redirect just hard drive C, you could use this command:

```
INTERSVR C:
```

Or you could do it by not redirecting to drives A and B:

```
INTERSVR /X=A /X=B
```

Figure 8.2.
INTERSVR
command reference.

INTERSVR

Format:

```
INTERSVR [drive ... ] [/X=drive ...]
[/LPT[n] ¦ /LPT:[address] ¦ /COM[n] ¦ /COM:[address]]
[BAUD:rate] [/B] [/V] [/RCOPY]
```

Parameters and Switches:

none	Loads the server program and displays the server screen.
drive	Identifies server drive(s) to redirect. By default, INTERSVR redirects all the server's drives.
/X=*drive*	Identifies server drive(s) not to redirect.
/LPT	Indicates that the cable is connected to a parallel port.
/COM	Indicates that the cable is connected to a serial port.
n	Identifies the number of the port that the cable is connected to.
address	Identifies the address of the port that the cable is connected to.
/BAUD:*rate*	Sets a maximum baud rate for data transfer. Values for *rate* may be 9,600, 19,200, 38,400, 57,600, and 115,200. The default is 115,200.
/B	Displays the INTERLNK server screen in black and white.
/V	Prevents conflict with the server computer's timer.
/RCOPY	Copies the INTERLNK programs from one computer to the other.

INTERSVR does not redirect network drives, CD-ROM drives, or any other drives that use a redirection interface.

When you don't include a port name on the command, INTERSVR scans all the server's ports looking for the cable. You'll use up more memory space this way, as it installs the routines for handling both serial and parallel ports, but the server's memory space is probably not a problem since it can't do anything else while INTERSVR is running. However, you should avoid scanning the serial ports if a mouse is attached to one of them; INTERSVR can damage the mouse driver in this situation. Suppose you have a serial mouse on COM1 and a cable to your laptop on COM2. You should enter the INTERSVR command this way:

```
INTERSVR /COM2
```

Suppose instead you have a serial mouse on COM1 and a cable to your laptop on LPT2. You could use either the /LPT switch to let INTERSVR scan your parallel ports or specify /LPT2.

With a serial connection, INTERSVR transfers data at 115,200 baud. If that's too fast for your computer, use the /BAUD parameter to set a lower baud rate.

> If one of your computers freezes up during the connection, use the /V switch the next time you try.

Figure 8.3 shows what the server computer's screen looks like when you first load INTERSVR and no connection has been established. You can see the drives and ports that will be redirected, but they have not received their client names yet. The Client column is filled in when INTERLNK completes the connection. Notice the instruction to press Alt+F4; this is how you break the connection later on.

Setting Up the Client

Figure 8.4 shows how you load the INTERLNK.EXE driver. INTERLNK scans for a server computer as soon as it is loaded. If it finds one, it completes the connection and you can begin accessing the server. If not, it merely loads itself and waits. Use the /AUTO switch if you want INTERLNK.EXE to load only if it can find a connection during booting.

Figure 8.3.
The INTERSVR screen.

```
              Microsoft Interlnk Server Version 1.00



              ┌─────────────────────────────────────────┐
              │ This Computer      Other Computer       │
              │   (Server)            (Client)          │
              ├─────────────────────────────────────────┤
              │ A:                                       │
              │ B:                                       │
              │ C: (84Mb)                                │
              │ LPT1:                                    │
              └─────────────────────────────────────────┘




  Transfer:          │      Port=        Speed=      │  Alt+F4=Exit
```

Inserting INTERLNK.EXE in your usual CONFIG.SYS file could change other drive assignments that come later in CONFIG.SYS, for RAMDRIVE.SYS and DRIVER.SYS commands, for example. If you don't insert it in its own configuration block, you might want to put it last in CONFIG.SYS so that the changed drive assignments don't invalidate your current batch programs and DOSKEY macros.

Figure 8.4.
INTERLNK.EXE Configuration command reference.

INTERLNK.EXE

Format:

DEVICE[HIGH]=[*path*]INTERLNK.EXE [/DRIVES:*n*] [/NOPRINTER]
[/COM[*n* ¦ *address*]] [/LPT[*n* ¦ *address*]] [/AUTO] [/NOSCAN]
[/LOW] [/BAUD:*rate*] [/V]

Parameters and Switches:

path	Identifies the location of the INTERLNK.EXE file. The default is the root directory of the boot drive.
/DRIVES:*n*	Specifies the number of server drives to be redirected to the client computer. The default is 3. If *n* = 0, INTERLNK redirects only printers.

/NOPRINTER	Inhibits redirection of printers. By default, INTERLNK redirects all available parallel printer ports.
/COM[n	address]	Specifies the port by which the client computer is cabled to the server computer; if neither n nor address is specified, INTERLNK scans all serial ports for the connection.
/LPT[n	address]	Specifies the port by which the client computer is cabled to the server computer; if neither n nor address is specified, INTERLNK scans all parallel ports for the connection.
/AUTO	Installs INTERLNK.EXE in memory only if it can establish an immediate link with the server computer. By default, INTERLNK.EXE is installed even if the connection can't yet be completed.
/NOSCAN	Installs INTERLNK.EXE in memory, but prevents it from establishing a connection. By default, INTERLNK tries to establish a connection with the server as soon as you install it.
/LOW	Loads the INTERLNK.EXE driver into conventional memory, even if upper memory is available. By default, INTERLNK.EXE loads into upper memory if available.
/BAUD:rate	Sets a maximum baud rate for serial communication. Valid values are 9,600, 19,200, 38,400, 57,600, and 115,200. The default is 115,200.
/V	Prevents conflicts with a computer's timer. Specify this switch if you have a serial connection between computers and one of them stops running when you use INTERLNK to access a drive or printer port.

Identifying the Connected Port

As with the server, you should not let INTERLNK.EXE scan the client's serial ports if you have a serial mouse. Specify /LPT to limit the scan to the parallel ports, or specify /COM*n* to identify a specific serial port. These switches also save memory space by loading only the port software that's actually needed. You can save more space with the /NOPRINTER switch if you don't plan to access the server's printers.

If you don't know which port you'll be using, specify /NOSCAN to prevent the scan. This forces you to use the INTERLNK command to complete the connection.

Redirected Drives

By default, INTERLNK redirects three of the server's drives. Include the /DRIVES parameter to request a different number of drives. INTERLNK redirects server drives starting with A unless the INTERSVR command specified the drives to be redirected. For example, suppose you want to access only drive C on the server. The INTERSVR command should look like this:

```
INTERSVR C:
```

The INTERLNK.EXE command should look like this:

```
DEVICE[HIGH]=C:\DOS\INTERLNK.EXE /DRIVES:1
```

Suppose the server has three hard drives (C, D, and E) and you want to access those drives but not the floppy drives. You don't need to do anything special in the INTERLNK.EXE command, which redirects three drives by default, but you do need to specify the drives to be redirected on the INTERSVR command, like this:

```
INTERSVR C: D: E:
```

To access only printer ports on the server, include /DRIVES:0 in the INTERLNK.EXE command.

If you need to use the /V switch on the INTERSVR command, include it in the INTERLNK.EXE command too.

If the link is successfully completed when INTERLNK.EXE is loaded, you'll see a
report like this on the client's monitor:

```
Microsoft INTERLNK Version n.nn

Port=LPT1
Drive letters redirected: 3 (D: through F:)
Printer ports redirected: 1 (LPT2:)
```

```
This Computer     Other Computer
  (Client)           (Server)
------------      --------------

      D:     equals    A:
      E:     equals    B:
      F:     equals    C: (80Mb MS-DOS 5)
   LPT2:     equals    LPT2:
```

This tells you that the cable is attached to the client's LPT1 port. The client should
use drive name D to access the server's drive A, drive name E for the server's drive
B, drive name F for the server's drive C, and LPT2 to access the server's LPT2. You
can also see that the server's drive C is 80 megabytes and is partitioned by DOS 5.
An equivalent table appears on the server's video screen and stays there as long as
the link is in force.

Only one computer needs to be running DOS 6. The other must have
DOS 3.0 or later. You can copy the necessary INTERLNK program files
to a computer that does not have DOS 6.

Completing the Connection with INTERLNK

If INTERLNK.EXE can't complete the connection when you boot the client computer, you need the INTERLNK command (see fig. 8.5) to complete it when the
server is set up.

Figure 8.5.
INTERLNK
command reference.

INTERLNK

Completes an INTERLNK connection of client and server computers; redirects server drives.

Format:

```
INTERLNK [drive1 = [drive2]]
```

Parameters:

none   Completes the link, if necessary; displays a status report, including the current drive and printer assignments.

drive1   Identifies a client drive name to be assigned to *drive2*.

drive2   Identifies a server drive to be acccessed by the name *drive1*.

When the connection is established, the report shown earlier appears on the client computer. You can enter an INTERLNK command at any time during the link to rework the drive name assignments. For example, suppose you want to refer to the server's drive C as drive D, not F, so that some batch programs work properly. You could enter this command:

```
INTERLNK D:=C:
```

INTERLNK displays a new drive assignment table to confirm the change. You can't use this feature to add new drive names to the list, merely to rework the names that were already reassigned. If you omit the second drive name, as in `INTERLNK D:=`, the redirection is canceled.

> Enter the INTERLNK command (without parameters) at any time during the link to redisplay the drive name table on the client computer.

If you want to print from Windows on a redirected parallel port, use Windows Control Panel to assign the port to LPT*n*.DOS.

You can't use any programs on the redirected drives that deal with drive architecture and clusters instead of directories and files. For example, you can't run FORMAT, UNFORMAT, CHKDSK, or DEFRAG. Even UNDELETE is forbidden.

Copying the INTERLNK Software

You can copy the INTERLNK software to any computer that's running DOS 3 or later. You can use diskettes to transfer the files, but you can also do it via the INTERSVR command with the /RCOPY switch. You must use the 7-wire, null-modem cable with this feature. After the two computers are cabled, enter this command on the computer that contains DOS 6:

```
INTERSVR /RCOPY
```

No other parameters can be used with /RCOPY. INTERSVR guides you through the process of setting up the target computer to receive the INTERLNK files. (The MODE command must be available on the target computer.)

Breaking the Link

When you're finished working with the linked computers, press Alt-F4 on the server computer's keyboard to break the link. The server computer returns to its normal mode.

DOS and the Environment

Introduction

DOS sets aside a memory buffer called the *environment* that it uses for storage of crucial variables such as the path and the prompt. Other programs also may store and access variables in the DOS environment. For example, Microsoft Windows uses the TEMP variable to locate its temporary files.

You also can create environment variables and access them in batch programs. In fact, you may find occasion to start up a second command interpreter just to obtain a new environment for a batch program.

Environment Variables

An environment variable has a name and a value. In the following example, TEMP is the variable name, and C:\ DOS is its value:

```
TEMP=C:\DOS
```

The name and value can be any length as long as they don't exceed the amount of space left in the environment. They can contain any characters, including spaces. DOS always translates and stores the name in uppercase letters, but the value will be stored exactly as entered.

Displaying Environment Variables

Figure 9.1 shows the SET command, which controls environment variables. SET with no parameters displays the full list of variables, as in the following:

```
C:\>SET
COMSPEC=C:\DOS\COMMAND.COM
PATH=C:\DOS;D:\NU;C:\WINDOWS;C:\WORD;C:\
PROMPT=$P$G
TEMP=C:\WINDOWS\TEMP
NU=D:\NU
```

No DOS command displays the value of a specific variable, but you can use the following batch program, where %1 is the name (or the value) of the variable you want:

```
@ECHO OFF
SET ¦ FIND "%1"
```

DOS's Environment Variables

DOS has a number of environment variables that it uses. Some of them are set automatically by DOS, and others are used by DOS if you set them.

SET

Sets or changes values of environment variables or displays current values.

Format:

SET [*variable*=[*string*]]

Parameters and Switches:

none   Displays the current values of all environment variables.

variable   Identifies the environment variable to be set.

string   Specifies a new value for an environment variable; if omitted, the current value is cleared.

Figure 9.1.
SET command reference.

PATH

The PATH variable is set when you enter a PATH command and shows your current search path. DOS accesses this variable whenever it must search for a program file. When no PATH variable is in the environment, there is no search path.

PROMPT

The PROMPT variable is set when you enter a PROMPT command and shows the current format of the command prompt. DOS accesses this variable every time it displays the command prompt. If no PROMPT variable exists, DOS displays the default command prompt, which is just the current drive name (not the current directory) followed by a right angle bracket. The PROMPT command and the meaning of the symbols it uses are discussed in Chapter 18.

TEMP

The TEMP variable, which you must create with a SET command, tells DOS where to store temporary files (such as pipe files). If no TEMP variable is available, DOS stores temporary files in the current directory. Microsoft Windows also uses the TEMP variable to locate its temporary files. Windows needs at least 2M of available space for its temporary files; if you direct TEMP to a drive that doesn't have enough room, you will have problems with Windows Print Manager.

One sure way to speed up Windows is to create a RAM drive of at least 2M in extended or expanded memory and set TEMP to point to it. That way, Windows can write its temporary files without doing any real disk access. However, SmartDrive gives you better performance improvement than a RAM drive, so don't steal space from SmartDrive to create a RAM drive. If you have expanded memory not needed by any other programs, or if you have more than 4M of extended memory so that SmartDrive can create a 2M cache and still have 2M left over, go ahead and create the RAM drive. If it turns out to be drive E, you would place the following command in CONFIG.SYS:

```
SET TEMP=E:\
```

DIRCMD

The DIRCMD variable, which you must create with a SET command, establishes default parameters for the DIR command. DOS accesses DIRCMD whenever a DIR command is entered. When no DIRCMD variable is available, DOS uses the default DIR parameters and switches.

COMSPEC

The COMSPEC variable is set by DOS to show the location of the command interpreter. DOS accesses this variable whenever it needs to reload the memory-resident portion of the command interpreter after some other program has overwritten it. You see how DOS decides on the value for COMSPEC later in this chapter.

Creating an Environment Variable

The following command creates an environment variable named TEMP and sets its value to C:\ DOS:

```
C:\>SET TEMP=C:\DOS
```

Because both the name and the value can have spaces, make sure that there is no space before or after the equal sign unless you want that space included in the name or the value. DOS sees "TEMP" and "TEMP " (with a trailing space) as two different variables. When looking for the place to store its temporary files, it accesses "TEMP" but not "TEMP ".

The preceding SET command receives no confirmation messages unless the environment space is exceeded, in which case the following message is displayed:

```
Out of environment space
```

Modifying and Deleting Environment Variables

To change a variable's value, enter a SET command with the same name and the new value. To delete an environment variable, enter a SET command with the same name and nothing after the equal sign, as in the following:

```
SET TEMP=
```

> Rebooting deletes all environment variables except the ones DOS sets and those set in AUTOEXEC.BAT.

Accessing Environment Variables

You can access environment variables from batch programs, much the same as you use replaceable parameters. Use a parameter in the following format:

```
%variable-name%
```

For example, to switch to the directory defined as TEMP from within a batch program, use the following command:

```
CD %TEMP%
```

> You can't access environment variables from the command prompt or from DOSKEY macros.

Adding to the Path

The following command uses the PATH variable to add the C:\PROGS directory to the end of the current search path:

```
PATH=%PATH%;C:\PROGS
```

The expression %PATH% causes the current value of the PATH variable (the current search path) to be filled into the command. Then C:\PROGS is appended to it. You could just as easily insert C:PROGS at the front of the search path.

Preserving and Restoring Environment Variables

If a batch program needs to reset the current prompt, you can preserve and restore the current one with commands like the following:

```
REM Save the current prompt:
SET SAVEPROMPT=%PROMPT%

REM Make sure we didn't run out of environment space
IF %SAVEPROMPT%=%PROMPT% GOTO CONTINUE

.
. (commands to deal with inadequate environment space)
.

:CONTINUE

.
. (the remainder of the program)
.

REM Restore the previous prompt:
SET PROMPT=%SAVEPROMPT%

REM Remove unneeded variable:
SET SAVEPROMPT=
```

The same technique can be used to preserve and restore any environment variable.

Environment Variables versus Replaceable Parameters

Using an environment variable instead of a replaceable parameter has several advantages:

- You can use as many variables as you want (up to the size limit of the environment).

- An environment variable is more permanent than a replaceable parameter. It outlasts the batch job and can be accessed by other batch jobs.

Using the CONFIG Variable

When you set up multiple configuration blocks in CONFIG.SYS, DOS sets the CONFIG environment variable to show which block was selected during booting. You can access that variable from AUTOEXEC.BAT (or any other batch program) to branch based on which configuration was chosen. For example, if CONFIG.SYS contains three blocks, PETER, JUDI, and RUTH, you could branch to different startup routines in AUTOEXEC.BAT in the following way:

```
@ECHO OFF
    commands for all blocks
GOTO %CONFIG%

:PETER
    commands that should be executed for the PETER block
GOTO ENDING

:JUDI
    commands that should be executed for the JUDI block
GOTO ENDING

:RUTH
    commands that should be executed for the RUTH block
:ENDING
```

Controlling the Command Interpreter and the Environment

The environment is established when the command interpreter is loaded during booting. To control the command interpreter and/or environment size, you must include a SHELL command (see fig. 9.2) in CONFIG.SYS.

Figure 9.2.
SHELL configuration command reference.

SHELL

Loads a command interpreter

Format:

SHELL=*filespec* [*parameters*][*switches*]

Parameters and switches depend on which command interpreter is indicated. The following are available for COMMAND.COM:

SHELL=[*path*]COMMAND.COM [*path*][*device*][/E:*nnn*][/P][/MSG]

Parameters:

filespec	Identifies the command interpreter.
path	Identifies the location of the command interpreter if not in the root directory of the boot drive.
device	Identifies a device to be used for standard input and output; default is CON.
/E:*nnn*	Identifies the size of the environment in bytes, from 160 to 32,768; the default is 256.
/P	Establishes the command interpreter as the primary command interpreter.
/MSG	Requests that error messages normally stored on disk should be loaded into memory; use when the command interpreter is located on floppy disk.

When no SHELL command appears in CONFIG.SYS, DOS loads COMMAND.COM from the root directory of the boot drive. (If it's not there, the message `Bad or missing command interpreter` appears, and booting is halted.) The default environment size is 256 bytes. You will quickly run out of environment space if you create and use your own environment variables in addition to those that DOS uses.

Use SHELL in any of the following cases:

- You want to use a command interpreter other than DOS's COMMAND.COM.

- The command interpreter is not located in the root directory of the boot drive.

- You want to use a nondefault environment size.

Environment Size

For a larger environment, you must include a SHELL command in CONFIG.SYS with the /E switch included in it. To use the default command interpreter and create a 1K environment size, use the following command:

```
SHELL=COMMAND.COM /E:1024 /P
```

The environment is located in conventional memory, which is valuable space, so don't request more environment space than you need.

If you omit the /P switch and subsequently enter an EXIT command, the system will hang up. If you include /P, EXIT is ignored.

Command Interpreter in Another Location

If the command interpreter is not in the root directory of the boot drive, you must specify its location twice:

- You must include its path with the first parameter (COMMAND.COM) so that DOS knows where to find the command interpreter during booting.

- You must include the path again (without the filespec) as the second parameter so that DOS knows where to find the command interpreter when it needs to reload the transient part of it. This parameter causes DOS to set the COMSPEC variable in the environment.

To use C:\DOS\COMMAND.COM as the command interpreter with the default environment size, you would put the following command in CONFIG.SYS:

```
SHELL=C:\DOS\COMMAND.COM C:\DOS /P
```

The second parameter causes DOS to create the following environment variable:

```
COMSPEC=C:\DOS
```

Using a Third-Party Command Interpreter

It's possible to use a command interpreter other than COMMAND.COM. For example, the Norton Utilities includes NDOS, with many more features than COMMAND.COM. The SHELL statement is used to establish an alternative command interpreter such as NDOS, in which case COMMAND.COM is not loaded.

Loading a Secondary Command Interpreter

Sometimes, the best way to solve a problem is to start up a secondary command interpreter, even if it's another instance of COMMAND.COM. Among other things, this gives you a second environment to use.

The COMMAND command (see fig. 9.3) starts up COMMAND.COM as a secondary command interpreter. The parameters and switches are the same as those on the SHELL command when it references COMMAND.COM. The following command starts up a secondary COMMAND.COM with a 2K environment; because no other location is specified, the COMSPEC variable will be inherited from the parent environment.

```
COMMAND /E:2048
```

As long as you don't use the /P switch, the secondary command interpreter is a child of the primary one. The primary command interpreter remains in memory and resumes control when you terminate the secondary one. To terminate the secondary command interpreter and return to the primary one, enter the following one-word command:

```
EXIT
```

Figure 9.3.
COMMAND
command reference.

COMMAND

Starts a new version of the DOS command processor COMMAND.COM.

Format:

```
COMMAND [path] [ctty] [/Ccommand] [/Kfilespec] [/E:n]
```

Parameters and Switches:

path	Identifies the location of the command processor.
ctty	Identifies the device for command input and output. The default is the current device.
/Ccommand	Loads a secondary command processor, performs *command*, and exits the secondary command processor.
/Kfilespec	Runs the specified program before displaying the DOS command prompt.
/E:n	Specifies the environment size in bytes for the new command processor, from 160 to 32,768.

Specifying COMSPEC

If you specify a location for COMSPEC, the new environment is empty except for the COMSPEC variable. You will have no PATH, PROMPT, or any other variable that existed in the parent environment. You should notice the difference immediately because your prompt changes to DOS's default prompt (that is, it shows only the current drive, not the current directory). You will not be able to start up programs from other directories until you establish a search path. One quick way to reset your path and prompt is to rerun C:\AUTOEXEC, but that also can load some TSRs for the second time, which may not be desirable.

Omitting COMSPEC

If you don't specify a location for COMSPEC, the secondary environment inherits the parent environment's variables. It can modify, add, and delete variables as desired without affecting those in the parent environment. When you return to the parent command interpreter, its environment is in exactly the same condition as when you left it. This is the main reason for starting up a secondary command interpreter. For example, suppose that you must create a batch program that changes the prompt, the search path, and the TEMP directory. You want to restore the original parameters before ending the batch program. The easiest way to do it is as follows:

```
@ECHO OFF
REM Preserve current environment:
COMMAND
    .
    .    (remainder of batch program)
    .
REM Restore original environment:
EXIT
```

Suppose that you are creating a batch program that needs a 2K environment. Starting a secondary command interpreter not only gives you the extra environment space temporarily, it also eliminates all extra environment variables automatically when you exit back to the parent command interpreter:

```
@ECHO OFF
REM Establish a larger environment:
```

```
COMMAND /E:2048
.
.     (remainder of batch program)
.
REM Return to original environment:
EXIT
```

Dynamic Environment Allocation

When COMMAND creates an environment, DOS initially allocates the default or requested amount of environment space. However, if you set variables in excess of that space and the adjacent memory area is available, DOS will dynamically allocate to the environment as many bytes as necessary to create the variables you request. You could set many thousands of bytes of environment variables this way, but keep in mind that you're removing available space from conventional memory, which could prevent programs from being loaded.

If /E is not specified, the default environment size is 256 bytes or the number of bytes necessary to inherit all the parent's variables, whichever is greater.

Starting COMMAND.COM When Another Command Interpreter Is Primary

Suppose that NDOS is loaded as the primary command interpreter and you now need to run COMMAND.COM. To start it up as a secondary command interpreter, enter the following command:

```
COMMAND C:\ [switches]
```

You need to specify the COMSPEC path so that the COMMAND environment doesn't inherit NDOS's COMSPEC variable, which could lead to trouble when

DOS attempts to reload the transient portion of COMMAND from the wrong directory. Because the COMSPEC path is specified, no variables are inherited from the parent environment, so you may want to set at least the path and prompt before continuing.

To return to NDOS again, enter the following command:

```
EXIT
```

Loading a New Primary Command Interpreter

Suppose that you want to replace the primary command interpreter with COMMAND.COM. You need to include the /P (for primary) switch as follows:

```
COMMAND  C:\ [switches] /P
```

This method has some effects similar to rebooting. AUTOEXEC.BAT is executed from the root directory of the current drive. (If you're not on drive C, you probably don't have an AUTOEXEC.BAT available, and the DATE and TIME commands will be executed instead.) The EXIT command will not terminate this interpreter. Although you can't get back to the previous command interpreter, it continues to take up space in memory, which could cause a shortage of memory space. If memory is tight, it's better to modify the SHELL statement in CONFIG.SYS and reboot to get the command interpreter and environment you want.

Executing a Command with COMMAND.COM

The /C *command-text* switch causes COMMAND to start up a secondary command interpreter just long enough to run the indicated command and then exit to the parent command interpreter again. You use this feature primarily to redirect output that can't otherwise be redirected.

Recall that you can't redirect the output of a batch program or pipe the output of a FOR command. However, you can redirect the output of COMMAND. Suppose that you want to redirect the output of a batch program called STYLIST to a file named SAVESTY.TXT. The following command will do it:

```
COMMAND /C STYLIST > SAVESTY.TXT
```

Chapter 7 showed you how to combine FIND with FOR to search a set of files for a specified phrase. However, you were unable to pipe the output to MORE because FOR can't be piped. Here again, COMMAND can be used to accomplish the redirection:

```
COMMAND /C FOR %F IN (*.DOC *.TXT) DO FIND "Carnival"
%F ¦ MORE
```

Unless you have directed TEMP to a RAM drive, this command could result in a long pause while MORE builds a temporary file of the entire output from the FOR command.

> If you redirect the COMMAND command without the /C switch, all standard output of the secondary command interpreter is redirected until you exit back to the primary interpreter again. This includes the command prompt, which no longer appears on the monitor but is recorded in the redirected output. You can still enter commands and data, even though you can't see the command prompt.

Circumventing DOS's Memory Limitations

10

Introduction

Even though it's not much more than 10 years old, DOS has been suffering from a lack of memory for many years. DOS was originally designed for Intel's 8088 microprocessor, the chip installed in the original IBM PC and compatibles.

It could accommodate up to 1M of memory, which seemed like a lot at the time. Intel (and Microsoft) decided to make 640K of that available for program use, providing 10 times as much space as any personal computer software of that day needed, and to reserve the upper 384K for system needs.

That was then... this is now. Today's huge applications are bumping up against the 640K ceiling with increasing frustration. It's not uncommon to attempt to start up a program and receive the message `Not enough memory`.

The 286 and later microprocessors used in modern personal computers are capable of accommodating huge memory areas, much larger than the original 1M. A 286-based computer, such as an AT, can access as much as 16M of memory, and a 386 or 486 can have as much as 4G (gigabytes)—more than four billion bytes. However, poor old DOS is stuck with its original design and can still access only 1M, with 640K available for program use, even if the computer it's running on has several gigabytes of memory installed in it.

Why not just upgrade DOS to accommodate the larger memory capacities of today's machines? Because that would make it incompatible with earlier DOS versions and the thousands of programs designed to run under them. (OS/2 is an attempt in this direction.) However, new versions of DOS have added several facilities to provide relief from the 640K barrier without changing its basic design, as you see in this chapter.

Memory Layout

When discussing DOS's memory layout, it's important to distinguish between memory address space and installed memory. Every byte in memory has a numerical address, which is used by programs to access that byte. Memory address space is a range of addresses set aside for memory, even if no memory chips have been installed for those addresses. The address space represents the computer's memory potential; it doesn't mean that the computer has that much memory. For example, under DOS, the address space from 0H to A0000H (see the following sidebar for an explanation of why computer addresses are always stated in hexadecimal) is the 640K range available for running programs. Even if you install only 512K of RAM in your computer, DOS still reserves the entire 640K address range for that purpose, starting the system area at address A0000H.

The Hexadecimal Mystique

Why do computers so often report addresses and other values in hexadecimal numbers instead of decimal? It's partly a tradition and partly a necessity for programmers.

Internally, a computer must store all data using the binary number system. With a base of 2, binary has only two digits, 0 and 1, which can be represented in an electronic circuit by a pulse or no pulse, on a disk by a magnetized spot or no spot, and so on. It takes a lot more binary digits (called *bits*) to represent a value. The number 20 in binary is 10100B; the number 500 is 111110100B.

When the computer displays or prints internal values, binary numbers take up too much room and are too difficult for humans to interpret at a glance. It's also easy for humans to skip or transpose digits in long strings of 1s and 0s. Therefore, the computer uses a larger number system for display purposes.

Any number system whose base is a power of 2 has a direct relationship with binary, and it's easy to translate back and forth between the two. This makes octal (base 8) and hexadecimal (base 16) the most likely candidates for displaying numbers that are really binary. Over the years, hexadecimal has squeezed out octal and is now used almost universally.

When you see a hex number, you really are seeing a binary number in shorthand. Because hexadecimal has 16 digits, the decimal digits 0 through 9 and the letters A through F are used to express hex numbers. The value 21C5H is actually 0010000111000101B.

Now for the $16 million question: Why not let the computer convert numbers into decimal? It's a lot better at calculations than people are. The answer is that programmers often need to see hexadecimal values to figure out what's happening internally. At one time, only programmers had to deal with hexadecimal output. With the advent of personal computers and nontechnical users, the conversions should be done, but that doesn't always happen. It's a particularly

strong tradition to display memory addresses in hexadecimal. If this
was a basic book, we would translate the addresses to decimal.
Because the book is designed for advanced readers, the addresses
have been left in hexadecimal because that's how they appear in
other places (such the MEM /D report).

Figure 10.1 shows the layout of DOS's total address space on a 286 or 386 computer.
8086/8088 machines have only the conventional and upper portions, not the extended. The following sections describe each type of memory in detail.

Figure 10.1.
Memory layout.

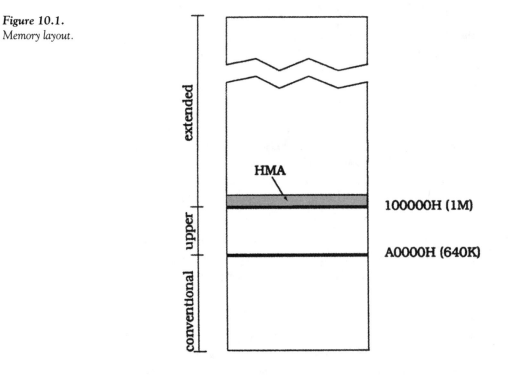

Conventional Memory

The address space from 0H to A0000H is called *conventional memory*—the everyday
workspace in which most programs must be loaded to work under DOS. This area is
random-access memory (RAM), which can be written again and again. It's cleared
when the power goes out and when you reboot.

DOS uses the first portion of conventional memory for system data. Traditionally, DOS resides in the next part; you see a little later how to load it higher up. The remainder of conventional memory is available for other programs.

Most systems need to load at least a few device drivers—programs that control hardware such as the printer and the mouse. Most systems also start up some TSRs—programs that stay resident in memory after they're started up—such as DOS's PRINT and DOSKEY. The more drivers and TSRs you load into conventional memory, the less space you have to start up an application. In fact, you can put yourself into a situation in which you can't start up some of your larger applications without removing some TSRs from conventional memory.

DOS 6 includes features that can help free up conventional memory by letting you load drivers, TSRs, and DOS itself in other parts of memory, if you have the right setup.

Upper Memory

The address space from A0000H to 100000H, which is called *upper memory*, is reserved so that DOS can access the memory built into controllers for devices such as a video monitor. ROM BIOS and ROM BASIC (if present) also are accessed through this address space. Most systems don't have enough devices to fill the address space and that provides a loophole through which DOS can access memory beyond the 1M limit.

Expanded Memory (EMS)

One way to provide extra memory in a PC is to add on a memory board and access it through upper memory as an external device. This early solution to the PC memory crunch, called *expanded memory*, can be used with any PC model. Expanded memory, like conventional memory, is RAM; it can be read and written, and it is cleared when the power goes out or you reboot. However, unlike conventional and upper memory, DOS can't execute programs from expanded memory. It can be used for data storage only.

Figure 10.2 illustrates the methodology DOS uses to access and manage expanded memory. A memory manager uses some available address space in upper memory to create a page frame, which is divided into 16K pages. All of expanded memory is divided into pages of the same size. You can access any expanded memory page by allocating to it a page of address space from the page frame. The process of continually reassigning the address space in the page frame on an as-needed basis is referred to as bank switching. Notice that you can't access all of expanded memory at the same time. You can access only as many pages as there are in the page frame.

Figure 10.2.
Accessing expanded memory.

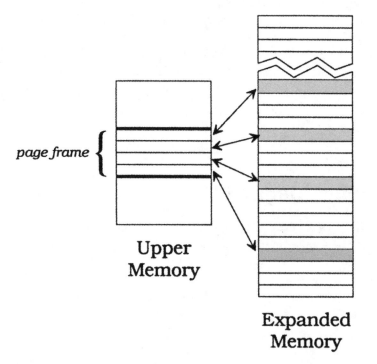

A program called an *expanded memory manager* keeps track of the pages, servicing the needs of all programs requesting expanded memory so that each program's data is protected from the others. Expanded memory boards usually come with their own management software, but you may find that you want to purchase a third-party manager with more features.

Chaos reigned in the early days of expanded memory management until Lotus, Intel, and Microsoft (LIM) created an Expanded Memory Specification (EMS), released as LIM 3.2 EMS. AST Research, Quadram, and Ashton-Tate developed an enhanced standard that was combined with the LIM 3.2 to produce LIM 4.0 EMS. Expanded memory that conforms to one of the LIM specifications is referred to as EMS memory.

LIM 3.2 and LIM 4.0 are in current use, and your expanded memory may conform to either one. LIM 3.2 limits the system to one 64K page frame with four 16K pages. LIM 4.0 permits any number of page frames, which may be smaller or larger than four pages and may appear in conventional as well as upper memory. LIM 4.0 also permits access to larger expanded memory areas (32M as opposed to 8M).

Extended Memory

A 286-based computer has a 16M address space, but a 386 or 486 has a 4G address space. Memory in the range above 1M is referred to as extended memory because it extends beyond the original PC's address space. As with conventional and expanded memory, any memory installed here is always RAM and is cleared when you reboot or lose power. DOS can use it for data storage only (with one exception, which is explained shortly).

Some people order a 286 or higher machine with 1M of RAM thinking that they will not have any extended memory because the first megabyte of memory will be used up by conventional and upper memory. However, the first 640K of RAM becomes conventional memory, but the remaining 384K goes into the extended range. Because the address space from 640K to 1M is reserved for device and ROM BIOS memory, it is not filled in with general-purpose RAM.

286 and higher machines have two basic modes of operation: protected and real. In *protected mode*, a program can directly address the entire memory range, from conventional through extended. (OS/2 runs in protected mode, and programs designed to run under OS/2 can do this.) Real mode forces the more advanced computer to emulate an 8086/8088 so that it can run DOS and all the thousands of programs designed to run under DOS. In real mode, only conventional and upper memory can be directly addressed, with one important exception.

Some programs attempt to access extended memory under DOS by switching the machine into and out of protected mode on an as-needed basis, but this solution is difficult to program, difficult to manage, and can cause conflicts (and data loss) if two programs attempt it concurrently.

High Memory Area (HMA)

Because of the way the memory addresses are handled in real mode (see the sidebar for details), DOS can actually access almost 64K of extended memory through the A20 address line. That area is called the High Memory Area (HMA) and is used to access and manage the rest of extended memory with a bank-switching technique similar to expanded memory's. It's not the ideal solution, but it's the best DOS can manage.

How DOS Exceeds the 1M Limit with a 286 or Higher Microprocessor

The 8086/8088 has a 16-bit architecture, meaning that its registers and words are 16 bits (2 bytes) long. It would be natural if its memory addresses were 16 bits, too, because that is the size that can be stored in a register or memory word. However, with 16-bit addresses, you can access only 64K of memory, which isn't enough, so the designers had to come up with some other way of addressing memory.

The solution lay in dividing memory into 64K segments and having two 16-bit values for each address: a 16-bit segment address and a 16-bit offset within the segment. The 8086/8088 creates a 20-bit address by shifting the segment address to the left four bits and adding the offset to it. If the segment address is 5CH and the offset is 23H, the actual memory address is calculated this way:

```
  005C0H
+ 00023H
  005E3H
```

The 8086/8088 has 20 memory address lines, named A00 through A19, to carry the 20 address bits from the microprocessor to the memory unit. With 20 bits, you can access an address range of exactly 1M.

However, this addressing technique can generate addresses above 1M. The maximum address that can be generated is larger than 1M by almost 64K:

```
  FFFF0H  (largest segment address)
+ 0FFFFH  (largest offset)
  10FFEFH  (largest address)
```

10FFEFH equals 1,114,095, which is 65,519 bytes more than 1M. However, the values from 100000H to 10FFEFH have 21 bits, not 20. Because the 8086/8088 has only 20 address lines, if such an address is generated, the twenty-first bit disappears.

The 286, 386, and 486 are designed to address much larger memory areas and have considerably more than 20 address lines. The twenty-first bit can be retained and used on address line A20. Therefore, DOS can actually address almost 64K over the 1M limit when operating on a 286 or higher machine operating in real mode. For convenience, this figure is rounded to 64K.

A familiar group—Microsoft, AST Research, Intel, and Lotus—have released an extended memory specification (XMS) that standardizes control of extended memory through the A20 line in real mode, preventing conflicts in much the same way as LIM EMS does for expanded memory. DOS provides an XMS manager called HIMEM.SYS with DOS. However, you may find that you want to buy an XMS manager with more features.

DOS 6's Memory Facilities

DOS 6 includes a number of facilities to help you manage memory, free up conventional memory, and use upper, expanded, and extended memory:

- The MEM program displays a list of what's currently in memory. MEM helps you find out how much of each type of memory your system has, how much of it is currently available, and what programs are currently loaded where.

- The HIMEM.SYS XMS manager gives your 286 or higher machine access to extended memory according to the XMS standard.

- If XMS memory is present, the DOS command loads DOS itself into the HMA.

- If you have a 386 or 486 with XMS memory, EMM386.EXE enables you to convert some (or all) XMS extended memory to EMS expanded memory. XMS also enables you to load drivers and TSRs into upper memory to free up conventional memory for applications.

● If you have a 386 or 486 with XMS memory, the MEMMAKER program can set up your CONFIG.SYS and AUTOEXEC.BAT files (as well as SYSTEM.INI if you are using Windows) to use upper memory blocks. Generally, MEMMAKER can do a better job at this than you can because it has access to internal information about the exact address ranges available in upper memory and how much space each program needs.

MEM

Figure 10.3 shows the format of the MEM command. When used without any switches, MEM displays a report similar to the following:

```
C:\>MEM
Memory Type        Total = Used  +  Free
---------------    ------   ------    ------

Conventional        640K      32K     608K
Upper               155K     155K       0K
Adapter RAM/ROM     229K     229K       0K
Extended (XMS)     4096K    3072K    1024K
---------------    ------   ------    ------

Total memory       5120K    3488K    1632K
Total under 1 MB    795K     187K     608K
Largest executable program size      608K   (622624 bytes)
Largest free upper memory block        0K       (0 bytes)
MS-DOS is resident in the high memory area.
C:\>
```

Figure 10.3.
MEM *command*
reference.

<hr>

MEM

Displays current memory use.

Format:

MEM [/CLASSIFY ¦ /DEBUG ¦ /FREE ¦ /MODULE *program*]
[/PAGE]

Parameters and Switches:

none   Displays summary information about your system's used and free memory.

/CLASSIFY   Lists currently loaded programs and their memory usage along with summary information. Abbreviate as /C. May be used with /PAGE, but not with any other switches.

/DEBUG   Lists programs and drivers currently loaded into memory. For each module, shows size, segment address, and module type. Displays summary information also. Abbreviate as /D.

/FREE   Lists the free areas of memory; shows the segment address and size of each free area of conventional memory and the largest free UMB in each region of upper memory. Displays summary information also. Abbreviate as /F.

/MODULE   Shows how a program is currently using memory. Lists the memory areas the program occupies and shows the address and size of each. Abbreviate as /M.

program   Identifies a program currently loaded in memory.

/PAGE   Pauses after each screen. Abbreviate as /P.

Notes:

Mem displays the status of extended memory if installed.

Mem displays the status of expanded memory only if your system has expanded memory that conforms to LIMS 4.0 EMS standards.

Mem displays the status of upper memory only if a UMB provider such as EMM386 is installed and if DOS=UMB is included in CONFIG.SYS. MEM does not display the status of upper memory if you run MEM under Windows 3.0.

Sometimes, you want to find out exactly what programs are loaded. The /CLAS-SIFY or /C switch lists all programs in conventional memory, as in the following example:

```
C:\>MEM /C
Modules using memory below 1 MB:
Name        Total      = Conventional + Upper Memory
--------  ------------   --------------   ------------
MS-DOS      16621  (16K)   16621  (16K)        0   (0K)
HIMEM        1152   (1K)    1152   (1K)        0   (0K)
EMM386       3120   (3K)    3120   (3K)        0   (0K)
COMMAND      3680   (4K)    3680   (4K)        0   (0K)
win386      91808  (90K)    2560   (3K)    89248  (87K)
WIN          1568   (2K)    1568   (2K)        0   (0K)
COMMAND      3856   (4K)    3856   (4K)        0   (0K)
SETVER        816   (1K)       0   (0K)      816   (1K)
ANSI         4240   (4K)       0   (0K)     4240   (4K)
MOUSE       13648  (13K)       0   (0K)    13648  (13K)
GRAPHICS     5872   (6K)       0   (0K)     5872   (6K)
SMARTDRV    27264  (27K)       0   (0K)    27264  (27K)
UNDELETE    13616  (13K)       0   (0K)    13616  (13K)
DOSKEY       4144   (4K)       0   (0K)     4144   (4K)
Free       622640 (608K)  622640 (608K)        0   (0K)
Memory Summary:
Type of Memory      Total      =    Used     +    Free
--------------  --------------   --------------   --------------
Conventional    655360  (640K)    32720  (32K)    622640  (608K)
Upper           158848  (155K)   158848 (155K)         0    (0K)
Adapter RAM/ROM 234368  (229K)   234368 (229K)         0    (0K)
Extended (XMS) 4194304 (4096K)  3145728 (3072K) 1048576 (1024K)
--------------  --------------   --------------   --------------
Total memory   5242880 (5120K)  3571664 (3488K) 1671216 (1632K)
Total under 1 MB 814208 (795K)   191568 (187K)   622640  (608K)
Largest executable program size 622624 (608K)
Largest free upper memory block      0   (0K)
MS-DOS is resident in the high memory area.
```

You probably will want to add the /PAGE or /P switch to break the report into pages.

The MEM /C display is not very detailed about exactly where each program and free block appear in memory. In particular, all free space tends to be shown at the end of the area, even though it's really scattered around in memory. Therefore, the largest executable program size is smaller than the total free space. Also, MEM /C does not show the MEM program itself; it shows you what the situation will be like after MEM terminates, so you can decide whether another program could be loaded.

If you need more specific information, which you may when debugging a program, use MEM /D, which shows you exactly where programs and free space are, including MEM itself; all addresses are in hexadecimal.

HIMEM.SYS

HIMEM.SYS is DOS's XMS manager. When loaded, it takes over the HMA and enables other XMS-compatible software to use extended memory. HIMEM.SYS is loaded from CONFIG.SYS with a command like this:

```
DEVICE=C:\DOS\HIMEM.SYS
```

If you have another XMS driver in your system, you must choose between it and HIMEM.SYS. If you decide to use HIMEM.SYS, remove the other driver's DEVICE command from your CONFIG.SYS file. (Place REM in front of the command until you are sure that HIMEM.SYS is the program for you and that you really don't want to use the other one. Then you can erase that command.)

You need to place HIMEM's DEVICE command before any other command that uses extended memory (such as a command that installs a RAM drive or a disk cache in extended memory). If the other programs require an XMS manager, they can't load without HIMEM being installed first. If they don't require an XMS manager and take over all or part of extended memory, HIMEM can't start up. An error message during booting warns you when HIMEM can't be loaded.

Problems in Using HIMEM.SYS

If you find that HIMEM doesn't work for you in its default configuration—for example, if HIMEM.SYS won't load or other programs can't access extended memory—you may need some switches on HIMEM's DEVICE command. Figure 10.4 shows the switches and their settings.

The most likely problem is the /MACHINE switch, which identifies the driver that controls the A20 line. Microsoft includes several A20 handlers in HIMEM.SYS. HIMEM.SYS attempts to load the correct handler for your system, but it can't sense the correct handler for some systems. When that happens, you have to use the /MACHINE switch to load the correct handler. If you're not sure which handler to use, it doesn't hurt to experiment. Your hardware dealer or Microsoft's Product Support team may be able to help you find the right one.

Figure 10.4.
HIMEM.SYS
configuration
command.

HIMEM.SYS

Manages extended memory, including the high memory area (HMA).

Format:

```
DEVICE=[path]HIMEM.SYS [/A20CONTROL:ON ¦ OFF]
[/CPUCLOCK:ON ¦ OFF] [/EISA] [/HMAMIN=size] [/INT15=x]
[/NUMHANDLES=n] [/MACHINE:machine] [/SHADOWRAM:ON ¦ OFF]
[/VERBOSE]
```

Parameters and Switches:

path	Identifies the location of the HIMEM.SYS file. The default is the root directory of your boot drive.

/A20CONTROL:ON | OFF	Specifies whether HIMEM is to take control of the A20 line even if A20 is already on. If you specify /A20CONTROL:OFF, HIMEM takes control of the A20 line only if A20 is not already in use when HIMEM loads. The default setting is /A20CONTROL:ON.
/CPUCLOCK:ON | OFF	Specifies whether HIMEM can affect the clock speed of your computer. If your computer's clock speed changes when you install HIMEM, /CPUCLOCK:ON may correct the problem but slow down HIMEM. The default setting is /CPUCLOCK:OFF.
/EISA	Specifies that HIMEM.SYS should allocate all available extended memory. This switch is necessary only on an EISA (Extended Industry Standard Architecture) computer with more than 16 MB of memory; on other computers, HIMEM allocates all available extended memory.
/HMAMIN=*size*	Specifies (in kilobytes) how large a program must be to use the HMA. Valid values are 0 through 63; the default is 0, which forces HIMEM to give the HMA to the first program that requests it. This switch has no effect when Windows is running in 386 enhanced mode.

Figure 10.4. *continued*	/INT15=*x*	Allocates (in kilobytes) extended memory for the interrupt 15h interface. Valid values are 64 through 65535 but not more than your system's available memory. The default value is 0. If *x* is less than 64, HIMEM uses 0.
	/NUMHANDLES=*n*	Specifies the maximum number of extended memory block handles that can be used simultaneously. Valid values are 1 through 128; the default value is 32. Each handle requires an additional 6 bytes of memory. This switch has no effect when Windows is running in 386 enhanced mode.
	/MACHINE:*machine*	Specifies which A20 handler to use.
	/SHADOWRAM:ON | OFF	Specifies whether or not to enable shadow RAM. If your computer has less than 2M of memory, the default is OFF (disabled).
	/VERBOSE	Directs HIMEM.SYS to display status and error messages while loading. By default, HIMEM.SYS does not display these messages. You can abbreviate /VERBOSE as /V.

Loading DOS into Extended Memory

Because the HMA is directly addressable by DOS, it is possible to run programs there. However, HIMEM.SYS enables only one program in the HMA; the first one that loads itself there is the king of the hill. Most DOS users load DOS itself in the HMA to get it out of conventional memory. If you don't do this, a smaller program may take up residence there, and you will not gain as much savings in conventional memory. (Moving DOS into the HMA saves about 45K in conventional memory.)

You can load most of DOS into the HMA by including the following command somewhere following the XMS manager's DEVICE command in CONFIG.SYS:

```
DOS=HIGH
```

Loading Programs in Conventional Memory with LOADFIX

When you move DOS into the HMA, other programs may be loaded into the low parts of conventional memory where DOS traditionally resides. A few programs don't work well when loaded in the first 64K of memory (DOS EDIT is one). If you receive the message `Packed file corrupt` when starting up a program, try inserting LOADFIX in front of the command, as in the following:

```
LOADFIX EDIT TRYME.BAT
```

LOADFIX forces the program to be loaded above the 64K line.

Using EMM386

Because expanded memory has been around longer and can be made available on any PC, many applications work with expanded but not extended memory. It's frustrating to have several megabytes of extended memory and have some applications suffering for lack of memory because they recognize only expanded memory. For 386 and 486 microprocessors with extended memory, EMM386.EXE has two functions:

● It makes some or all of your extended memory emulate expanded memory.

● It lets you load programs into upper memory instead of conventional memory.

Figure 10.5 shows the format of EMM386's DEVICE command, which must be placed somewhere after HIMEM's DEVICE command in CONFIG.SYS. If used without any parameters, it converts 256K of XMS extended memory into expanded memory but does not provide access to the upper memory area. Most of the parameters provide solutions to rare problems and can be ignored if you have no trouble emulating expanded memory or loading programs into upper memory. You may find use for the memory-size, RAM, and NOEMS switches, however.

Emulating Expanded Memory

If you have an application that wants expanded memory but your 386 or 486 has only extended memory, you may be able to use EMM386.EXE combined with HIMEM.SYS to provide the expanded memory you need.

> Some programs, notably Windows 3.0, have their own emulators and don't work well with EMM386.

Suppose that you have two megabytes of extended memory that is not needed by any of your applications. You also have an application that will use as much expanded memory as you can provide. The following CONFIG.SYS command will convert your entire range of extended memory into expanded memory:

```
DEVICE=C:\DOS\EMM386.EXE 2048
```

> Although EMM386.EXE will not work with a 286, you can purchase third-party memory managers that will accomplish the same functions (and more) on a 286.

EMM386.EXE

Provides access to the upper memory area and uses extended memory to simulate expanded memory.

Format:

```
DEVICE=[path]EMM386.EXE [ON ¦ OFF ¦ AUTO]
[expanded-memory] [MIN=size] [W=ON ¦ W=OFF]
[Mx ¦ FRAME=address1 ¦ /Paddress1] [Pn=address2]
[[X=mmmm1-nnnn1]...] [[I=mmmm2-nnnn2]...] [B=address3]
[L=minXMS] [A=altregs] [H=handles] [D=nnn]
[RAM[=mmmm3-nnnn3]] [NOEMS] [NOVCPI] [NOHIGHSCAN]
[/VERBOSE] [[WIN=mmmm4-nnnn4]...] [NOHI] [ROM=mmmm5-nnnn5]
```

Parameters and Switches:

path	Identifies the location of the EMM386.EXE file. The default is the root directory of the boot drive.
ON l OFF l AUTO	ON loads and activates the EMM386 driver; OFF loads the driver but deactivates it; AUTO places the driver in automatic mode, which enables expanded-memory support and upper memory block support only when a program calls for it. Use the EMM386 command to change this value after the driver has been loaded.
expanded-memory	Specifies (in kilobytes) the maximum amount of extended memory that you want EMM386.EXE to provide as expanded memory. Values are 64 through 32768 (or the amount of free extended memory). The default value is the amount of free extended memory unless you specify NOEMS. EMM386.EXE rounds the value down to the nearest multiple of 16.

Figure 10.5.
EMM386.EXE
configuration
command reference.

Figure 10.5. *continued*	MIN=*size*	Specifies (in kilobytes) the minimum amount of expanded memory that EMM386.EXE will provide. Values are 0 through *expanded-memory*. The default value is 256 unless you specify NOEMS.
	W=ON | W=OFF	Enables or disables support for the Weitek coprocessor. The default is W=OFF.
	M*x*	Specifies the base address of the expanded-memory page frame. Valid values are 1 through 14. If your computer has less than 512K of memory, *x* must be less than 10.
	FRAME=*address1*	Specifies the page-frame base address directly. Valid values are 8000H through 9000H and C000H through E000H, in increments of 400H. You may specify FRAME=NONE, but this could cause some programs to malfunction.
	/P*address1*	Specifies the page-frame base address directly. Valid values are 8000H through 9000H and C000H through E000H, in increments of 400H.
	P*n*=*address2*	Specifies the base address of page *n*. Valid values for *n* are 0 through 255. Valid values for *address* are 8000H through 9C00H and C000H through EC00H, in increments of 400H. The addresses for pages 0 through 3 must be contiguous to maintain compatibility with version 3.2 of LIM EMS. If you use M*x*, FRAME, or /P*address1*, you can't specify addresses for pages 0 through 3 with the /P*n* switch.

X=*mmmm1-nnnn1*	Prevents EMM386.EXE from using a particular range of segment addresses for an EMS page or for UMBs. Valid values for *mmmm1* and *nnnn1* are in the range A000H through FFFFH and are rounded down to the nearest 4-kilobyte boundary. This parameter takes precedence over the I parameter if two ranges overlap.
I=*mmmm2-nnnn2*	Specifies a range of segment addresses to use for an EMS page or for UMBs. Valid values for *mmmm2* and *nnnn2* are in the range A000h through FFFFh and are rounded down to the nearest 4-kilobyte boundary. The X parameter takes precedence over the I parameter if two ranges overlap.
B=*address3*	Specifies the lowest segment address available for EMS bank-switching. Valid values are in the range 1000H through 4000H. The default value is 4000H.
L=*min*XMS	Ensures that *min* kilobytes of extended memory will still be available after you load EMM386.EXE. The default value is 0.
A=*altregs*	Specifies how many fast alternate register sets (used for multitasking) you want to allocate to EMM386.EXE. Valid values are in the range 0 through 254. The default value is 7. Every alternate register set adds about 200 bytes to the size of EMM386.EXE in memory.
H=*handles*	Specifies how many handles EMM386.EXE can use. Valid values are in the range 2 through 255. The default is 64.

Figure 10.5. *continued*	D=*nnn*	Specifies how many kilobytes of memory to reserve for buffered direct memory access (DMA). Discounting floppy-disk DMA, this value should reflect the largest DMA transfer that will occur while EMM386.EXE is active. Valid values for *nnn* are in the range 16 through 256. The default value is 16.
	RAM[=*mmmm3-nnnn3*]	Requests both expanded memory and UMB support and specifies a range of segment addresses in extended memory to use for UMBs. If you do not specify a range, EMM386.EXE selects the addresses.
	NOEMS	Provides UMB support but not expanded memory support.
	NOVCPI	Disables support for VCPI (Virtual Control Program Interface) applications. This switch may be used only with the NOEMS switch. When you specify both switches, EMM386.EXE disregards the *expanded-memory* and MIN parameters.
	NOHIGHSCAN	Limits scanning of the upper memory area for available memory. Specify this switch only if you have trouble using EMM386.EXE.
	/VERBOSE	Directs EMM386.EXE to display status and error messages while loading. By default, EMM386.EXE does not display these messages. You can abbreviate /VERBOSE as /V.
	WIN=*mmmm4-nnnn4*	Reserves a range of segment addresses for Windows instead of for EMM386.EXE. Valid values for *mmmm4* and *nnnn4* are in the range A000H through FFFFH and are rounded down to the nearest 4 kilobytes. The X parameter takes precedence over the WIN

	parameter if two ranges overlap. The WIN parameter takes precedence over the RAM, ROM, and I parameters if their ranges overlap.
NOHI	Prevents EMM386.EXE from loading into the upper memory area. Normally, a portion of EMM386.EXE is loaded into upper memory. Specifying this switch decreases available conventional memory and increases the upper memory area available for UMBs.
ROM=*mmmm5-nnnn5*	Specifies a range of segment addresses that EMM386.EXE uses for shadow RAM. Valid values for *mmmm5* and *nnnn5* are in the range A000H through FFFFH and are rounded to the nearest 4 kilobytes. Specifying this switch may speed up your system if it does not already have shadow RAM. (See HIMEM.SYS for an explanation of shadow RAM.)

You can disable your system by using the EMM386.EXE parameters incorrectly. If that happens, you can reboot and bypass the EMM386.EXE command in CONFIG.SYS and then edit the command.

EMM386.EXE takes up a small amount of conventional memory for its own software; it can't be loaded into upper memory. It also needs to borrow 64K from extended memory to create the upper memory page frame. EMM386.EXE also takes whatever extended memory is necessary to create the EMS memory. (If there isn't enough XMS to create the requested amount of EMS, it creates as much as it can, rounded down to the nearest multiple of 16K.)

Turning Expanded Memory On and Off

After you have installed EMM386 from CONFIG.SYS during booting, you can turn it on and off with the EMM386 command (see fig. 10.6) as long as it isn't currently in use. You may want to turn it off to make more extended memory available to an application and then turn it on again when you're ready to run an application that needs expanded memory.

You can load EMM386.EXE but turn it off (or place it in AUTO mode) by including the OFF or AUTO parameter in the CONFIG.SYS command that loads it. Then you can use the EMM386 command to turn it on when it's needed.

If you try to turn EMM386 off when it is providing access to upper memory blocks or when some program is using its expanded memory, you see the following message:

```
Unable to de-activate EMM386 as UMBs are being provided
and/or EMS is being used.
```

Using Upper Memory Blocks (UMBs)

Trying to load programs into upper memory blocks can lock up your system. If that happens, reboot and bypass the startup files until you can locate and fix the problem.

Because various devices have fixed address ranges in upper memory, free space appears in chunks located here and there rather than in one contiguous piece. The free chunks are called upper memory blocks or UMBs. No RAM is associated with UMBs unless you use a program like EMM386 to fill the address space with actual memory borrowed from extended memory.

Figure 10.6.
EMM386
command reference.

EMM386

Controls expanded memory support.

Format:

```
EMM386 [ON ¦ OFF ¦ AUTO] [W=ON ¦ W=OFF]
```

Parameters and Switches:

none	Displays the status of EMM386 support.
ON	Enables the EMM386.EXE driver.
OFF	Disables the EMM386.EXE driver without unloading it.
AUTO	Lets programs control enabling and disabling of EMM386.EXE driver.
W=ON	Enables Weitek coprocessor support.
W=OFF	Disables Weitek coprocessor support. Default is W=OFF.

Notes:

You must have a 386 or higher processor and must have installed the EMM386.EXE device driver before you can use this command.

You cannot turn EMM386 off when it is providing UMBs or when any program is currently using expanded memory.

After UMBs have been associated with actual memory, you can load and run programs from UMBs just as you can from conventional memory. By loading drivers and TSRs in upper memory, you can free up conventional memory for applications.

To set up EMM386 to manage UMBs, you must use the NOEMS or the RAM parameter on EMM386's DEVICE command. Use RAM if you want to use both of EMM386's functions; you get both EMS memory and upper memory access. Use NOEMS if you want upper memory access only and don't care to emulate expanded memory.

You also must include DOS=UMB somewhere in CONFIG.SYS. If you're already using DOS=HIGH, combine both commands in one as follows:

```
DOS=HIGH,UMB
```

Remember—to make all this work, you have to have a 386 or 486 with extended memory, and you have to include three commands in CONFIG.SYS:

```
DEVICE=C:\DOS\HIMEM.SYS
DEVICE=C:\DOS\EMM386 RAM (or NOEMS)
DOS=UMB (or HIGH,UMB)
```

You will find these as the first three commands in many CONFIG.SYS files. Don't forget that you have to reboot to put changes in CONFIG.SYS to work.

Controlling the Page Frame Address

Most systems don't use upper memory starting at address E0000H for any hardware purpose, but EMM386 will not use this portion unless you tell it to. When you are using EMM386.EXE to access UMBs and expanded memory, it pays to force the expanded memory page frame to start at E0000H, which moves the page frame out of an area that EMM386 will use as an UMB, freeing up another 64K of UMB space.

You can force the page frame to start at E0000H in several ways, all equally effective, but the easiest is as follows:

```
DEVICE=C:\DOS\EMM386.EXE M9 ...
```

Loading Programs into UMBs

Now that you have set up the UMBs, you can load programs into them. Device drivers and TSRs are the natural choice for a number of reasons. They are generally smaller than applications and can fit in the smaller spaces available in upper memory. They also are not transient, so they will not leave unusable holes in upper memory when they terminate.

Any driver normally loaded with the DEVICE command in CONFIG.SYS can be loaded into a UMB with the DEVICEHIGH command instead (except for HIMEM.SYS and EMM386.EXE). DEVICEHIGH works just like DEVICE except it causes the driver to be loaded into a UMB if a large enough one is available. If DOS cannot find a UMB large enough for the program, it loads the driver into conventional memory with no warning. After you set up your CONFIG.SYS with DEVICEHIGH commands and reboot, you can use MEM /C to see which programs were actually loaded into upper memory.

TSRs can be loaded into UMBs using the LOADHIGH command, which is abbreviated LH. All you have to do is insert LH in front of the command that normally starts up the TSR, as in the following command:

```
LH DOSKEY
```

Problems with UMBs

Not all programs work well in UMBs. Some try to expand themselves after loading and can't get the space to do so. Some make assumptions about where they are located in memory. If your system locks up during or after booting, bypass the startup files and see whether you can figure out which program(s) caused the problem.

All TSRs and device drivers included with DOS 6 run from UMBs with no problems.

You can see how much space a program actually takes up in memory by loading the program in memory (conventional or upper) and using the following command:

```
MEM /MODULE:program-name
```

For example, to find out how much space DOSKEY is using in memory, you could use the following command:

```
MEM /MODULE:DOSKEY
```

The report looks something like the following:

```
DOSKEY is using the following memory:
   Segment  Region       Total         Type
   -------  ------   ---------------   --------

    0D5EB       1        4144    (4K)  Program
                     ---------------
   Total Size:          4144    (4K)
```

From this report, you can see that DOSKEY occupies 4,144 bytes. The Region number appears only if the program is in upper memory. Sometimes, you see that a program is occupying two or more locations in memory, perhaps in different regions in upper memory. The `Total Size` shows how much space the program needs altogether.

Using MEMMAKER

The MEMMAKER program can do all the upper memory decision making for you. In fact, if you're having trouble fitting all your drivers and TSRs into upper memory, it can do more, because it will generate switches on the DEVICEHIGH and LOADHIGH commands to specify exactly where to place a program in upper memory.

Enter MEMMAKER (with no parameters) to start up MEMMAKER. It communicates with you through a series of dialog boxes, much like Setup does. Your first choice is whether to do a Custom or EXPRESS setup. You may as well try the Express setup the first time. If you end up not being able to boot or if some of your programs will not run with the new setup, you can try a Custom setup (see Table 10.1). In either case, you get to specify whether or not you need EMM386 to convert some extended memory into expanded memory.

When you run MEMMAKER, it reboots your system several times, trying out new settings in upper memory. If it ever gets stuck, do a cold start to help it along. MEMMAKER will resume control when the system reboots and offer you the option of trying again with more conservative settings (such as not doing an aggressive scan).

Table 10.1. Custom Setup Options

Option	Description
Specify drivers and TSRs	Choose this option if you want to exclude some of your drivers and TSRs from being loaded into upper memory.
Aggressive scan	Choose this option if you want MEMMAKER to use the upper memory range from F000-F7FF, which is otherwise excluded. The Express setup will use this memory range; if you have trouble after the Express setup, you could try turning this option off.
Optimize for Windows	Choose this option if you never run DOS-based programs under Windows. If you don't use Windows, or if you run DOS-based programs under Windows, turn this option off.
Use monochrome region	Choose this option if you don't have a monochrome or SuperVGA monitor. If you're having trouble after MEMMAKER uses the monochrome region, rerun MEMMAKER and turn this option off again.
Keep current inclusions and exclusions	If your EMM386.SYS driver is currently set up to include or exclude certain areas of upper memory, choose this option to retain them. Turning this option off gives MEMMAKER freer reign in upper memory, but it may not work well with your system.
Move extended BIOS data area to upper memory	Choose this option to move the EBDA to upper memory. If you have problems after MEMMAKER uses this option, rerun MEMMAKER and turn it off.

When MEMMAKER is finished, your CONFIG.SYS and AUTOEXEC.BAT will look something like the following:

```
[CONFIG.SYS]
DEVICE=C:\DOS\HIMEM.SYS
DEVICE=C:\DOS\EMM386.EXE NOEMS D=64
BUFFERS=15,0
FILES=50
DOS=UMB
LASTDRIVE=E
FCBS=4,0
DOS=HIGH
STACKS=9,256
DEVICEHIGH /L:1,12048 =C:\DOS\SETVER.EXE
DEVICEHIGH /L:1,9072 =C:\DOS\ANSI.SYS
SHELL=C:\DOS\COMMAND.COM C:\DOS\ /E:1024 /P
[AUTOEXEC.BAT]
PATH C:\DOS;C:\WINWORD;C:\NDW;C:\WINDOWS
LH /L:1,20304 MOUSE\MOUSE BON
PROMPT $P$G
SET TEMP=C:\WINDOWS\TEMP
LH /L:1,20560 C:\DOS\GRAPHICS LASERJET /R
LH /L:0;1,42448 /S C:\DOS\SMARTDRV
LH /L:1,53936 UNDELETE /SC
LH DOSKEY
```

MEMMAKER inserted or adapted the HIMEM.SYS and EMM386.EXE commands in CONFIG.SYS and then changed appropriate DEVICE commands into DEVICEHIGH. The /L switches specify exactly where to load the programs in upper memory. It also added the DOS=UMB, LASTDRIVE, and FCBS commands. In AUTOEXEC.BAT, it converted commands that load TSRs into LH commands, adding /L switches as before. The /S switch in the SMARTDRV command also was inserted by MEMMAKER; it shrinks the UMB after loading SMARTDRV to make more room for other programs.

Handling TSRs

A TSR (terminate-and-stay-resident) program is a program that stays in memory after it is loaded, whether it is active or not. Many TSRs scan keyboard input for commands or hotkeys pertaining to their functions. DOSKEY provides a good example: when you press the up-arrow key at the command prompt, it recalls the preceding command from the command history.

When you press a key with no TSRs installed, DOS sends the keystroke to its own keystroke handler for processing. When you load a TSR that scans keyboard input, the TSR inserts itself in the normal chain of keystroke processing so that it looks at the keystrokes first, processes what it recognizes, and passes unfamiliar ones on to DOS's keystroke handler.

When you load a second TSR that scans keyboard input, it inserts itself in the chain after the first one. The chain gets longer and longer as you load more TSRs:

```
TSR #1 → TSR #2 → TSR #3 → DOS's keystroke handler
```

It's this chain that prevents you from unloading any TSR except the last one loaded. If you were able to unload a TSR in the middle of the chain, the chain would be broken and your keystrokes would never reach DOS's keystroke handler. In fact, the system would probably freeze up.

Not all TSRs behave as they should in the chain, and you may find that your system locks up anyway. Usually this is because two (or more) TSRs don't get along well together. Perhaps one is stealing the other's keystrokes or is not passing the correct information along. If this starts happening in your system, try installing your TSRs in a different order. If that doesn't work, bypass TSRs one at a time until you find the one that is causing the problem. Talk to its developers about how to load it with your other TSRs; they probably are aware of the problem and have found (or are working on) a solution.

Speeding Up Your System

11

Introduction

When you consider how much more you can accomplish in a few minutes at your personal computer than you could with a typewriter, white out, scissors, and paste, it's amazing that the computer sometimes seems so slow.

You can do a lot of things to speed it up. Some of them are quite expensive, such as upgrading your system board, installing math coprocessors, or adding several megabytes of extended memory.

However, you can do some things with your present system and DOS that have a surprising impact on speed. All of them fall into the area of optimizing and buffering your hard disk to reduce access time as much as possible. (Although floppy disk drives are 10 times slower than hard disks, you don't use them as much, and their impact on system performance isn't as significant.)

Why So Slow?

A hard disk consists of a stack of metal platters with read-write heads that move between them. The heads are attached to an arm that must move in and out to position the heads at the various cylinders on the disk. (A cylinder is a vertical configuration of the same track on every surface on the hard disk. That is, cylinder 0 consists of side 0, track 0; side 1, track 0; side 2, track 0; and so on.) When the heads have reached the cylinder, they must wait for the desired sector to roll into position.

Anything mechanical moves at agonizingly slow speeds compared to the lightning quickness of solid state circuitry. If the microprocessor had to wait for the hard disk to find and read the data it requests or to locate a place to write data, system efficiency would plummet right through the floor! System architecture is designed to avoid most of the waiting and to keep the microprocessor working, but the architecture can't do some things that you can.

Generally, your goal is to minimize the number and distance of read-write arm movements. The more you can do that, the faster your hard disk access times will be, and the more efficiently all your programs will run. Disk-intensive programs, such as word processors and database managers, will benefit the most. You have three basic ways to minimize arm movements:

- Organize the directories and data on your hard disk for optimum access.

- Eliminate file fragmentation from the disk.

- Buffer disk access so that DOS reads from memory as much as possible instead of from the disk.

DOS offers a number of features to help you with these tasks.

How DOS Accesses a File

DOS can't read a file in one arm movement. It takes several movements, perhaps dozens. Figure 11.1 shows why. First, DOS must find the directory entry for the file, which involves reading the root directory and then making several trips between subdirectories and the FAT until the desired subdirectory is found. When DOS finds the file's directory entry and knows the first cluster number, it must travel back and forth between the FAT and the file until all fragments are located and read.

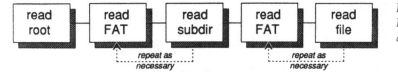

Figure 11.1.
DOS strategy in accessing a file.

As if all those arm movements weren't bad enough, some of them can be quite a long distance. Figure 11.2 diagrams the architecture of a hard disk. The first track contains only the partition table, which is accessed during booting but is not needed to locate or write files. The second track contains the remaining system data, so DOS can move between the root directory and the FAT with no arm movements; it just has to wait for the correct sector to roll around. (DOS maintains the second FAT as a duplicate of the first; it uses the second if the first develops problems.) All subdirectories and files are located in the data area, which starts on the third track. A subdirectory or file may be located anywhere in the data area. To locate a particular file, DOS may need to visit cylinder 227, the FAT, cylinder 412, the FAT, cylinder 7, the FAT, and so on.

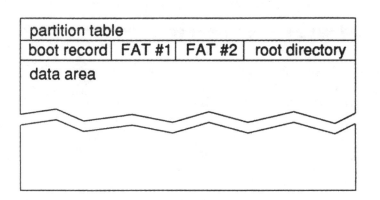

Figure 11.2.
Hard disk layout.

Arm Movement Factors

Several factors add to number and the distance of arm movements:

- *The length of a file's path:* Remember that DOS must read every directory in a file's path every time it opens the file. The longer the path, the more subdirectories DOS must read.

- *The size of a subdirectory:* The larger a subdirectory is, the more likely it is to be fragmented. The more fragments DOS must access, the more arm movements (perhaps long ones) are needed.

- *Subdirectory locations:* When subdirectories are located all over the data area, DOS must move around more to follow a file's path.

- *File fragmentation:* The more fragments the file is divided into, the more arm movements (perhaps long ones) DOS must use to read or write it.

- *File location:* The farther a file fragment is located from the FAT, the farther the arm must move to access it.

- *Disk interleave factor:* The arrangement of the segments around a track has a dramatic influence on access time. Interleave factors are explained in the next section.

You can control all these factors, partially with DOS, partially by setting up your disk and its subdirectories to facilitate access, and partially with third-party utilities.

Getting Ready To Defragment Files

DOS 6 includes a utility called DEFRAG that defragments the files on a drive, but you should take several steps to get ready for it. Some of these steps need to be done only once; some need to be done every time you run DEFRAG.

Setting the Interleave Factor

A disk's interleave factor determines how quickly data can be read from successive sectors. When the read-write head is positioned over a track, it must wait for the correct sector to roll around before starting to read. It reads one sector, transfers that to DOS, and then waits for the next sector to arrive. Depending on the speed that the disk is spinning compared to the length of time before the system is ready for the next sector, the ideal location for the next sector may be immediately next to the current one, one sector away from it, two sectors away from it, or even farther away.

The spacing of the sectors on a track is known as the disk's interleave factor. With an interleave factor of 1, the sectors are located sequentially in the track. With an interleave factor of 2 on a disk with 17 sectors per track, the sectors are arranged as follows:

1 10 2 11 3 12 4 13 5 14 6 15 7 16 8 17 9

An interleave factor of 3 means that they are arranged three apart, as follows:

1 7 13 2 8 14 3 9 15 4 10 16 5 11 17 6 12

The interleave factor is established during the low-level format of the disk, which, for a hard disk, is usually done at the factory. You may be surprised how often an inefficient factor is selected! The wrong interleave factor can double or triple the time it takes to access files on the disk. Therefore, it's worth finding out whether yours is correct.

DOS does not include any facility to analyze or correct the interleave factor. However, you can get third-party utilities that test the interleave factor, find the ideal one for your hard disk, and set it up without destroying any of the data on your hard disk.

Even if an interleave utility promises not to harm data, do a complete backup of your hard disk before trying it out.

Don't spend a lot of money on an interleave utility until you're sure it can work with your hard disk. Some hard disks can't be manipulated by interleave utilities.

Optimize the Directory Structure

It can be a long process, but reorganizing the directory structure to shorten paths and keep subdirectories to a reasonable length may be worth it. This is most easily done in Windows or DOS Shell, where you can see the whole directory tree and one or more directory listings at the same time, and you can drag files around as necessary.

If you need to reorganize your directory structure, do it now so that the new directory structure is used as you optimize your files.

Delete Unnecessary Files

Deadwood builds up quickly on a hard disk. Not only do you forget to delete files that you don't need anymore, but your applications create backup and temporary files that aren't necessarily deleted.

While you're working with your directory structure in Windows or the Shell, question the files you find there. Delete any files you know you don't need any more. Table 11.1 lists DOS (and some Windows) files that can be deleted if you don't use their functions.

Table 11.1. Files To Delete

Filename	Description
HIMEM.SYS	Delete this file if your system does not have extended memory. (If you use DOS's HIMEM.SYS, you can delete Windows' version, and vice versa.)
LOADFIX.EXE	Delete this program if you don't have extended memory or if you don't load DOS into the HMA.
EMM386.EXE	Delete this if your computer is not a 386 or 486.

Filename	Description
RAMDRIVE.SYS	Delete this file if you don't want to use it to create RAM drives.
SMARTDRV.SYS	Delete this hard disk caching system if you don't want to use it, if your system has no extended memory, or if you use a newer version provided with Windows. (If you use DOS's version, you can delete Windows' version.)
DRIVER.SYS	Delete this file if you don't want to redefine or rename your disk drives.
GRAPHICS.COM GRAPHICS.PRO	These files let you print graphics screens under DOS and can be deleted if you don't need that function.
NLSFUNC.EXE KEYB.COM	Delete these files if you are in the COUNTRY.SYS DISPLAY.SYS U.S. and don't need international language support.
DEBUG.EXE	Delete this file if you are not a programmer.
MSHERC.COM	Delete this file if you don't plan to use QBasic or if you don't have a Hercules graphics adapter.
*.TXT	Delete these documentation files (from the DOS directory only) when you don't need them anymore.
FASTOPEN.EXE	Delete this file if you don't plan to use it to cache hard disk directories in RAM.
SHARE.EXE	Delete this file if you don't need it in a networking or multitasking environment.

continues

Table 11.1. continued

Filename	Description
DOSSHELL.* EGA.SYS	Delete these files if you don't plan to use DOS Shell.
ASSIGN.COM, BACKUP.EXE, COMP.EXE, CV.COM, EDLIN.EXE, EXE2BIN.EXE, GRAFTABL.COM, JOIN.EXE, 4201.CPI, 4208.CPI, 5202.CPI, LCD.CPI, MIRROR.COM, MSHERC.COM, PRINTER.SYS, PRINTFIX.COM REMLINE.BAS	These files are left over from DOS 5 and are obsolete with DOS 6. However, they will still work with DOS 6 if you need them. Delete them when you no longer need them.

If you installed DOS 6 from scratch, you don't have the last set of files. You can order them from Microsoft if you need them for some reason. See your User's Guide for ordering information.

Every file you delete leaves room so that you can move your active files closer to the system area, which helps to shorten arm movements. Clean out unnecessary files often to keep your hard disk optimized.

Run CHKDSK

The next step in optimizing your hard disk is to run CHKDSK to recover any lost allocation units and fix any problems in the drive's directory structure. Chapter 17 explains in detail how to use CHKDSK for this process.

A lost allocation unit is a cluster that contains valid data, but DOS can't figure out to what file it belongs. Most lost allocation units belonged to files that were deleted; you can safely delete them after you know what they contain. Getting rid of the lost allocation units can free up thousands of bytes on your hard disk, giving you space to move active files closer to the directories and FAT.

CHKDSK also detects problems in the drive's directory tree and FAT. It can fix most of the problems it finds if you include the /F switch on the CHKDSK command. DEFRAG can't cope with errors in the directory structure or FAT, so it's important to fix them before you run DEFRAG.

> Repeat this procedure often to keep your hard disk optimized.

Delete PCTRACKR.DEL

The deletion-tracking file will be invalid after defragmenting. Because it is a hidden file, DEFRAG would be forced to work around it if you don't delete it.

Exit All Programs

DEFRAG would make a terrible mess out of your hard drive if it moved the clusters belonging to open files. Be sure to exit all programs such as Windows and DOS Shell and run DEFRAG from the primary command prompt. In addition, disable any caching program (SmartDrive doesn't have to be disabled) as well as any TSR that may write to the hard drive while DEFRAG is working.

Defragmenting Your Hard Drive

DOS's DEFRAG program optimizes the files on your hard drive by moving clusters around to minimize or eliminate fragmentation. You also can ask it to move all the free space to the end of the drive, which helps to minimize future fragmentation. In addition, it sorts directory entries; a sorted directory doesn't affect access speed, but it determines the order in which files are processed by commands such as XCOPY and BACKUP.

Because DEFRAG moves data around in the clusters, it destroys any leftover data in available clusters. You can't undelete files after running DEFRAG unless they are protected by Delete Sentry.

Figure 11.3 shows the format of the DEFRAG command. You can use DEFRAG in an interactive graphics mode or in batch mode. Either way, it pays to include the /B switch to do an automatic reboot when DEFRAG is done. This clears out any buffers or caches that may be holding old directory information; if a program tries to access the drive using invalid directory information, some files could be severely damaged.

Figure 11.3.
DEFRAG
command
summary.

DEFRAG

Reorganizes files on a drive to optimize file performance; sorts directory entries.

Format:

```
DEFRAG [drive] [/F ¦ /U] [/Sorder] [/V] [/B] [/SKIPHIGH]
```

Parameters and Switches:

none	Opens the DEFRAG dialog box so that you can select the drive and options.
drive	Identifies the drive to optimize.
/F	Defragments files and free space.
/U	Defragments files only.
/Sorder	Sorts directory entries; *order* specifies the sort field (see "Notes").
/V	Verifies data after moving it.
/B	Reboots when DEFRAG ends.
/SKIPHIGH	Loads the DEFRAG program in conventional memory.

Notes:

The values for *order* are as follows:

N	by name (alphanumeric order)
N-	by name (reverse alphanumeric order)

E	by extension (alphanumeric order)
E-	by extension (reverse alphanumeric order)
D	by date and time, earliest first
D-	by date and time, latest first
S	by size, smallest first
S-	by size, largest first

You can't use DEFRAG to optimize network drives or drives created with INTERLNK.

DEFRAG's Interactive Windows

To start DEFRAG in interactive mode, enter a command as follows:

```
DEFRAG /B
```

You can include other switches and parameters in the command if you want. You can select the drive to be optimized, the optimization method, and the sort order in the interactive menus and dialog boxes, but the remaining switches have no equivalents. If you want DEFRAG to verify the data that it writes, use the /V switch; if you use DOS's verify function, the /V switch is unnecessary. Use /SKIPHIGH to prevent DEFRAG from loading itself into upper memory. Generally, you should let DEFRAG run from upper memory, as it's more efficient that way. However, if it stumbles over something in your system, you may need to use the /SKIPHIGH switch to force it into conventional memory.

DEFRAG starts by performing a memory test to make sure that it can safely move data around at high speeds. If your system fails the memory test, you can't run DEFRAG until you get it fixed.

Next, DEFRAG asks you to select the drive to be optimized. You can work on only one drive at a time. When you choose a drive, DEFRAG analyzes that drive and displays a window similar to the one in Figure 11.4. The Recommendation dialog box is displayed on top of DEFRAG's main window, which includes a map of your drive.

Figure 11.4.
DEFRAG window.

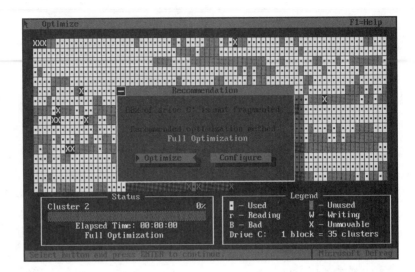

DEFRAG always shows the entire drive in one screen, so the number of clusters represented by each map block varies according to the size of the drive. In the example, each block represents 35 clusters, as you can see in the Legend box. The Legend box also explains the symbols that are used in the map. In cases where a block contains some used clusters, some unused clusters, some unmovable clusters (clusters containing hidden or system files), and so on, DEFRAG displays the most significant symbol pertaining to the block. For example, a bad cluster is the most significant because DEFRAG must work around it; whereas an unused cluster is the least significant because DEFRAG is free to use it at will.

DEFRAG will recommend no optimization, defragment files only, or full optimization. If you decide to go with the recommended method, press Optimize to start. Otherwise, press Configure to clear the recommendation dialog box and pull down the Optimize menu (see fig. 11.5).

Choose Optimization Method to open a dialog box from which you can choose from the two methods: full optimization or defragment files only. Choose Drive to select a different drive. Choose Map Legend to see a complete legend for the symbols used in the drive map. File Sort lets you select a sort order for the directory entries. When you're ready to run the optimizer, choose Begin Optimization.

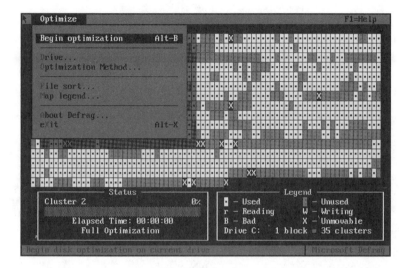

Figure 11.5.
DEFRAG's
Optimize menu.

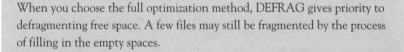

When you choose the full optimization method, DEFRAG gives priority to defragmenting free space. A few files may still be fragmented by the process of filling in the empty spaces.

During the optimization, the DEFRAG window acts as an animated progress box. The letters r (for "read") and W (for "write") appear and disappear in the map blocks to show you exactly where DEFRAG is currently working. The message line at the bottom of the Window also explains the current activity, but it may flash past too quickly to read. The Status box shows you how much of the job has been completed, as a percentage and as a bar graph. Defragmenting an entire hard drive could take anywhere from a few minutes to half an hour or so, depending on system speed, the size of the hard drive, and the optimization method.

Using DEFRAG in Batch Mode

You can avoid opening the DEFRAG dialog box by including the drive name and the optimization method in the DEFRAG command. For example, to do a full optimization of drive D with verification, you could enter the following command:

```
DEFRAG D: /F /V /B
```

DEFRAG begins optimizing immediately when you enter a command like this. This would be a good way to defragment a drive from a batch program (such as a weekly housekeeping program).

Disk Caching

After the hard drive has been optimized, you are ready to set up some systems that will speed it up even more. The single most beneficial technique is disk caching, which stores hard disk data in memory so that you can substitute memory-to-memory transfers for disk reads and writes.

If you have extended memory, you can install DOS 6's intelligent caching system, SMARTDRV.SYS. If not, you can install extra disk buffers to reap some of the benefits of caching, as explained under "Disk Buffers" later in this chapter.

A number of third-party caching systems provide even more features and more flexibility than SMARTDRV.

SMARTDRV Features

SMARTDRV sets up a disk cache in extended memory. Everything you read from or write to disk is copied to the cache. When you read from a disk, SMARTDRV intervenes and looks in the cache first. If the desired material can be found in the cache, the disk access is avoided. The same sectors are reread more often than you may expect; for example, imagine how many times an hour the root directory is accessed.

If you have both Windows 3.1 and DOS 6, you have two versions of SMARTDRV.SYS. Examine their date/time stamps and use the most recent one (which isn't necessarily the last one you purchased).

SMARTDRV.SYS also includes a look-ahead feature. When you read a sector from disk, SMARTDRV copies the next group of sectors into a special look-ahead cache. If you are reading data in sequence, as when loading a file, those are the sectors you will access next (as long as the file isn't fragmented).

SMARTDRV tracks your use of cached data. When the cache is full, it replaces the least-used data with the next read or write. This way, your most active data (such as that root directory) stays in the cache, and something you read only once, such as a program file, is soon replaced with something more useful.

SMARTDRV also caches data written to the disk and delays writing it for up to five seconds. This feature gives priority to reading and processing data; deferred-writes are written whenever the system is not busy with other tasks. As a safeguard against losing data, SMARTDRV immediately writes deferred-writes in the following cases:

- If you press Ctrl-Alt-Delete to reboot.

- If you enter the command SMARTDRV /C, which you use to force deferred-writes to be written before shutting down.

- When the data has been delayed for five seconds.

- When SMARTDRV needs room for new data in the cache.

There's a good chance of losing deferred-writes if the system goes down. If something hangs up in your system, try to free it with Ctrl-Alt-Delete before taking any other measures. If it works, it forces deferred-writes to be written before rebooting.

It's easy to lose data by removing a floppy disk before the deferred-writes are completed. For this reason, SMARTDRV by default does not use deferred-writes on floppy disk drives, just hard drives. However, you can request deferred-writes for floppy disk drives and/or suppress them for hard drives.

Starting SMARTDRV

You start up SMARTDRV with a SMARTDRV command (see fig. 11.6). Windows also uses SMARTDRV and can reduce the size of the cache when it starts up to give itself more room in extended memory. You can specify the initial size of the cache and the minimum size when Windows is running. If you run only Windows, give it free reign to manage the cache by specifying a 0 minimum size. However, if you go back and forth between Windows and DOS, save some cache space so that not all your DOS data will be eliminated when you start up Windows. Table 11.2 shows the default cache sizes.

Table 11.2. Default Cache Sizes

Extended Memory	Initial Cache	Smallest Cache (when Windows is running)
Up to 1M	All extended memory	0 (no cache)
Up to 2M	1M	256K
Up to 4M	1M	512K
Up to 6M	2M	1M
6M or more	2M	2M

The bigger the cache is, the better, so give it as much space as you can. For example, if you have three megabytes of extended memory not used for any other purpose, you could install SMARTDRV with the following command:

```
SMARTDRV 3072 512
```

Figure 11.6.
SMARTDRV
command.

SMARTDRV

Starts or configures SmartDrive, which creates a disk cache in extended memory; writes cached data.

Format:

```
SMARTDRV [drive[+¦-]...] [/E:element] [InitCache] [WinCache]
[/B:buffer] [/R] [/L] [/Q]
```

Parameters and Switches:

none   If SmartDrive is not already loaded, loads the TSR portion
                of the program with default values. Displays caching status
                of drives.

---

drive	Identifies a disk drive for which you want to control caching (do not follow the drive letter with a colon).
+ | -	+ enables both read and write caching for drive; - disables both read and write caching for drive. See Notes for defaults.
/E:*element*	Specifies in bytes the amount of the cache that SmartDrive moves at one time; may be 1024, 2048, 4096, or 8192; the default is 8192. The larger the value, the more conventional memory SmartDrive uses.
InitCache	Specifies in kilobytes the size of the cache when SmartDrive starts and Windows is not running. The default depends on your system's memory (see Notes).
WinCache	Specifies in kilobytes the smallest size to which SmartDrive reduces the cache when Windows starts. The default depends on your system's memory (see Notes).
/B:*buffer*	Specifies the size of the read-ahead buffer; may be any multiple of element; the default is 16K.
/R	Clears the contents of the cache.
/L	Prevents SmartDrive from automatically loading into upper memory, even if there are UMBs available.
/Q	Prevents SmartDrive from displaying error and status messages.
/S	Displays additional information about the status of SmartDrive.

If the specified cache doesn't fit in extended memory, SMARTDRV adjusts the cache size to fit the available space.

Specifying Drive Caching

By default, SMARTDRV reads-caches and writes-caches hard drives, read-caches floppy drives, and doesn't cache other types of drives. You can specify different drive caching by including drive switches in the SMARTDRV command. A *drive* switch with no suffix turns on read caching but not write caching for the indicated drive; *drive+* turns on both read-and-write caching; whereas *drive-* turns off caching. For example, suppose that you want to read-cache but not write-cache drive C and eliminate caching altogether for your floppy drives; you would start up SMARTDRV with the following command:

```
SMARTDRV C+ A- B-
```

If you have other hard drives, they would be read-cached and write-cached by default because this command does not specify otherwise.

You can alter the type of caching for a drive after SMARTDRV has started by entering the SMARTDRV command with the *drive*[+/-] switch, as in SMARTDRV A- to turn off caching for drive A.

SMARTDRV's Double-Buffering Feature

Some drives do not function well with SMARTDRV's normal setup. For such drives, SMARTDRV needs to use a double-buffering technique that slows it down a bit but protects your system from data loss.

Drives with bus-mastering controllers that do not conform to Microsoft's Virtual DMA Services (VDS) standard need double-buffering. This group includes SCSI drives, some ESDI drives, and a few other types of drives.

Don't install double-buffering automatically; some drives won't function with double-buffering in place. You can use the SMARTDRV status report to see whether your system needs to use double-buffering. Enter a SMARTDRV command with the /S switch to see a status report similar to the following:

```
Microsoft SMARTDrive Disk Cache Version 4.1
Copyright 1991,1993 Microsoft Corp.
Room for 128 elements of 8,192 bytes each
There have been 5,727 cache hits
          and 3,111 cache misses
Cache size: 1,048,576 bytes
Cache size while running Windows: 262,144 bytes
          Disk Caching Status
drive   read cache   write cache   buffering
------------------------------------------------
A:      yes          no            no
B:      yes          no            no
C:      yes          yes           no
For help, type "Smartdrv /?".
```

If any line in the buffering column says yes, you definitely need double-buffering. If a line says –, SMARTDRV is unable to determine whether you need it or not, and you had best install it for safety's sake. Install it by loading the SMARTDRV.EXE driver from CONFIG.SYS with a command like the following:

```
DEVICEHIGH=C:\DOS\SMARTDRV.SYS DOUBLE_BUFFER
```

You still need the SMARTDRV command to start up SMARTDRV, as explained earlier.

SMARTDRV Hit Ratios

The status report also includes "hit ratio" information. In the example, SMARTDRV has accomplished 5,727 *hits*; that is, it has supplied data from the cache 5,727 times. It has missed only 3,111 times; DOS had to access the disk for each miss. As you can see, SMARTDRV really does make a difference. In this example, SMARTDRV has prevented about 65 percent of the disk accesses. The longer you work, the higher the percentage becomes as SMARTDRV manages to identify and retain your most active data. The hit ratio can actually achieve 90 percent or higher in a typical system.

Tailoring SMARTDRV

The /E, /L, and /B parameters can be used to adjust the balance between SMARTDRV efficiency and the amount of memory space it uses. These parameters can be used only on the command that starts up SMARTDRV; you can't change these features after SMARTDRV is loaded.

If you need SMARTDRV to use less conventional memory space, set /E to less than the maximum 8K. This setting causes SMARTDRV to move less data at the same time, hence slowing it down, but it also uses that much less space in conventional memory. You also can cut down on conventional memory usage by reducing the size of the read-ahead buffer, which is 16K by default. If you usually access large sequential files that are not fragmented, increasing the size of the read-ahead buffer can increase your hit ratio, if you can afford the space in conventional memory.

Ordinarily, SMARTDRV loads itself into upper memory if possible. In some systems, especially when double-buffering is needed, loading SMARTDRV in upper memory could actually slow it down. If you're using double-buffering and upper memory blocks and if you have the room in conventional memory, try the /L switch to see whether this switch affords even more performance improvement.

> Don't install two caching systems. Double-caching wastes time and memory space and can cause data loss.

Disk Buffers

You can't use SMARTDRV.SYS without extended memory. But, you can set aside some disk-buffering space in conventional memory to speed up disk access a little. Disk buffers are somewhat like a dumb cache.

DOS always reads from disk into a buffer before transferring the data to the program that requested it. Similarly, DOS always writes data from a program into a buffer before writing it to disk. If only one buffer is allocated, it must be used for all reads and writes, so it's unlikely that the data DOS wants next is already present in the buffer. However, if 30 buffers are allocated, the probability of finding desired data in a buffer goes up dramatically. If 99 buffers are allocated (the maximum), the probability goes up even more, but generally, system performance goes down because DOS spends more time searching the buffers for desired data than it would take to access the disk.

If you also allocate some look-ahead buffers, DOS will read additional sectors when a program requests one. This practice increases the probability of finding the next desired sector in a buffer when unfragmented files are read sequentially.

Figure 11.7 shows the format of the BUFFERS command, which belongs in CONFIG.SYS. If you don't specify BUFFERS, DOS allocates a default number of buffers based on your system configuration. It's a sure bet that the default number is not what you want. If you are using a more intelligent caching system, such as SMARTDRV, cut the number of buffers back to about 15. If not, use Table 11.3 to determine the number of buffers to allocate. Include some look-ahead buffers if you tend to read unfragmented files in sequential order.

Generally, the buffers are located wherever DOS is located. If DOS is loaded into the HMA, the buffers also are created there. However, if extended memory doesn't have enough room for all the buffers you have requested, they are all moved to conventional memory. You can usually fit around 40 buffers along with DOS in the HMA; each buffer is the size of a sector, half a kilobyte. If conventional memory is tight in your system, it pays to experiment with the number of buffers you can get away with in the HMA. Use the MEM /D /P command to determine whether they are in conventional memory. You'll see the line BUFFERS=nn in the report. If the size of that area is only 512 bytes, the buffers are in the HMA.

BUFFERS

Specifies the number of disk buffers.

Format:

BUFFERS=read-write[,look-ahead]

Parameters:

read-write   Specifies the number of read-write buffers. Range is 1 to 99. Default (if the BUFFERS command is omitted) depends on your system configuration.

look-ahead   Specifies the number of look-ahead buffers. Range is 0 to 8. Default is 0. If either *read-write* or *look-ahead* is outside its range, *look-ahead* defaults to 0.

Figure 11.7.
BUFFERS
configuration
command reference.

Table 11.3. Buffer Allocation Recommendations

Disk Size	Number of Buffers
< 40M	20
40M to 79M	30
80M to 119M	40
> 119M	50

RAM Drives

A RAM drive is a pseudo drive (often called a virtual drive) in RAM instead of on disk, with lightning-fast access times as a consequence. You can store directories and files on it just as you can on a real drive, but all its data disappears when you reboot or the power goes out—and that's the main drawback. Most people use RAM drives for temporary files so that they don't have to worry about losing any data when the power goes out. Even at that, RAM drives can be a great boost to your system.

However, you shouldn't take space away from a disk-caching system to create a RAM drive. Disk caching gives you much better performance improvement for the same amount of memory space. Set up a RAM drive in unused expanded memory or in extended memory if you have some space left over after creating a disk cache.

Creating a RAM Drive

DOS includes the RAMDRIVE.SYS driver (see fig. 11.8) to create and manage RAM drives. It runs well in upper memory; use DEVICEHIGH if UMBs are available on your system.

RAMDRIVE.SYS

Uses an area of your computer's random-access memory (RAM) to simulate a hard disk drive.

Format:

```
DEVICE[HIGH]=[path]RAMDRIVE.SYS [DiskSize [SectorSize
[NumEntries]]] [/E ¦ /A]
```

Parameters and Switches:

path	Identifies the location of the RAMDRIVE.SYS file. The default is the root directory of the boot drive.
DiskSize	Specifies, in kilobytes, how much memory to use for the RAM drive. Valid values are 4 to 32,767 or available memory, whichever is smaller. The default is 64.
SectorSize	Specifies disk sector size in bytes. May be 128, 256, or 512 (the default). Microsoft recommends that you use 512. If you include *SectorSize*, you must include *DiskSize*.
NumEntries	Specifies the number of files and directories you can create in the root directory of the RAM drive. May be 2 to 1,024; the limit you specify is rounded up to the nearest sector size boundary. The default is 64. If you include *NumEntries*, you must also include *SectorSize* and *DiskSize*.
/E	Creates the RAM drive in extended memory.
/A	Creates the RAM drive in expanded memory.

Notes:

If you omit /E and /A, the RAM drive uses conventional memory. This is recommended only on a system with no extended memory, no expanded memory, and no hard disk.

If you use Windows and set TEMP to a directory on a RAM drive, be sure that *DiskSize* is at least 2,048 (2M) to allow enough space for Window's temporary print files.

Figure 11.8.
RAMDRIVE.SYS
DEVICE
command.

Figure 11.8.
continued

> If there is not enough room to create the RAM drive as specified, RAMDRIVE.SYS tries to create a drive with a limit of 16 entries in the root directory.

Determining RAM Drive Size

The bigger the RAM drive, the better. After determining what other programs need extended or expanded memory, including your disk cache, give the rest to the RAM drive.

Number of Directory Entries

If you want to be able to store more than 64 files in the RAM drive, you can increase the size of the root directory or create subdirectories, which is done just as on any other drive. The space for the root directory and FATs is taken out of the RAM drive's total size. (A RAM drive doesn't have a partition table or boot record.)

Determining Sector Size

You have little reason to use a sector size other than 512 bytes. Some people feel that you can save slack space if you use a smaller sector size, but DOS works best with the 512-byte size.

You can create multiple RAM drives. Just include a separate DEVICE statement in CONFIG.SYS for each one.

Using the RAM Drive

DOS assigns the RAM drive the next available drive letter during booting. A message tells you the drive name. If you miss it, start up DOS Shell and you'll see it in the drive list.

> You don't need to use LASTDRIVE to make a RAM drive name available. DOS automatically expands the number of available drive names to include RAM drives.

About the best thing you can do with a RAM drive is to store temporary files on it. Temporary files are those files written by programs for their own internal purposes and deleted automatically when they are no longer needed. For example, DOS creates a temporary file when you pipe something. Windows and Windows applications write a lot of temporary files; if they can write them on a RAM drive instead of a hard drive, they save a great deal of time. Both DOS and Windows look for an environment variable named TEMP to tell them where to write temporary files. (Chapter 9 explains environment variables.) To direct DOS's and Windows' temporary files to RAM drive E, include the following statement in AUTOEXEC.BAT:

```
SET TEMP=E:\
```

> If you omit the switch to create the RAM drive in extended or expanded memory, DOS will try to create it in conventional memory. If it's too large for conventional memory, DOS issues the message `Configuration too large for memory` and freezes. You need to reboot and bypass the RAM drive statement until you can fix the problem.

DoubleSpace

Introduction

DOS 6's new Double-Space compresses disk data so that you can store a lot more files on one drive. DoubleSpace works on both hard drives and floppies, so you can compress the drives that you work with every day as well as the disks that you use for vault storage.

You can even send compressed data to other personal computer users if they also have DoubleSpace to decompress it again. When you install DoubleSpace, it becomes part of the core DOS system so that it doesn't cause the booting problems that third-party compression utilities experience.

About Compression

Data compression reduces the amount of space it takes to store a file by eliminating repetitive data. Repeated strings of bytes are replaced by codes pointing back to the first appearance of the string. Compression saves much more space than you might imagine. A typical word processing file can by reduced by 50 percent. Bit-mapped graphics files, such as a TIF file, may be reduced by more than 90 percent.

DoubleSpace Features

DoubleSpace does not compress files individually. Instead, it creates a *compressed volume file* (CVF) on the host drive. The CVF is in fact a file, but it looks to DOS like another drive. DoubleSpace manages this compressed drive. Any files that you write to the drive are automatically compressed. Files read from the drive are automatically decompressed. The compression and decompression processes are transparent to the user, who simply sees more space on the drive than was there before. You can create compressed drives on hard drives and floppy disks.

The small amount of time that compression and decompression take impedes some time-sensitive applications, such as animators and sound synthesizers. Such applications should not be stored on compressed drives.

Sector Allocation

DoubleSpace manages to save even more space on the compressed drive by allocating file space in sectors instead of clusters. DOS's smallest allocation unit is a cluster, which might be 2K on a hard drive. If a file fills only a few bytes of its last cluster, the rest of the cluster goes to waste; that could be nearly 2K of space. By allocating space in smaller increments, DoubleSpace throws away less space at the ends of files.

The DoubleSpace Core Program

When you install DoubleSpace, the DBLSPACE.BIN program file becomes the third file in DOS's kernel, joining the traditional IO.SYS and MSDOS.SYS. If it is present on the boot drive when you boot, it is loaded along with the other two core files, before CONFIG.SYS is processed. It immediately seizes control of its compressed volumes, so that by the time CONFIG.SYS is processed, the compressed drives are already available. This avoids the boot problems experienced by third-party compression software, which must be loaded via CONFIG.SYS.

DOS initially loads DBLSPACE.BIN at the top of conventional memory. A program called DBLSPACE.SYS then moves it to a more appropriate location. If your system is set up to use upper memory blocks and if DBLSPACE.SYS is loaded with a DEVICEHIGH command, DBLSPACE.SYS moves DBLSPACE.BIN into upper memory. (DOS loads it at the top of conventional memory to start with so that it won't leave an unusable gap in conventional memory when it's moved to upper memory.) If DBLSPACE.BIN can't be moved to upper memory, DBLSPACE.SYS moves it lower down in conventional memory. After installing DoubleSpace, you'll find the following command in CONFIG.SYS; this is the command that loads DBLSPACE.SYS, whose only function is to move DBLSPACE.BIN:

```
DEVICE=C:\DOS\DBLSPACE.SYS /MOVE
```

If your system is set up for upper memory, run MEMMAKER after installing DoubleSpace to convert this command into a DEVICEHIGH command that will load DBLSPACE.BIN into upper memory.

Manipulating Drive Names

There are two basic ways to create a CVF on a drive. You can make a CVF out of the existing data, or you can leave the existing data alone and make a CVF out of the empty space. If you choose to create a CVF out of empty space, DoubleSpace assigns a new drive letter to the CVF. For example, suppose your current drive names are A,

B, and C. If you create a CVF out of the empty space on drive C, the new compressed drive might be assigned the name D. DoubleSpace suggests a name for the new drive, but you can select a different name if you like.

If you create a CVF by compressing the existing files on a drive, DoubleSpace assigns the host drive's name to the new compressed drive. That way, any programs that refer to those files are still valid. The host drive receives the new drive name. For example, if you have only drives A, B, and C, and you compress the existing data on drive C, the compressed drive becomes drive C and the host drive becomes drive D (or some other letter).

This process of assigning drive names to a compressed drive and its host is called *mounting* the compressed drive. DoubleSpace automatically mounts all hard disk compressed drives during booting. But if you have a compressed drive on a floppy disk, you must ask DoubleSpace to mount it whenever you want to use it.

You can *unmount* a compressed drive, which restores the host drive's original name and eliminates the compressed drive's name, but there's very little reason to do so. Sometimes DoubleSpace unmounts a compressed drive while maintaining it, but it always remounts the drive again.

Files on the Host Drive

DoubleSpace leaves a certain amount of space on the host drive for storing uncompressed files. By default, it leaves 2M, but you can specify the amount of space to leave when the compressed drive is first created, and you can resize the compressed drive later on.

Even if the host drive had only 1.2M of free space when DoubleSpace compressed its data, after compression there will be enough space to leave 2M or more for the host drive.

If the host drive is the boot drive, the three DOS core system files will be stored in the uncompressed area along with DBLSPACE.INI. All these files are hidden, but you can see them by including the /A switch with DIR. You'll also see DBLSPACE.*nnn*, which is the compressed volume file. The *nnn* is 000 if you compressed the existing data; otherwise, it's a higher number.

> Don't delete, move, or otherwise manipulate the DBLSPACE files. You could lose contact with your compressed drive and all its data.

If you compress a drive containing the Windows permanent swap file, DoubleSpace places the swap file in the uncompressed space because it won't work if it's compressed. If you have any other files that should not be compressed, you'll have to move them from the compressed drive to the uncompressed drive after DoubleSpace finishes. If you discover later that one of your programs doesn't work properly on the compressed drive, you can move it to the host drive, resizing the compressed drive to make more room on the host drive if necessary. You might have to reconfigure or even reinstall the program to reflect the changed drive name.

> You might have to reinstall copy-protected programs that make note of the location where they were installed. Such programs might refuse to run after being compressed, not because they have been compressed but because they have been moved.

Installing DoubleSpace

Don't install DoubleSpace just to see whether or not you like it. There is no uninstallation feature, and although it can be done, it's not easy to decompress a drive or uninstall DoubleSpace.

You must exit Windows or DOS Shell to install DoubleSpace. You'll probably want to turn off VSAFE or any other virus monitor, also. DoubleSpace must reboot a couple of times during the setup process, so if these programs are started up via AUTOEXEC.BAT, insert REM in front of their commands and reboot before starting up DoubleSpace.

DoubleSpace takes every precaution to protect existing data during the
compression process, but you would be wise to back up your data before
starting DoubleSpace, just in case.

To compress the boot drive, it must have 1.2M of free space; other drives must have
665K of free space before compression begins.

To install DoubleSpace and compress a hard drive, enter the DBLSPACE command
with no parameters at the command prompt. After displaying a welcome screen,
DoubleSpace gives you the choice of an Express or Custom setup (see fig. 12.1). The
Express setup offers no more choices; it compresses the existing data on drive C
using default settings for the amount of space to leave on the host drive and the
host drive's name.

Figure 12.1.
Choosing Express
Setup or Custom
Setup.

```
Microsoft DoubleSpace Setup

    There are two ways to run Setup:

    Use Express Setup if you want DoubleSpace Setup to compress
    drive C and determine the compression settings for you. This
    is the easiest way to install DoubleSpace.

    Use Custom Setup if you are an experienced user and want to
    specify the compression settings and drive configuration
    yourself.

    ┌──────────────────────────────────────────────────────────┐
    │ Express Setup (recommended)                              │
    │ Custom Setup                                             │
    └──────────────────────────────────────────────────────────┘

    To accept the selection, press ENTER.

    To change the selection, press the UP or DOWN ARROW key
    until the item you want is selected, and then press ENTER.

 ENTER=Continue  F1=Help  F3=Exit
```

The Custom setup gives you more options:

- You can choose the hard drive you want to compress. (The first time you
  use DoubleSpace, you must compress a hard drive.)

- You can choose whether to compress the existing data or the empty space
  on that drive.

- If you choose to compress the existing data, you can choose how much
  space to leave on the host drive for uncompressed data (see fig. 12.2).

● As you can see in Figure 12.2, you can choose the new drive name.

```
Microsoft DoubleSpace Setup

   DoubleSpace provides two ways to create more disk space:

   To compress the files on an existing drive so that the drive
   has more free space, choose 'Compress an existing drive.'
   This method provides the most free space, and is
   particularly useful if the drive is getting full.

   To convert the free space on an existing drive into a new
   compressed drive, choose 'Create an empty compressed drive.'
   You might want to use this method if the drive has a lot of
   free space.

   ┌────────────────────────────────────────────────────────┐
   │ Compress an existing drive                             │
   │ Create a new empty compressed drive                    │
   └────────────────────────────────────────────────────────┘

   To change the selection, press the UP or DOWN ARROW key
   until the item you want is selected, and then press ENTER.

ENTER=Continue  F1=Help  F3=Exit  ESC=Previous screen
```

Figure 12.2.
Custom setup compression settings.

The Compression Process

After you have made your decisions, DoubleSpace begins the compression process. It could take a few minutes or several hours, depending on whether you're compressing existing data, how much data, and how fast your system is. DoubleSpace displays a time estimate, but it might not even be close to the actual time.

First, DoubleSpace defragments the drive to put all the free space together. Then it begins compressing data if you've chosen to do so. The compression process is designed to protect your data as much as possible. DoubleSpace validates each file after compressing it. It flushes buffers and caches frequently so that nothing is lost in a power outage. If it's interrupted by a power outage or some other event, it continues where it left off when the computer restarts.

When it's done, a summary screen tells you how long the compression took and how much free space the compressed drive contains. You can begin using the compressed drive just as you use any other drive.

SMARTDRV continues to cache the host drive, not the compressed drive. This causes the compressed data to be cached also. FDISK (see Chapter 23) does not show a compressed drive in its list of logical drives; the host drive does appear in the list, however.

Compression Ratios and Space Estimates

The compression ratio shows how much space was saved by compression. For example, a compression ratio of 2.3:1 means that, for every 2.3 bytes in the uncompressed file, only 1 byte was written in the compressed file. Some types of files compress more than others. A typical word-processing document, for example, achieves a compression ratio around 2:1. A bit-mapped graphic might compress as high as 20:1. Other types of files might compress at only 1.3:1. The overall compression ratio on your compressed drive depends on the mixture of file types you have stored there. It will probably be around 2:1.

When a program such as DIR or CHKDSK reports the available space on a compressed drive, the actual number of bytes would be meaningless. What's more important is how much data you can still store on that drive. To compute this, DoubleSpace calculates an estimated compression ratio based on the data that's already on the drive, then multiplies that by the number of free bytes on the drive. The result estimates how many bytes of *uncompressed data* you can write to the drive. It may or may not be accurate, depending on the nature of the files that you write to the drive. DIR, CHKDSK, and other programs that report available space use the estimated space figure provided by DoubleSpace.

In addition, the DIR command includes a new switch that displays compression ratios on a compressed drive. The /C switch displays compression information based on an 8K cluster size. If you add an H to it, as in /CH, it displays compression information based on the host drive's cluster size, which is more accurate. A DIR /CH listing looks something like this:

```
Volume in drive D has no label
 Volume Serial Number is 13EF-2218
 Directory of D:\FRENCH

 .              <DIR>      02-21-93  12:28p
 ..             <DIR>      02-21-93  12:28p
 CHKLIST  MS          54  12-22-92   3:58p    4.0 to 1.0
 FLASHCRD BAS      30896  05-05-92  10:42a    2.3 to 1.0
 FLASHCRD EXE      91084  05-05-92  10:43a    1.3 to 1.0
 VOCAB    BAS      31265  05-05-92  11:42a    2.2 to 1.0
 VOCAB    EXE      91242  05-05-92  11:42a    1.3 to 1.0
```

```
WORK      BAS     13054 05-04-92  11:59a    1.6 to 1.0
                       1.4 to 1.0 average compression ratio
        8 file(s)      257595 bytes
                     21102592 bytes free
```

You can see the compression ratio for each file as well as the average compression ratio for the listed files. The size listed for each file is the uncompressed size; this tells you how much space the file will take up when you read it into memory or copy or move it to an uncompressed drive. The space estimate on the last line is provided by DoubleSpace.

You can also sort the DIR listing by compression ratio. The /OC switch lists files from lowest to highest ratio, and /O-C lists them from highest to lowest.

If you apply the SUBST command to a compressed drive, DoubleSpace no longer provides space estimates for the drive, and the actual number of bytes will be shown.

Compressing Additional Hard Drives

After DoubleSpace is installed and the first compressed drive is created, the DBLSPACE command opens the window shown in Figure 12.3. All your compressed drives are shown in the list. You use this window to perform maintenance on a compressed drive, such as resizing the drive, and to compress more drives.

You can compress additional hard drives by using the commands on the Compress menu: Compress Existing Data or Create New Drive (to compress the free space). DoubleSpace asks you to choose the drive to be compressed, then compresses the drive as before. When it's done, you'll see the new compressed drive in the drive list in the main DoubleSpace window.

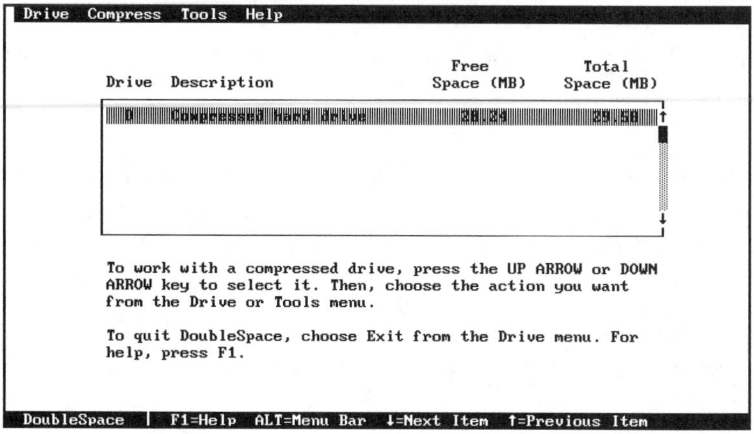

Figure 12.3.
DoubleSpace
window.

```
 Drive  Compress  Tools  Help

                                          Free         Total
        Drive  Description            Space (MB)    Space (MB)

         D    Compressed hard drive       28.23        29.58  ↑




                                                              ↓

        To work with a compressed drive, press the UP ARROW or DOWN
        ARROW key to select it. Then, choose the action you want
        from the Drive or Tools menu.

        To quit DoubleSpace, choose Exit from the Drive menu. For
        help, press F1.

 DoubleSpace  |  F1=Help  ALT=Menu Bar  ↓=Next Item  ↑=Previous Item
```

Alternatively, you could enter a command in this format at the DOS command prompt:

```
DBLSPACE /COMPRESS drive1 [/NEWDRIVE=drive2] [/RESERVE=megabytes]
```

This command compresses the existing files on a drive. The *drive1* parameter identifies the host drive; *drive2* identifies the new name for the host drive, if you don't want to use the DoubleSpace default. Use the /RESERVE parameter to specify how much uncompressed space to keep on the host drive; if you omit it, DoubleSpace leaves only the minimum on the host drive.

To create a compressed drive out of the free space on a drive, enter a command in this format:

```
DBLSPACE /CREATE drive1 [/NEWDRIVE=drive2]
[/SIZE=megabytes ¦ /RESERVE=megabytes]
```

For example, to create a compressed drive out of 10M of free space on drive D, you would enter this command:

```
DBLSPACE /CREATE D /SIZE=10
```

Compressing a Floppy

You can create a compressed drive on a floppy disk. Suppose that you need to ship a large group of files to a client who also has DoubleSpace. You'll save a lot of disk space by compressing them. Or suppose you want to back a finished project off your hard drive but keep a vault copy on floppy disks for a year or so. You'll need a lot fewer vault disks if you compress them.

You could use Backup for these tasks, but DoubleSpace offers some real advantages. With DoubleSpace, you simply copy files back and forth; you don't have to deal with backup catalogs when you want to access files on the floppies. Furthermore, you can add, delete, and modify files on the floppies. With Backup, once the backup set is made, it can't be modified. But there are tradeoffs. DoubleSpace doesn't offer many of Backup's bells and whistles, such as error correction code. Furthermore, since DoubleSpace automatically decompresses any data that you read from a compressed drive, you can't telecommunicate the data in compressed form. With Backup, you can.

To be compressed, a floppy must be formatted and have at least .65M of free space. Also, DoubleSpace can't compress a 360K floppy. If the floppy drive doesn't show up in DoubleSpace's drive list, the disk that's currently in it doesn't meet these requirements.

To create a compressed drive on a new floppy, insert the disk in the drive and select the Compress Existing Drive command. (You can't use the Compress Create New Drive command on a floppy.) DoubleSpace displays a list of drives that are available for compression (see fig. 12.4). Select the floppy drive and press Enter. After you confirm the command, DoubleSpace converts nearly the entire disk into a compressed drive, mounts the drive, and adds it to the drive list in the DoubleSpace window.

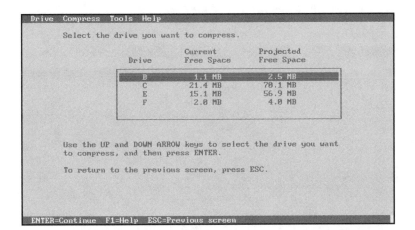

Figure 12.4.
Compress Existing
Drive screen.

Alternatively, you could enter the DBLSPACE /COMPRESS command shown in the preceding section.

As with hard drives, the floppy disk receives a new name for the host drive, and the CVF takes on the old drive name. For a disk in the first floppy disk unit, drive A accesses the compressed volume, whereas the host drive might be called drive L.

The drive is automatically unmounted when you remove it from the disk unit. The next time you want to use it, you must mount it. You can mount it from the DoubleSpace window by choosing Drive Mount. Or you could enter the following at the DOS command prompt:

```
DBLSPACE /MOUNT A:
```

When it creates the drive, DoubleSpace installs in the uncompressed portion of the disk a READTHIS.TXT file that explains that the disk contains a compressed drive and how to mount it. If you list the directory of the unmounted disk, you'll see the READTHIS.TXT file. You'll see the DBLSPACE.000 file only if you include the /A switch to see hidden, read-only, system files. There will be almost no space available on the drive because the DBLSPACE.000 file is taking up most of it.

Once you mount the floppy, the directory of drive A shows a markedly different result. You can't see the READTHIS.TXT file, which is on the host drive. But you can see the files on the compressed drive, and the drive no longer appears full (unless there's no more room in the compressed drive).

The complete format of the DBLSPACE /MOUNT command is

```
DBLSPACE /MOUNT[=nnn] drive1 [/NEWDRIVE=drive2]
```

The *nnn* identifies the extension of the CVF to be mounted; 000 is the default. In other words, if there is more than one CVF on the indicated drive and you don't specify *nnn*, DoubleSpace mounts DBLSPACE.000, the CVF that was originally created from the existing files on the drive.

The NEWDRIVE parameter specifies the new drive name to be assigned to the host drive if you're mounting the 000 volume; for any other volume, it specifies the name to be assigned to the compressed volume.

The Drive menu contains an Unmount command that you can apply to both hard drives and floppies, but there's very little reason to use it. There's also an /UNMOUNT switch for the DBLSPACE command.

CVF Maintenance

The Drive menu and the Tools menu contain several options for maintaining compressed drives. Most of these options are also available as switches on the DBLSPACE command.

Viewing Compressed Drive Information

Figure 12.5 shows the dialog box that opens when you select a compressed drive and choose the Drive Info command. You can also see this information at the command prompt by entering a command in this format:

```
DBLSPACE [/INFO] drive
```

The /INFO switch is optional because if you enter a DBLSPACE command with a drive name and no switch to identify the desired function, /INFO is the default. (If you also omit the drive name, the DoubleSpace window opens.)

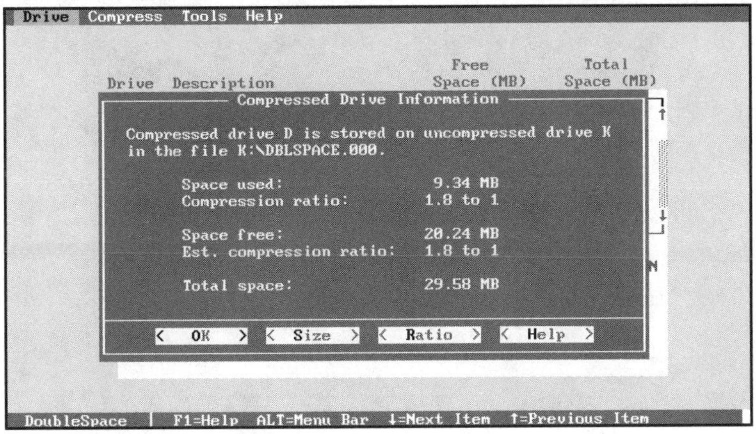

Figure 12.5.
Compressed Drive Information dialog box.

For information about all your non-network drives, compressed and otherwise, use this command instead:

```
DBLSPACE /LIST
```

The list indicates whether each drive is a local hard drive, compressed drive, floppy drive, removable media with no disk inserted, available for DoubleSpace, and so on. (RAM drives are described as local hard drives.) Space used and free space are shown for each drive if appropriate. For each mounted compressed drive, the report shows the compressed volume name (and its host drive). This function is not available via the DoubleSpace window.

Resizing the Drive

You can press the Size button in the Information dialog box or choose the Drive Change Size command to open a dialog box that lets you change the size of the currently selected drive (see fig. 12.6). To change the size from the command prompt, enter a command in this format:

```
DBLSPACE /SIZE=megabytes drive
```

or

```
DBLSPACE /SIZE /RESERVE=megabytes drive
```

Figure 12.6.
Change Size
dialog box.

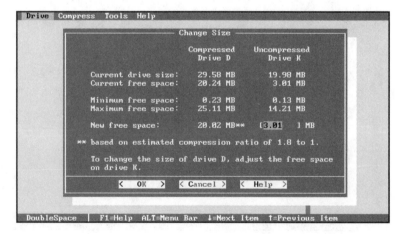

For example, to change the size of drive C to 60M, enter this command:

```
DBLSPACE /SIZE=60M C:
```

The specified size refers to the size of the CVF on the host drive, not the estimated capacity. If you don't specify a size, as in DBLSPACE /SIZE C, DoubleSpace makes the drive as small as possible.

To change drive C so that there are 20M left on the host drive, enter this command:

```
DBLSPACE /SIZE /RESERVE=20 C:
```

If you specify /RESERVE=0, DoubleSpace makes the compressed drive as large as possible.

If you want to make the drive smaller, and especially if you want to shrink it to its smallest possible size, you should defragment it first, as explained in the next section.

Defragmenting a Compressed Drive

Defragmenting a compressed drive will not improve its access speed as it does with a regular drive. But defragmenting can help to bring all the empty space together when you want to make the drive smaller. To defragment a compressed drive, choose the Tools Defragment command or enter a command in this format:

```
DBLSPACE /DEFRAGMENT [drive]
```

If you omit the drive name, the current drive is defragmented. As with most of the drive maintenance functions in this section, you can't use the regular DOS commands because they see the compressed drive as a file, not a drive. If you try to apply a regular DOS DEFRAG command to a compressed drive, DoubleSpace intervenes and uses its own defragmenting function.

Changing the Estimated Compression Ratio

As you've seen, the estimated compression ratio determines how much free space commands such as DIR and CHKDSK report. DoubleSpace updates the estimated compression ratio to match the actual compression ratio every time it mounts the drive. But you can change the estimated compression ratio if you think you know something that DoubleSpace doesn't. For example, suppose you move 40M of TIF files to a compressed drive that has a current compression ratio of 2.1:1. Since TIF files compress at about 20:1, this makes a dramatic difference in the compression ratio. If you want to see more accurate space estimates during this work session, without waiting until the next time the drive is mounted, you can change the estimated compression ratio.

To change the estimated ratio, press the Ratio button in the Information dialog box or choose Drive Change Ratio (see fig. 12.7). Or you can enter this command:

```
DBLSPACE /RATIO[=r.r] [drive ¦ /ALL]
```

The ratio can range from 1.0 to 16.0. If you omit it, DoubleSpace adjusts the estimated ratio to the current ratio. /ALL sets the specified compression ratio for all mounted compressed drives. If you don't specify either a drive name or /ALL, DoubleSpace sets the ratio for the current drive.

Figure 12.7.
Change Compression Ratio dialog box.

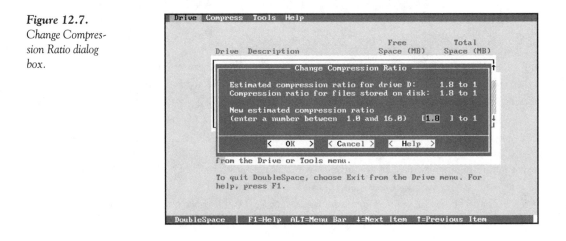

To adjust the estimated ratios for all mounted drives to match their actual ratios, you would enter this command:

```
DBLSPACE /RATIO /ALL
```

Formatting a Compressed Drive

When you first create a compressed drive, it doesn't need to be formatted. But you can reformat it to delete all its data. You must use DoubleSpace's format function, not DOS's FORMAT program.

You can't unformat a compressed drive.

To format a compressed drive, choose the Drive Format command or enter a command in this format:

DBLSPACE/FORMAT *drive*

DoubleSpace's Chkdsk Function

To check the directory structure on a compressed drive, choose the Tools Chkdsk command or enter a command in this format:

DBLSPACE /CHKDSK [/F] [*drive*]

Use the /F switch if you want DoubleSpace to correct any errors it finds.

Freeing Up Memory

Two DoubleSpace options can help to free up some of the memory space that DoubleSpace uses: Last Drive and Removable Media Drives.

DoubleSpace automatically reserves a number of drive names on your system so that it can mount drives as necessary, but it usually reserves many more drive names than you need. Since each drive name it reserves takes up 24K of memory space, it pays to eliminate some of the extra names. Choose the Tools Options command to see and change the last drive name. For example, suppose you have created only one compressed drive and don't intend to create any more. Furthermore, you're not using any RAM drives or other psuedo drives, so that your highest drive name, not counting the names assigned by DoubleSpace, is C. You could safely change the DoubleSpace's last drive name to D and save 168K of memory space.

The Tools Option command also lets you change the number of removable media drives you have. DoubleSpace counts all your floppy drives, removable cartridge drives, and Flash memory card drives and sets aside enough memory space so that you could mount a compressed drive on each one. You can save some memory space by cutting the number back to the number of removable media drives that you actually intend to use compressed drives on. For example, suppose you have two floppy drives and no other removable media drives. If you want to use compressed drives on drive A but not drive B, you could reduce the number of removable media drives to 1. If you plan never to create compressed drives on floppy disks, cut the number to 0.

Deleting a Compressed Drive

If you want to delete a complete compressed drive with all its data from the host drive, choose the Drive Delete command or enter a command in this format:

```
DBLSPACE /DELETE drive
```

Deleting the drive also unmounts it. If it was created by compressing existing data and assigned the host drive's original name, the host drive resumes its original name. If it was created out of free space and assigned a new drive name, that drive name is now available for other uses.

A deleted CVF can be recovered by UNDELETE just like any other file in DOS. If you recover it, you'll have to mount it to use it again.

Decompressing a Drive

You can decompress a drive if you can find enough room for its data. First, copy all the data that you want to keep to another location. If you're going to put it in a temporary location, Backup is a good tool because its own compression function enables the data to take up less space in the temporary location. Next, delete the compressed volume. You can then restore data to the original drive as necessary.

If you want to uninstall DoubleSpace altogether, follow the preceding steps to remove every compressed volume. Don't forget any volumes on floppy disks. Then delete DoubleSpace's files (DBLSPACE.BIN and DBLSPACE.INI) from the root directory of your boot drive. Also remove the DBLSPACE.SYS command from CONFIG.SYS.

Converting from Stacker

If you're currently using Stacker and want to change to DoubleSpace, you can convert your Stacker volumes to DoubleSpace volumes using a command in the following format:

```
DBLSPACE /CONVSTAC=stacvol drive1 [/NEWDRIVE=drive2] [/CVF=ext]
```

The /CONVSTAC=*stacvol* parameter identifies the Stacker volume to be converted. The *drive1* parameter identifies the host drive. /NEWDRIVE identifies the new drive name to be assigned, if you don't want to use DoubleSpace's default. The /CVF=*ext* specifies the extension to be assigned to the new CVF, from 000 to 254. If you assign 000, DoubleSpace treats the volume as if it were created from the existing data on the drive; that is, it receives the host drive's name when it is mounted. Any other number causes the volume to be treated as if it were created from free space. If you omit this parameter, DoubleSpace assigns the extension.

Backing Up and Restoring Files

Introduction

DOS's new backup system offers a number of features that weren't available in the old one.

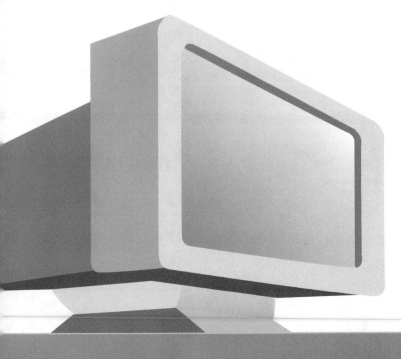

- A graphic user interface lets you select options and files from dialog boxes by using either your mouse or your keyboard.

- Backup setup files let you define backup parameters once and then use them time and time again. After your first backup session, you should be able to run your standard backup with just a couple of keystrokes or mouse clicks. Backup setup files can be transferred to other computers, so you can create setups to give to less experienced users or to standardize the backup procedures for your group.

- You can back up to floppy disks, tape, or any device that can have a DOS drive and directory name (such as a tape drive or removable cartridge).

- If you have two identical floppy drives, you can use both of them in one backup, alternating between them so that Backup doesn't have to wait for you to insert disks.

- A setup can cover several hard drives if desired.

- Several options are available to guarantee the accuracy of the backup files, including a read and compare verification that corrects any errors immediately.

- Backup can compress the backup files to save both space and time.

- Backup is designed to facilitate creating a backup cycle consisting of a full backup followed by differential or incremental backups.

- Automatic backup catalogs keep track of the contents of backup sets. Your latest backup catalogs are maintained on your hard drive so that they can be accessed easily if you want to compare or restore files.

- A COMPARE function compares backup files to their originals on the hard drive and notifies you of changed files. (You can also compare to files on other computers.)

- The RESTORE function lets you select files to be restored and load a backup catalog. You can restore to the original drive and directories or to different ones.

- A CONFIGURE function helps to make sure that Backup will work properly with your hardware and software configuration.

● Backup is available in a Windows version (called MWBACKUP) and a DOS version (called MSBACKUP). The two versions can read each other's files. This chapter describes the DOS version; the Windows version has the same features, although the dialog boxes are more attractive.

For convenience, this chapter assumes that the backup medium is floppy disk. If you're using tape, a removable cartridge, or a second hard drive, there won't be much difference except that you won't have to feed disks into the backup drive.

Backup Cycles

A backup cycle generally starts by archiving all the files on your hard drives that need backup protection—your important data files, but perhaps not program files or casual data files. This is called a *full backup*. The full backup turns off the archive attributes of all the files it handles in preparation for the next part of the cycle.

After you've done a full backup, the cycle continues with some sort of partial backup on a daily basis. The partial backup archives only those files that have been created or modified since the last backup, as identified by their archive attributes. The full backup plus the subsequent partial backups represent all the files that you need to restore your important data files to your hard disk. Backup offers two types of partial backups:

● The *differential backup* backs up only those files that have positive archive attributes; it does not turn off the archive attributes. Each differential backup backs up all files that have been created or modified since the last full backup. Therefore, each differential backup replaces the preceding differential backup; you can use the same disks over again unless you want to be able to fall back to earlier versions of files. The last full backup plus the last differential backup represent the complete set of up-to-date files you need to restore your hard disk. Differential backups are the better choice if you work on the same few files every day.

● The *incremental backup* also backs up files with positive archive attributes, but it turns off the archive attributes of every file it copies. Therefore, each incremental backup archives only those files that have been created or modified since the last incremental backup (or the last full backup). You have to keep all your incremental backups until you do the next full backup. The last full backup plus all subsequent incremental backups make up the complete set of backups you need to restore your hard drive. Incremental backups are the better choice if you work on different files every day.

Don't intermix incremental and differential backups for the same set of files. Because an incremental backup turns off archive attributes, it interferes with the basic premise of a differential backup. You might find that you want to create several backup cycles for different sets of files, in which some files are best handled by a differential cycle and others work best with an incremental cycle.

Managing Backup Sets

After your first full backup, you'll have a set of disks that you add to with each partial backup. Where will you store these disks? How long will you keep them? When will you reuse them for a new backup? The answers depend on several factors.

If a hard disk crash is your only concern, you can keep your backup disks right by your computer for convenience. But if you're worried about fire, flood, and other disasters, you might want to keep your backups at a separate site or in a fireproof, waterproof container. As a compromise, you could copy your backup disks, keep one set nearby for convenience, and keep the other one in a safer location.

There's some justification for keeping old backup disks for a while, even after you have completed the cycle with a new full backup. An old backup may help you restore a file that was deleted a long time ago and has long since disappeared from the deletion-protection system. You also have the ability to fall back to an earlier version of a file that has become corrupted for some reason. If these capabilities are important in your system, you might want to keep an old backup set for a month or longer.

Backup is also good for making vault copies of files that you are removing from your hard drive at the end of a project, the end of the fiscal year, or whenever. Back the files up one last time, label the backups carefully, and store them in a safe place until you're sure you'll never need them again.

DOS 6 includes the old RESTORE program so that you can restore files from vault copies made by earlier versions of DOS. You can delete RESTORE.EXE from your DOS directory when you no longer need to restore files from earlier backups.

Overview of the Backup Procedure

The first time you start Backup, you must configure it. You can't access any other functions until you pass the configuration tests. After it is configured, you select the BACKUP function and create at least one setup file, which identifies the drive(s) to back up from, the drive to back up to, the files to be backed up, the type of backup (full, incremental, or differential), and the BACKUP options (such as compression). Then you press the Start Backup button and insert floppy disks according to the directions on the screen.

The next time you want to run the same backup setup, you start the BACKUP function, open the desired setup if it isn't already open, press Start Backup, and insert disks. That's all there is to it.

Configuring Backup

When you start Backup for the first time, a message tells you that you must do the configuration tests. Your only choice is to start the tests or cancel. If Backup ever senses that you have changed your configuration, you must redo the configuration tests in the same manner. This can happen not just because you have changed your hardware, but also because you have installed a new driver or TSR.

You should redo the configuration tests any time you change your configuration, even if Backup doesn't detect the change. Don't take the chance of depending on an imperfect backup.

Backup performs the following configuration tests:

- It identifies your system's hardware; you must confirm or modify its assessments.

- It determines whether or not it can detect floppy disk changes. If so, you won't have to press Enter each time you insert a new disk. You must remove all disks from your floppy drives for this test.

- It tests the speed of your memory and hard drive.

- It performs a compatibility test on your system by making a small backup involving two floppy disks; then it compares the backup files to the originals. This test identifies any problems with the disk drives as well as any incompatibilities with your current TSRs. Backup tells you whether you need to remove any TSRs.

At the end of successful configuration tests, you'll see the Configure dialog box with the Save button highlighted. Press Save to record the results of the tests, or you'll have to repeat them the next time you start Backup. If your system passes everything but the compatibility test, you're no longer blocked from making backups, but you shouldn't do so until you can be sure that they're reliable.

When you have successfully completed the compatibility tests, you can reuse the two floppy disks and delete the two catalog entries from your DOS directory. The catalog names are COMPAT.CAT and xxymmddA.FUL, where x is the drive that was backed up; y is the last digit of the year; and mmdd is the month and day.

When you're done with the Configure dialog box, press Exit to close the dialog box and see Backup's main menu (see fig. 13.1). This isn't necessary in the Windows version, where you can go directly from one function to another by pressing the function buttons at the top of the window.

You can return to the Configure dialog box at any time to change the Video and Mouse or Backup Devices settings or to rerun the compatibility test.

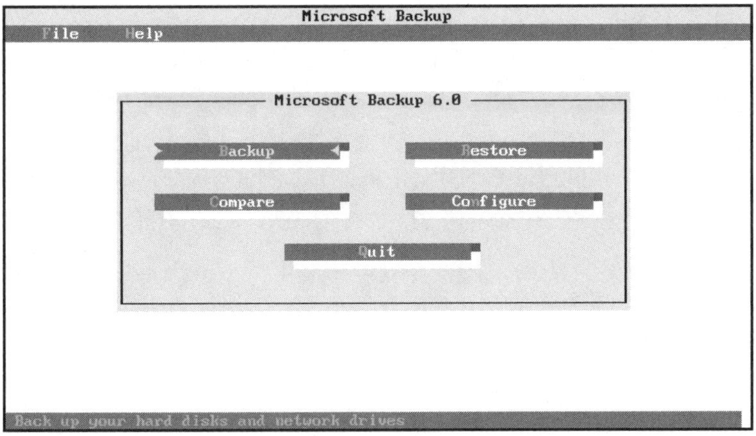

Figure 13.1.
Backup's main menu.

Creating a Backup Setup

Press the Backup button to open the Backup dialog box (see fig. 13.2). This is where you'll create backup setups. The default setup, named DEFAULT.SET, is automatically open. You use this setup as a basis for the other setups you create. Don't modify DEFAULT.SET, or you won't have a plain vanilla setup to act as a basis for a new setup.

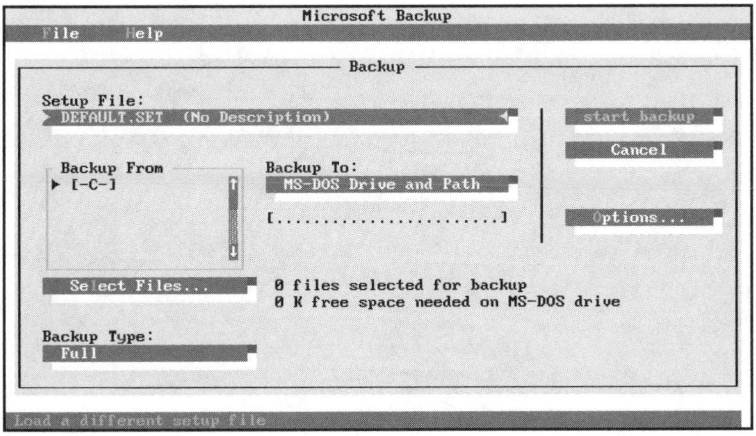

Figure 13.2.
Backup dialog box.

Choose File Save Setup As to save a copy of DEFAULT.SET with a new name, such as DAVIDA'S.SET. The extension must be SET. Save it in the DOS directory unless you want to create different groups of setup files for different users.

When the new setup file is open, select the Backup To drive. If you're using a floppy drive, be sure to select the one you tested in the compatibility test. If you choose to back up to an MS-DOS Drive and Path, enter the path name in the box below the Backup To button.

Press the Backup Type button to choose between Full, Incremental, and Differential backups. Because the backup setup defines the files to be archived, you probably want to use the same setup for your full and partial backups. When you create it, set it up to do a full backup for the first run. The second time you run it, you can switch it to Differential or Incremental. From then on, you need to switch it to Full only once a week or so and then switch it back again (or don't save the modified setup).

Backup Options

Pressing the Options button opens the dialog box shown in Figure 13.3, from which you can select the options for the setup you are creating.

Figure 13.3.
Disk backup
options.

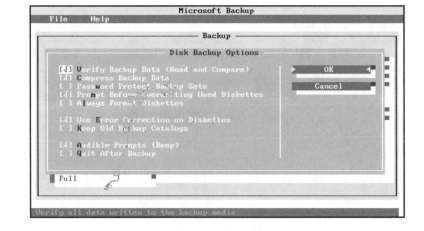

Verify Backup Data

The BACKUP function's verification option rereads each backed up file and compares it to the original on the hard disk. BACKUP attempts to correct any mistakes that are found. If the problem lies with a faulty floppy, BACKUP asks you to insert a different disk, and it rewrites the data to that disk. As you might expect, the verification option makes the backup take longer, but it helps to ensure a problem-free backup.

Compress Backup Data

BACKUP can compress the data on the backup disks using the same compression techniques that DoubleSpace uses. Not only do the compressed files take up less space on the backup disks, which can be a significant savings when you're backing up 40M or more of data, but the backup also takes significantly less time because there's less data to write.

> The amount of space you'll save depends on the type of files being backed up. A program file compresses about 40 percent, but a TIFF bit-mapped graphic compresses more than 90 percent.

When you complete your definition of the backup setup, Backup predicts how much time and how many floppy disks are needed. This prediction does not take compression into account, so if you have selected the compression option, you can count on using far fewer disks and much less time. (Other options may increase the time and space requirements, however.)

Password Protection

If you choose to password protect confidential backup data, you must provide a short password (up to seven characters) each time you run BACKUP using the protected setup. The password is case-sensitive. You must provide the same password to restore or compare files from the backup set.

A password-protected backup data set can be deleted or overwritten without supplying the password.

Prompt before Overwriting

BACKUP destroys all existing data on each floppy disk it uses. Check this option if you want BACKUP to warn you when a floppy already contains data—whether it's a former backup disk or a regular data disk. BACKUP tells you what's on the disk and lets you insert another disk or overwrite the current one.

If you plan to reuse your backup disks on a regular basis, this option really slows BACKUP down. Every time you insert a disk, it must examine the disk for data, display a message, and wait for you to respond. You might want to disable this option if you think you won't insert any disks by mistake. But if there's a chance that you might occasionally grab the wrong disk, you're best off checking this option. BACKUP's time estimate does not take this option into account.

Formatting the Backup Disks

A freshly formatted disk is less likely to encounter read-write errors and `sector not found` errors than is a disk that was formatted a while ago. Choosing the Always Format Diskettes option helps to create trouble-free backups, but your backup time will be more than doubled. BACKUP's time estimate does not take this option into account.

Error Correction Code

BACKUP can write on each backup disk *error correction code* that can be used to recover data from a disk even if it has been damaged. The error correction code adds less than 10 percent to the space needed and takes longer to write, but it increases the reliability of your backup data sets. BACKUP does take this option into account in its time and space predictions.

Old Backup Catalogs

Each time you make a backup, BACKUP stores a backup catalog on your hard drive as well as on the backup disks themselves. The hard drive version makes it convenient to open a catalog quickly to compare or restore files.

BACKUP automatically deletes old backup catalogs from the hard drive as you make new backups. For example, when you run a new full backup, any previous catalogs for that setup are deleted. When you run a differential backup, any former differential catalogs for the setup are deleted. So, by default, the catalogs on the hard drive represent the current backup cycles only.

You don't need the hard drive catalogs. If you want to work with an older backup set, COMPARE and RESTORE can retrieve the catalog from the backup disks. But if you plan to keep your old backup sets and want the convenience of maintaining their catalogs on the hard drive, you can prevent BACKUP from deleting out-of-date catalogs by choosing Keep Old Backup Catalogs. You will then be responsible for deleting catalogs yourself when you eliminate the backup sets.

Audible Prompts

If you want BACKUP to beep when it displays a message that you must respond to, such as when it asks for another disk, check Audible Prompts (Beep). Uncheck this option to suppress the beeps.

Quit after Backup

When you check Quit after Backup, BACKUP terminates itself when the backup is completed. Otherwise, you return to the Backup dialog box.

Selecting Files

You can't run a backup until you have selected at least one file to be backed up. The Start Backup button is dimmed when no files are selected. When you're creating a setup, selecting files might involve several stages. You should be careful to set it up to affect future directories and files, not just the present directory structure. This is especially true if you're creating a setup to be transferred to other users who might have different directory names and filenames.

Selecting Whole Drives

The Backup From box in the Backup dialog box lists all your hard drives that are eligible for backup. You can select an entire drive for backup—including all its directories and files—by selecting it in this box. In fact, you can select all the drives, if that's what you want.

It's rarely appropriate to back up every file on a drive. You would be backing up temporary files, BAK files created by applications, program files that you already have copies of, and so on. But you might want to start by selecting every file on the drive, then eliminate the files that you don't want to back up.

Figure 13.4 shows the dialog box that opens when you press the Select Files button. The drive list at the top is used merely to indicate which drive you want to work with now. You don't select any files by selecting a drive in this list. You must use the Backup From box in the previous dialog box to select whole drives for backup.

Figure 13.4.
Select Backup Files
dialog box.

```
┌──────────────────── Select Backup Files ────────────────────┐
│ [-C-]                                                        │
│ C:\DOS\*.*                                                   │
│ »C:\          ▒▐│√ appnotes.txt     9,058  12-06-92   6:00a  .... ◀▒│
│   ┌─COLLAGE     │√ dosshell.ini     17,001  3-02-93   6:16p  ....│
│   ►DAS          │√ msav    .ini       248   2-26-93   2:50p  ....│
│     ┌►DEMO      │√ msbackup.ini        43   2-22-93   2:12p  ....│
│     ├─FONTS     │√ mwav    .ini       354   1-09-93   8:15p  ....│
│     ├─»LIBRARY  │√ networks.txt    21,234   1-28-93   6:00a  ....│
│     ├►MORGUE    │√ qbasic  .ini       132   3-04-93   2:20a  ...a│
│     ├─SOUNDFX   │√ readme  .txt    53,669   1-28-93   6:00a  ....│
│     └►UNTITLED.LBM│√ undelete.ini    239   3-03-93  12:29p  ...a│
│       └»FALL.LBM │√ ~$readme.txt       51   2-28-93   5:23a  .h..│
│   »DOS          ▒│  untools .grp    3,741   1-28-93   6:00a  ...a ▒│
│ Total Files: 2,487 [   79,240 K]   Selected Files:    728 [   19,593 K]│
│ ┌ Include ┐ ┌ Exclude ┐ ┌ Special ┐  ┌ Display ┐ ►┌ OK ┐◀ ┌ Cancel ┐│
│ Select entire directories with right mouse button or Spacebar        │
└──────────────────────────────────────────────────────────────┘
```

Including and Excluding Files

The Include and Exclude buttons are used to create generic statements of which files should be included and excluded in the backup setup. For example, you might want to include all the files on drive C and then exclude COM, EXE, and SYS files but include CONFIG.SYS. The include/exclude statements affect future files as well as the current ones. Figure 13.5 shows the dialog box that opens when you press the Include button; the Exclude dialog box is similar to this. The default values depend on which directory or file is currently selected in the directory tree or file list.

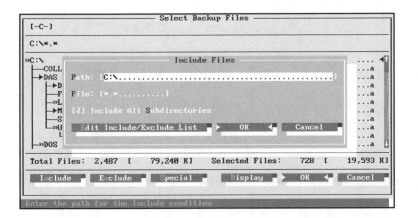

Figure 13.5.
Include Files
dialog box.

When you select a whole drive in the Backup From box, BACKUP creates an include statement for *d*:*.* with Include All Subdirectories checked.

The order of include/exclude statements is important. Each statement overrides preceding ones. So if you exclude COM files first and then include all files, COM files will be included. You can edit the include/exclude list to change the order of the statements. Figure 13.6 shows the dialog box that opens when you press Edit Include/Exclude List from either the Include or the Exclude dialog box. Highlight an entry and press Edit to modify it, Del=Delete to delete it, or Ins=Copy to copy it. Move an entry by copying it to a new location and then deleting it from the old.

Figure 13.6.
Edit Include/
Exclude List
dialog box.

```
┌──────────────── Select Backup Files ─────────────────┐
│                Edit Include/Exclude List              │
│                                                       │
│     Inc/Exc        Directories        Files   Subdirs │
│   1. Include C:\                       *.DOC    Yes    │
│   2. Include C:\                       *.SCR    Yes    │
│   3. Include C:\                       *.HSG    Yes    │
│   4. Include C:\                       *.TXT    Yes    │
│   5. Include C:\                       *.DRW    Yes    │
│   6. Include C:\                       *.INI    Yes    │
│   7. Include C:\                       *.PCX    Yes    │
│   8. Include C:\                       *.CFT    Yes    │
│   9. Include C:\                       *.SEC    Yes    │
│  10. Include C:\                       *.LBM    Yes    │
│                                                       │
│    Edit      Del=Delete     Ins=Copy          OK      │
│                                                       │
│  Select an include/exclude item to edit, delete, or copy │
└───────────────────────────────────────────────────────┘
```

Tailoring the Inclusions and Exclusions

As you create and edit include and exclude statements, you can see the results in the directory tree and file list. A selected file is checked. A directory that has some selected files has a chevron (») pointing to it. A directory with all files selected has a solid arrowhead pointing to it.

You might want to select or deselect specific directories or files without creating include/exclude statements. For example, even though you're excluding program files in general, you might want to include all the programs in the DIAGS directory because that was installed by your hardware manufacturer and you have no floppy disk backups for it. You can select the DIAGS directory to include all the files in the directory, or you can select individual files in the file list. If you select the entire directory, any files added to that directory will be included in future backups using this setup.

Selecting and deselecting individual directories and files overrides the include/ exclude list for those directories and files. After you have done this, you can change the selection status of a directory or file, but you can't return it to the control of the include/exclude list.

File selection information for a setup is stored in a file called *setup*.SLT. If you really want to return directories and files to the control of the include/exclude list, you can delete the SLT file. This eliminates your include/exclude list as well as individual selections and deselections.

To select or deselect a directory or file, double-click it or highlight it and press Enter. The directory entry turns red as a reminder that some of its files are no longer under the control of the include/exclude list.

Special Selections

Figure 13.7 shows the dialog box that opens when you press the Special button. This dialog box lets you exclude files based on date, attributes, or copy protection status. These exclusions override all other inclusions and selections.

Figure 13.7.
Special Selections dialog box.

If you specify a date range, any files outside that date range are excluded. Files within the date range are included only if they have been selected by some other means. If you check Exclude Copy Protected Files, you can enter up to five filespecs in the boxes to the right.

Files that would normally be included but have been specially excluded have a dot next to them in the file list. A dot also indicates files that are normally included in a full backup but will not be backed up because the Differential or Incremental type is selected and their archive attributes are not on.

Other Selection Functions

The Display button opens a dialog box in which you can choose the sort order for the file list, enter a filename filter for the file list, or ask that all the selected files be displayed at the beginning of the list. You'll find this last option very handy when you're trying to review the files that have been selected so far. The pointers in the directory tree tell which directories to look in, but it's often inconvenient to have to scroll through long directories to find the selected files.

The Print button prints out the entire setup: backup type, backup drive, options, selected files, and so on.

Running the Backup

When you return to the Backup dialog box after selecting files, you should see the number of files that will be written, an estimate of the number of floppy disks needed, and a time estimate. Press Start Backup to run the backup. A progress box keeps you informed of the progress of the backup.

If BACKUP can sense disk changes in the floppy drive, it displays a request for the next diskette directly in the progress box. The drive light remains lit while it waits for a new disk. If you don't respond within a few seconds, BACKUP displays a real dialog box. Then you'll have to press Enter to continue the backup.

Managing Backup Setups

BACKUP opens DEFAULT.SET by default unless you specify a setup name in the MSBACKUP command, as in

```
MSBACKUP WEEKLY.SET
```

You can change setups from the Backup dialog box either by pressing the Setup File button or by choosing File Open Setup. The latter command works from anywhere in Backup.

Whenever you modify a setup, you can save your changes by choosing File Save Setup. If you don't, Backup asks whether you want to save changes when you exit. If you say no, the changes are discarded from the setup.

The Backup Catalogs

For each backup you make, BACKUP creates a backup catalog with a name in the format *xxymmdda.typ*, in which the first letter indicates the first drive that was backed up, the second *x* indicates the last drive that was backed up, *ymmdd* indicates the date, *a* is simply a letter used to form a unique name (in case you run more than one backup in one day), and *typ* is FUL, DIF, or INC. The catalog name appears in the progress box. You should write the catalog name along with the setup name and the floppy disk number on the label of each floppy disk. The RESTORE and COMPARE functions ask for disks by catalog name and number.

BACKUP also creates and maintains on the hard disk a *master catalog* for each setup, with the name *setup*.CAT. The master catalog lists setup's description along with the names of the individual catalogs belonging to the current cycle for the setup. It's an ASCII file that you can view, print, edit, and so on. A typical master catalog might look like this:

```
Correspondence and other WP files
CC31010A.FUL
CC31011A.INC
CC31012A.INC
```

Unless you check the Keep Old Backup Catalogs option, BACKUP maintains the contents of this file for the current cycle only. As you'll see in the next sections, you can restore and compare from a master catalog when you want access to all the files covered by the setup rather than just the latest backup.

Restoring Files

Figure 13.8 shows the Restore dialog box. Backup's cataloging system makes it simple to restore files. In most cases, you open the desired catalog, select the files you want to restore, and press the Start Restore button. Backup tells you which disks to in-stall, and everything else is automatic.

If the backup set is damaged and contains error correction code, RESTORE will correct as much damage as possible. The progress box tells you how many corrections were made.

Figure 13.8.
Restore dialog box.

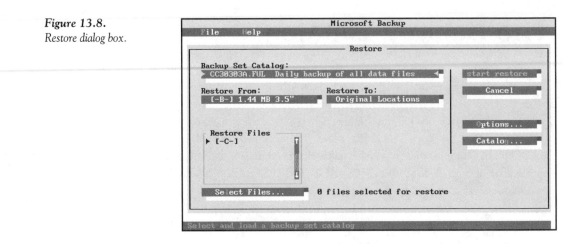

Opening the Backup Catalog

Figure 13.9 shows the dialog box that opens when you press the Backup Set Catalog button. As you can see, you can select a master catalog or an individual catalog. When you open a master catalog, RESTORE merges its individual catalogs into one file list, showing the latest version of each file.

Figure 13.9.
Backup Set Catalog dialog box.

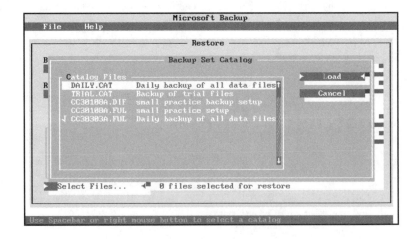

If the catalog you want to use is no longer on the hard drive, you can retrieve it from the backup disks. Place the last disk of the set into the floppy drive and press the Catalog button. In the next dialog box, press the Retrieve button. After the catalog has been retrieved, select it and press the Load button.

If your backup set is damaged and the built-in catalog is missing or corrupted, you can ask RESTORE to rebuild as much of it as possible by scanning what's left of the backup set. To do this, press the Catalog button and then press Rebuild and follow the directions. When the catalog has been rebuilt, press Load to open it.

Restore Options

The RESTORE function also offers a number of options. Several of them deal with how much prompting RESTORE will do as it restores the selected directories and files. The options are:

Verify Restore Data (Read and Compare)	If you want RESTORE to reread each file that it writes, compare it to the backup version, and correct any errors it finds, turn this option on.
Prompt before Creating Directories	If RESTORE finds it necessary to re-create a directory that was deleted in order to restore some files to it, it prompts you for permission to restore the directory if this option is turned on.
Prompt before Creating File	If RESTORE is restoring a file that is not overwriting an existing file, it prompts you for permission if this option is turned on.
Prompt before Overwriting Existing Files	If RESTORE is restoring a file that will replace an existing file on the hard drive, it prompts you for permission if this option is turned on.
Restore Empty Directories	If you want RESTORE to restore the drive's former directory structure even if some of the directories will be empty, turn this option on.

Audible Prompts (Beep)	If you want RESTORE to beep when it displays a prompt, turn this option on.
Quit after Restore	If you want RESTORE to terminate itself when the restoration is finished, turn this option on.

If you change any of the restore options, RESTORE asks whether you want to save changes to the setup file when you exit Backup. If you say yes, the changes are stored in the currently open setup file, which may not be related to the currently open catalog. (Remember that DEFAULT.SET is opened by default.) You can open a different setup file by using the File Open Setup command.

If you'll be using the same options for all your restorations, you might as well save them in DEFAULT.SET. That way, they'll always be available.

Selecting Restore Files

You select files for restoration in much the same way as you select them for backup, except that there is no include/exclude list. You can select all the files on a drive by selecting the drive in the Restore Files box, and you can select/deselect individual directories and files by pressing the Select Files button.

RESTORE does not save your file selections because they will probably be different for every restore job.

The RESTORE directory tree shows the entire directory structure of the drive at the time the backup was made. Some directories are empty if none of their files were included in the backup set. As mentioned earlier, you can restore the entire structure by checking the Restore Empty Directories option. This might be an appropriate thing to do when restoring a hard drive after a crash.

Selecting Versions

When you open a master catalog, some file might have several versions available. A plus at the right end of a file entry indicates that multiple versions are available. Only the latest version is listed by default. Press the Version button to see a list of all available versions for the highlighted file. If you select another version, it appears in the file list and is selected.

Pressing the Print button prints the entire file list. If a master catalog is selected, the right column indicates how many versions of each file are available.

Restoring to a Different Computer

There might be times when you need to restore files to a different computer than you backed them up from. You might be using Backup to copy very large files or a large set of files from one computer to another, for example, or you might simply have upgraded your equipment since you made the backups.

In the Restore dialog box, you can press the Restore From button to select a different floppy drive for the backup disks. You can press the Restore To button to ask RESTORE to restore files to Other Drives or Other Directories than they were backed up from. As RESTORE restores the files, it asks you for the names of the drives and/or the directories that you want to use.

Comparing Files

The COMPARE function (see fig. 13.10) can be used to verify a backup set immediately after it is made, but Backup's read and compare verification is a better verification technique because it fixes errors as it goes. COMPARE has other applications, however. For example, you could use it to compare the files backed up from one computer with files of the same name on another computer. The Compare From and Compare To buttons work just like the Restore From and Restore To buttons.

Figure 13.10.
Compare dialog box.

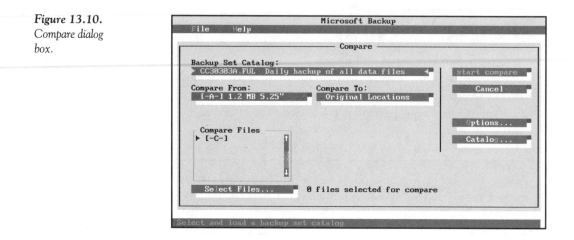

The COMPARE function is nearly identical to RESTORE. You open the desired catalog, select the files, and press Start Compare. A progress box keeps you informed of how many files were compared, how many were found to be different, and so on. The only COMPARE options are Audible Prompts and Quit after Compare.

> If the backup set is damaged and contains error correction code, COMPARE will correct as much damage as possible.

Maintaining Separate Backup Directories

By default, Backup stores configuration information, backup catalogs, and setup files in the same directory as the Backup program. You can specify a different location for these files for the DOS version of Backup by setting the MSDOSSDATA environment variable to point to a different directory. If several people share the same computer and have separate configuration blocks in CONFIG.SYS, you could set a different MSDOSDATA path for each of them so that they will see only their own setup files and catalogs when working with Backup. If your backup program is on a read-and-execute-only network drive, you would need to use MSDOSDATA to store your local configuration, setup, and catalogs on a local drive.

Microsoft's Anti-Virus programs also use MSDOSDATA, as explained in Chapter 15.

Restoring from Backups Made before DOS 6

If you need to restore files made by an earlier DOS backup, use the RESTORE command shown in Figure 13.11. For example, suppose you want to restore the CHAP*.TXT files from an old backup set to drive C. You would enter the following command:

```
RESTORE A: C:\CHAP*.TXT /S
```

Figure 13.11.
RESTORE
command reference.

RESTORE

Restores files backed up by BACKUP from previous DOS versions (DOS 2.0 through 5.0).

Format:

```
RESTORE drive1 target [/S] [/P] [/B:date] [/A:date]
[/E:time] [/L:time] [/M] [/N] [/D]
```

Parameters and Switches:

drive1	Identifies the drive containing the backup files.
target	Identifies the files to be restored, and the drive to which they are to be restored. *Target* must include a drivename; it may specify files by including a path and/or filename(s).
/S	Restores files to all subdirectories.

Figure 13.11.
continued

/P	Prompts for permission to restore read-only files or those changed since the last backup.
/B:*date*	Restores only those files last modified on or before *date*.
/A:*date*	Restores only those files last modified on or after *date*.
/E:*time*	Restores only those files last modified at or earlier than *time*.
/L:*time*	Restores only those files last modified at or later than *time*.
/M	Restores only those files modified since the last backup.
/N	Restores only those files that no longer exist on the destination.
/D	Displays a list of files that would be restored but does not restore any. Even though no files are restored, you must specify *target* when you use /D.

Notes:

RESTORE does not restore the system files IO.SYS and MSDOS.SYS. RESTORE does not work with drives that have been redirected with ASSIGN or JOIN.

A Pound of Protection

14

Introduction

Backing up your files isn't the only thing you can do to protect your data, although backups are the most effective. DOS includes a number of other features to prevent data loss and to facilitate data recovery. This chapter also discusses a couple of important tools that are missing from DOS and that you may want to get from some other source.

Format Protection

In early DOS versions, when you formatted a floppy disk with DOS's FORMAT program, any previous data on it was gone for good. Because every disk has to be formatted before it can be used, and reformatting is an effective way to remove data from a used disk, everyone sometimes reformats disks in error. Now FORMAT gives you protection even against itself.

The FORMAT Command

The FORMAT command prepares a new disk for use (see fig. 14.1). It also comes in handy to clear a used disk to hold other files.

Disks can be formatted in three ways. Table 14.1 compares the effects of the three different format styles. An *unconditional format* (with the /U switch) does low-level formatting, which means that it lays out the sectors and tests the surface for bad sectors. This process obliterates any previous data on the disk. Then FORMAT installs a boot record, root directory, and two FATs, marking the FATs for any clusters that contain bad sectors. A disk formatted unconditionally is like a brand new disk; any previous data can't be recovered. An unconditional format is the same as DOS's standard diskette format before DOS 5.

A *safe format*, which is the default, does an unconditional format on a new disk. However, if the disk has been formatted before, all it does is zero the FAT, clear the root directory, and check the entire disk for bad clusters (without destroying existing data in the clusters). It takes a lot less time than an unconditional format, and any previous data can potentially be recovered with UNFORMAT.

A *quick format* (with the /Q switch) just zeros the FAT and clears the root directory; it doesn't check for bad clusters. A quick format is the fastest format process, but it can be used only on previously formatted disks, as it will not switch into unconditional mode for a new disk.

FORMAT

Prepares a disk for use or reuse.

Format:

FORMAT *drive* [/Q] [/U] [V[:*label*]] [/S ¦ /B] [/F:*size*]
[/T:*tracks* /N:*sectors*] [/1] [/4] [/8]

Parameters and Switches:

drive   Identifies the drive to format.

/Q   Does a quick format.

/U   Does an unconditional format.

/V[:*label*]   Specifies the volume label for the formatted disk. *Label* can be
               up to 11 characters. If you omit /V or use /V but omit *label*,
               DOS prompts you for the volume *label* after formatting is
               complete. Do not use with /8.

/S   Makes the disk bootable.

/B   Reserves space for system files on a newly formatted disk.

/F:*size*   Overrides the default capacity of the disk. Specify *size* in bytes,
               as 360K or 1.2M. Don't use this switch with /T, /N, /1, /4, or /8.

/T:*tracks*   Specifies the number of tracks on the disk; must be used with
               /N. Don't use with /F.

/N:*sectors*   Specifies the number of sectors per track; must be used with
               /T. Don't use with /F.

/1   Formats a single-sided disk. Don't use with /F.

/4   Formats a 360K disk in a 1.2M drive. If used with /1, formats
               180K disk in a 1.2M drive. Don't use with /F.

/8   Formats a 5.25-inch disk with 8 sectors per track (for DOS 2.0
               or earlier). Don't use with /F or /V.

Figure 14.1.
FORMAT
command reference.

Table 14.1. Format Option Comparison

Function	Unconditional	Quick*	Safe
Clears FAT	✓	✓	✓
Clears root	✓	✓	✓
Redoes sector layout**	✓		
Identifies bad clusters	✓		✓
Saves unformat info		✓	✓
Speed	slow	fast	medium

*Can be used only on previously formatted floppy disks.

**Redoing the sector layout deletes all previous data on the disk.

Saving Unformatting Information

As an additional aid in unformatting, the safe and quick formats save a copy of the existing FAT and root directory before clearing them. The UNFORMAT program can use this information to recover the disk.

The quickest way to reformat an old disk is to combine the /U and /Q switches. FORMAT then doesn't check for bad clusters (because of /Q) or save unformatting information (because of /U). It would be difficult to recover previous information reliably after running this command because there is no unformatting information. If you are sure that you don't want to recover previous data and if you haven't any reason to suspect bad clusters (such as read or write errors), this combination of switches is safe.

Unconditional FORMAT Guidelines

You should do an unconditional format if you have experienced any read, write, or `sector not found` errors when using an old disk. Redoing the sector layout and blocking out bad clusters should clear up any problems. If the FORMAT summary shows too many bad clusters, throw the disk away. (If this happens very often, you should suspect that there is something wrong with your disk drive or with the way you are handling your disks.)

Unconditional formatting also provides security when you are disposing of confidential or sensitive files; because the data is no longer present on the disk, no one can access it using normal means.

> There are ways to access old data from a disk after unconditional formatting. If you are trying to destroy highly confidential data, you need a government-approved data wiping utility. (Or try shredding the disk.)

If you format a disk to a different capacity than it had before, you must do an unconditional format as the sectors have to be repositioned for the new capacity. If you try to do a safe format in this case, you will be given a choice of canceling the format or continuing in unconditional mode. (A quick format will ignore the capacity change.)

Recoverable Formats

When you do a safe or quick format, you see the following messages:

```
Checking existing disk format.
Saving UNFORMAT information.
```

The last line tells you that the disk will be recoverable. A quick format is fine for previously used disks that haven't had any problems. It is much quicker than a safe format, because the sectors aren't checked. However, if you have had trouble reading or writing files, a safe or unconditional format is a better choice. (If you've encountered `sector not found` errors, choose an unconditional format.)

> Chapter 15 discusses techniques for rescuing data from a disk with bad sectors. If you don't have good backups, you may need to do this before reformatting the disk.

If a disk is completely full, FORMAT can't find space to write its unformat information. You see a message like the following:

```
Checking existing format.
Saving UNFORMAT information.
Drive A error. Insufficient space for the MIRROR
image file. There was an error creating the
format recovery file. The disk cannot be
unformatted. Proceed with format (Y/N)?_
```

The problem is just that the disk is full. If you are sure that you do not want to unformat it, press Y, and the format continues without recording the image file. If you aren't sure, press N. After you delete a file or two, you should be able to do a safe or quick format.

Verifying Files

Your system provides several levels of protection to ensure that the data it reads and writes is not corrupted by hardware or media problems.

CRCs

In normal use, a drive controller does a cyclic redundancy check (CRC) each time it writes a sector. It performs a calculation on all the bytes in the sector and stores the result in the sector control area immediately preceding the sector. Then it re-reads the sector, recalculates the value, and compares it to the stored value. If they differ, the controller reports a write error to DOS. Later, when the sector is read, the CRC is performed again. If the calculated value doesn't match the stored value, a read error is reported. The CRC will catch all errors that occur after the data is transferred to the disk controller, but you may want to be even more exacting than that.

DOS's Verification

You also can ask DOS to verify each sector it writes. When DOS verifies, it makes sure that each sector is written correctly by comparing it to the data in memory. If verification fails, DOS reports a write error to you.

General Verification

Normally, DOS depends on the hardware's CRC verification and doesn't verify what it writes to disk. You can force it to verify all writes by using VERIFY ON at the command prompt. To find out the current state of verification, enter VERIFY (with no parameters). To turn verification off, enter VERIFY OFF.

General verification will slow down your entire system but not noticeably. However, you may prefer to verify only in specific instances.

Specific Verification

The COPY, XCOPY, and DISKCOPY commands let you use the /V switch to request verification for a single command. This switch works regardless of the setting of VERIFY, but it's redundant when VERIFY is ON. As with VERIFY ON, it takes a bit more time, but the delay may be worth it to you in some cases.

Comparing Files

Because DOS's verification compares the written file only to the memory version, mistakes can still creep in during a copy operation. The best protection is afforded by comparing the source and destination files. File comparison solves more problems than just ensuring that a copy is accurate. For example, if a program runs strangely, you could compare it to the original on its distribution disk. If they aren't identical, you could make a new copy from the original.

The FC Command

The FC command (see fig. 14.2) compares two files. When it does an ASCII comparison, FC compares two files line-by-line (a line is delineated by a carriage return). When it finds a mismatch, it checks later lines trying to find a point where the files match up again. If FC finds a rematch within a certain line limit, the matching lines are used as the starting point for continuing the comparison.

A successful FC job displays the following message:

```
FC: no differences encountered.
```

The output from an unsuccessful ASCII comparison displays the lines that don't match. The set of mismatched lines is preceded by the last line that matches and is followed by the first line that matches again (if FC was able to resynchronize the files). If the /A switch is used, you see only the first and last line for each set of differences. By default, two successive lines must match before FC considers the files resynchronized. In the following example, the two files have a single difference—one file is missing a line.

```
C:\>FC AUTOEXEC.BAT AUTODIFF.BAT
Comparing files AUTOEXEC.BAT and AUTODIFF.BAT

***** AUTOEXEC.BAT
REM SET COMSPEC=C:\DOS\COMMAND.COM
VERIFY OFF
PATH C:\DOS;D:\WINDOWS;C:\WS5;C:\;C:\WORD

***** AUTODIFF.BAT
REM SET COMSPEC=C:\DOS\COMMAND.COM
PATH C:\DOS;D:\WINDOWS;C:\WS5;C:\;C:\WORD
*****

C:\>
```

Notice that the matching lines appear in the list of lines from each file. When looking for a matching set of lines after a mismatch, FC uses the contents of the resynch buffer, which holds about 100 lines by default. If no match is found within the buffer, you are notified that the resynchronization failed. You can use /LB*lines* for a larger buffer if necessary; if resynchronization fails, try /LB200 and see whether that works.

You can use the /*resynch* parameter switch to change the number of lines that must match to resynchronize the file. /1 sets the number to 1, so only one line must match; /5 requires five successive matching lines. You may see identical lines identified as mismatches in the output if any number other than 1 is used. If one matching line isn't enough to resynchronize the file, those lines aren't considered a match.

FC

Compares two files and displays lines or bytes that don't match.

Format:

```
FC [/A] [/C] [/L] [/LBlines] [/N ¦ /B] [/T] [/W] [/resynch]
filespec1 filespec2
```

Parameters and Switches:

filespec1	Identifies the first file to compare.
filespec2	Identifies the second file to compare.
/A	Abbreviates output by showing only the first and last line for a series of mismatched lines; the default shows all mismatched lines.
/C	Ignores case.
/L	Compares files in ASCII mode, comparing line-by-line and attempting to resynchronize after finding a mismatch. This is the default mode for files that do not have the extensions EXE, COM, SYS, OBJ, LIB, or BIN.
/N	Displays line numbers when showing mismatched lines during an ASCII comparison.
/B	Compares files in binary mode, byte-by-byte, without attempting to resynchronize after a mismatch. This is the default mode with files having the extensions EXE, COM, SYS, OBJ, LIB, or BIN. Don't use any other switches in binary mode (all other switches pertain to ASCII mode).
/LB*lines*	Specifies the number of lines in the resynch buffer; the default is 100.
/T	Does not expand tabs to spaces. The default is to expand tabs with stops at each eighth character position.
/W	Ignores white space.
/resynch	Specifies the number of lines that must match before files are resynchronized; the default is 2.

Figure 14.2.
FC command reference.

Figure 14.3 shows part of the output from the following command:

```
FC /C /W REMLINE.BAS NEWLINE.BAS
```

Figure 14.3.
FC output.

```
Comparing files REMLINE.BAS and NEWLINE.BAS
***** REMLINE.BAS
'    the output lines in Sub GenOutFile. An example is shown
in comments.
DEFINT A-Z
***** NEWLINE.BAS
'    the output lines in Sub GenOutFile. An example is shown
in comments.
'    Set all default variable names to integer
DEFINT A-Z
***** REMLINE.BAS
' Function and Sublprocedure declarations
DECLARE FUNCTION GetToken$ (Search$, Delim$)
DECLARE FUNCTION StrSpn% (InString$, Separator$)
***** NEWLINE.BAS
' Function and Sublprocedure declarations
' Declare statements inserted automatically
DECLARE FUNCTION GetToken$ (Search$, Delim$)
' Rest also automatic
DECLARE FUNCTION StrSpn% (InString$, Separator$)
```

The comparison ignores any case differences and compresses white space. Two lines (the default) are required for resynchronization; notice that an apparently matching line appears in the middle of the second set.

The DISKCOMP Command

When you copy disks, you may want to make absolutely sure that they are identical before storing or shipping the copies. The /V switch on the DISKCOPY command makes sure that the data is written correctly from memory, but you need a command like DISKCOMP (see fig. 14.4) to make sure that the data was read and written correctly.

DISKCOMP

Compares two floppy disks.

Format:

DISKCOMP [*drive1*] [*drive2*] [/1] [/8]

Parameters and Switches:

drive1   Identifies one drive that holds a disk for comparison.

drive2   Identifies a second drive that holds a disk for comparison.

/1   Compares only the first side of the disks, even if they are double-sided.

/8   Compares only the first 8 sectors per track, even if the disks contain 9 or 15 sectors per track.

Figure 14.4.
DISKCOMP
command reference.

If you compare disks that were just DISKCOPYed and find errors, the problem may be the drive itself, a memory chip, or one of the disks. Hardware and media do wear out eventually.

Write Protection

Still another way to protect data is with write protection. It will not protect against sabotage, because any somewhat knowledgeable person can turn it off. It does protect against accidental overwriting, however.

A disk can be write-protected by placing a write-protect tab over the notch (5 1/4-inch) or sliding the write-protect plastic tab to open the hole (3 1/2-inch). Hard disks can't be write-protected through DOS, although some third-party software allows this.

Files can be protected somewhat by setting the read-only or system attribute. A file with one of these attributes can't be changed or deleted by many programs that run under DOS. Anyone can change the attribute, however, and some DOS utilities, such as Backup and REPLACE, will overwrite or delete read-only or system files without warning.

Read-only files are listed in DIR listings just like other files unless you exclude them with an /Ax switch. System files aren't normally listed in directories, but you can include them with /A or /AS.

By default, the Shell includes read-only files but not system files in directory lists. You can include hidden and system files by choosing `Options File Display Options` and checking `Display hidden/system files`.

Read-only files and system files can be deleted through the Shell. A message warns you when a file is read-only and asks whether you really want to delete it. If you choose Yes, DOS removes the read-only attribute and deletes the file. System files will be deleted without warning.

Parking Your Disk Heads

When you turn off your computer, the hard disk stops spinning and the read/write heads have to settle somewhere. Many hard disks move the heads to a safe landing zone, but others just let the heads land wherever they happen to be, which can damage the disk surface over time. If your hard drive does not park its heads automatically (check its manual to find out), you should use a program to park the heads in a safe place before shutting down.

DOS does not include a parking program. Several third-party utility packages include one, or you may be able to get one from your dealer for a slight charge (make sure it's virus-free). If your system arrived with one already installed on the hard disk, be sure to use it.

Additional Protection Facilities

The next two chapters discuss two of DOS 6's most important protection facilities: UNDELETE protects deleted files for a few days so that you can undelete them easily, and Microsoft Anti-Virus detects and removes viruses from your system.

Microsoft
Anti-Virus

15

Introduction

Ten years ago, computer viruses were virtually unheard of. Now, the latest virus is front-page news. DOS's new Anti-Virus facility can help keep your system virus-free.

Anti-Virus includes three major components:

● Microsoft Anti-Virus (MSAV) scans memory and your drives for viruses. If it detects a virus, it may be able to remove it. Otherwise, you might need to delete the infected file.

● Microsoft Windows Anti-Virus (MWAV) is the Windows version of the virus scanner.

● VSAFE is a TSR that monitors system activity looking for suspicious behavior, such as an attempt to do a low-level format on a hard drive. It blocks the attempt and lets you decide what to do next.

Between the virus scanner and the virus monitor, your system should be safe from most viruses. But keep your backups up-to-date, just in case.

About Viruses

A virus is a program that is capable of entering your system without your knowledge, hiding on your hard disk (probably in another program file or the partition table), and spreading itself to other computers whenever it has the opportunity. Some viruses seem to do nothing at all except take up residence in your system. Many viruses do something silly, just to let you know they're there; they might display a message or graphic or play a short tune. Or they might play jokes on you. Some viruses with a more malicious intent set out to damage as much of your system as possible. But with so many variations on hardware and software in the PC world, even a virus that was meant to be harmless might damage some systems. It requires advanced programming techniques to get a program to sneak into a system, hide itself from easy discovery, and spread itself to other systems. Many viruses have not been thoroughly debugged and can do considerable harm to your system beyond whatever harm the virus creator intended. No virus is "cute"; for the safety of your data, you should treat the possibility of infection very seriously.

Viruses generally invade your system hidden in software or in the boot record of a diskette. You might download one from a BBS, copy one over a network, install one with a new application, or borrow one from a friend. Your computer might even have arrived with a virus, especially if it's second-hand or a rental.

> Name-brand software in its original, shrink-wrapped packaging *should* be virus-free. The major software developers go to great lengths to ensure that their products are shipped without viruses. Nevertheless, scan any software before you install it.

Many viruses spread themselves quickly. If you have one in your system, it might infect every diskette you insert in a floppy drive. When an infected diskette is carried to another system, it infects the hard disk of that system. From there it spreads to every diskette inserted in that system, and so on until the virus becomes an epidemic.

Viruses usually hide in your system inside other program files or in the hard disk partition table. They might be loaded into memory when you boot or when you start up an infected program. A virus might lie dormant for a long time, then when a specific event triggers it (such as the system date indicating a Friday the 13th), it springs into action.

Known and Unknown Viruses

The Microsoft virus scanners can detect both known and unknown viruses. A known virus is one that has already been identified and analyzed. It can be recognized by its *signature*, a string of bytes contained in the program that serve to uniquely identify it. MSAV and MWAV can recognize over 1,000 known viruses, plus a multitude of virus *strains* (slight variations). Many of them can be removed from their host without damaging the system area or file they were in. But others damage the host when they invade it and can't be effectively removed.

New virus definitions become available all the time. You can—and should—obtain updates of the latest virus signatures periodically from Microsoft. You'll see how to do that under "Upgrading Your Virus Definitions" later in this chapter.

The newest viruses have not yet been identified, of course. Microsoft's virus scanners can detect the presence of an unknown virus by looking for changes in program files that might signal a virus invasion. If you choose to establish a watch for unknown viruses, the virus scanner creates a file called CHKLIST.MS in every directory that you scan. CHKLIST.MS contains an entry for each program file in the directory. It records the file's size, date/time stamp, and attributes along with a checksum—a unique value calculated from the file's contents. If the file changes in any way, its checksum should change even if the virus manages to invade it without causing a change to the size, date/time stamp, or attributes. If you scan for unknown viruses, the scanner compares all program files against their CHKLIST.MS entries and reports any files that have changed.

A new class of unknown viruses is capable of invading program files without triggering changes even in checksums. This type of virus is called a *stealth virus* for obvious reasons. Microsoft's Anti-Virus scanners are also capable of detecting stealth viruses. Stealth-virus scanning takes a little longer, but the extra measure of protection is probably worth the few additional seconds per day.

Some program changes are legitimate. You might have upgraded an application, for example. When the scanner reports that the program files have changed, you can tell it to update CHKLIST.MS with the new information. Or you might have a program that writes configuration changes in the program file instead of some type of INI file. After a while, you'll learn to ignore reports of changes in that program's files. But when you suddenly get a report that a program file has changed for no apparent reason, you must pay serious attention to the possibility of a virus.

If an unknown virus is already in your system the first time you scan for viruses (when the CHKLIST.MS files are built), or if an unknown virus arrives with a new or upgraded program, the virus scanner has no way of detecting it. That's when the virus monitor becomes important, because it can prevent the unsuspected virus from doing any damage to your system.

MSAV

The DOS version of the virus scanner can be run in interactive mode or in batch mode. Figure 15.1 shows the command that you use to start up MSAV. If you just enter MSAV with no parameters, the window shown in Figure 15.2 opens, and you can select the parameters that you want to use.

Figure 15.1.
MSAV command reference.

MSAV

Scans memory and disks for viruses; removes viruses if possible.

Format:

```
MSAV [drive ... ¦ path ¦ /A ¦ /L] [/S ¦ /C] [/R] [/A] [/L]
[/N] [/P] [/F] [/VIDEO] [/videomouse ...]
```

Parameters and Switches:

none	Opens the Microsoft Anti-Virus window so you can select drives and options.
drive	Identifies a drive to scan; all program files on the drive are scanned.
path	Identifies the top of a branch; all program files in the branch are scanned.
/A	Scans all drives except A and B.
/L	Scans all drives except A, B, and network drives.
/S	Scans without removing viruses. This is the default.
/C	Scans and removes any viruses found.
/R	Creates a report file (MSAV.RPT) that lists the number of files checked, number of viruses found, number of viruses removed, and names of files suspected of containing unknown viruses.
/N	Turns off the information display while scanning.
/P	Runs MSAV in nongraphic, command-line mode.
/F	Turns off the display of filenames being scanned. Use this switch only with the /N or /P switch.
/VIDEO	Displays a list of video and mouse options. This option does not perform any virus scan or load the dialog box; to scan for viruses you must enter Msav again after you see the list.
videomouse	Uses the indicated video or mouse option.

Figure 15.2.
Microsoft Anti-Virus window.

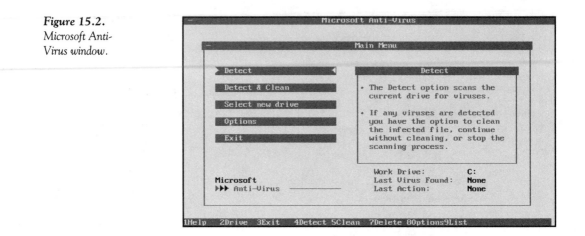

Some command-line options are not available within the window. If you want to scan multiple drives or limit the scan to a specific branch, you must specify the necessary parameters in the startup command. Once you're in the window, you can select only one drive at a time, and you can't select directories.

The video and mouse options also are not available in the window. If you need to use a monochrome color scheme, suppress the graphic mouse pointer. You'll have to include the appropriate switches on the startup command. Enter this command to see a complete list of the video and mouse options:

```
MSAV /VIDEO
```

Using MSAV in Interactive Mode

Press the Select New Drive button or choose the Drive command from the bottom of the window (which you can do by pressing F2) to display a list of drives so that you can select a different drive to scan. The drive list appears in the upper left corner of the window.

The Options button opens a dialog box that offers nine options. You can choose any combination of options, although some combinations make more sense than others. The options are

Verify Integrity	Turn this option on to scan for unknown viruses.
Create New Checksums	Turn this option on to create the CHKLIST.MS files in the first place and to add new program files to the existing CHKLIST.MS files.
Create Checksums on Floppy	The preceding option creates CHKLIST.MS files on hard drives only unless you also turn this option on.
Disable Alarm Sound	MSAV buzzes when it detects a possible virus. Turn this option on to eliminate the buzz.
Create Backup	Turn this option on if you want MSAV to create backup copies of infected files before cleaning them. The copies receive the VIR extension.
Create Report	Turn this option on to create a disk report named \MSAV.RPT showing the results of the scan.
Prompt While Detect	Turn this option on to cause MSAV to display an alert box for every virus it detects so that you can decide what to do with each one. When this option is off, MSAV handles viruses on its own.
Anti-Stealth	Turn this option on to scan for stealth viruses.
Check All Files	Turn this option on to scan data files as well as program files. MSAV will tell you when it has detected a virus that is known to infect data files too.

Using the Create Backup Option

In general, creating a backup of an infected file is not a good idea. What's the point of cleaning a virus out of a program file if you're going to make a copy of it first? However, making backup copies of infected files gives you the chance to decide what to do about the files after the scan finishes. In cases where the virus was successfully cleaned from the program file, you can delete the VIR file. In cases where the program file had to be deleted and you have no backup of the program, you might want to move the VIR file to a floppy for safe storage while you look for additional means to remove the virus from the file. For example, the next virus definition's upgrade might include a new definition that can remove the virus from the infected file.

A file with the extension VIR is not executable under DOS, so the virus should be inhibited while you look for a solution.

Using the MSAV.RPT Report

MSAV displays a summary report at the end of its scan showing the number of files scanned, number of known viruses detected, number of known viruses cleaned, and so on. But it doesn't include any information about unknown viruses in the report. And the only way you can record a permanent copy of the report is to capture a screen print of it.

Figure 15.3 shows a copy of the report that MSAV stores in the root directory when you choose the Create Report option. You can see every file that was suspected of containing an unknown virus as well as the results of the known virus scan. This report can be especially useful when you do not use the Prompt while Detect option and haven't seen a separate dialog box for every virus found.

If you're setting up a virus scanning procedure for inexperienced DOS users, you might want to generate the report on their systems. Then you'll be able to examine the results of their scans to see if any further actions need to be taken.

Interactive Prompts

When you turn on the Prompt while Detect option, MSAV displays an alert box for every virus it detects or suspects. You must decide what to do in each case. You'll see examples of some alert boxes later in this chapter.

If you turn Prompt while Detect off, MSAV's actions depend on how you start the scan. If you press the Detect button or choose the Detect command, MSAV simply notes viruses without attempting to handle them. How it notes them depends on what other options are, in effect. In all cases, you'll see brief descriptions under Last Virus Found in the Microsoft Anti-Virus window (if you stay at your computer during the scan). And the number of known viruses found will appear in the displayed report. If you don't disable the alarm sound, you'll hear a buzz for each detected or suspected virus. And if you generate the MSAV report, you'll see the list of files suspected of unknown viruses as well as the number of files containing known viruses.

If you start the scan with the Detect & Clean button or the Clean command, MSAV cleans every known virus that it can. Other viruses are handled just as they are when you use the Detect button or command.

The first scan you execute after starting MSAV also scans memory for viruses.

```
 File   Edit   Search   Options                                    Help
┌─────────────────────────── MSAV.RPT ──────────────────────────────┐
│Microsoft Anti-Virus.                                               │
│Virus search report for date: 03-05-93, Time 11:44:03.             │
│                                                                    │
│Verify error in file:                                              │
│ C:\INSTALL.EXE                                                     │
│                                                                    │
│                                                                    │
│Total boot sector viruses     FOUND  : 0                           │
│Total boot sector viruses     REMOVED: 0                           │
│                                                                    │
│Total Files                   CHECKED: 346                         │
│Total File viruses            FOUND  : 0                           │
│Total File viruses            REMOVED: 0                           │
│                                                                    │
│                                                                    │
│END OF REPORT.                                                      │
│                                                                    │
│                                                                    │
│                           ▌                                        │
│                                                                    │
└────────────────────────────────────────────────────────────────────┘
 MS-DOS Editor  <F1=Help> Press ALT to activate menus      N 00001:001
```

Figure 15.3.
Sample MSAV report.

Other MSAV Commands

The Delete command deletes all the CHKLIST.MS files from the selected drive. You might want to do this every so often to eliminate obsolete entries from the files.

Create new files by using the Create New Checksums option the next time you scan the drive.

The List command lets you review the list of known viruses that MSAV can detect. This list comes in handy when a virus is going around and you want to make sure that your scanner is capable of detecting and cleaning it. If the virus in question is not on the list, you can probably upgrade your virus definitions to include it.

Using MSAV in Batch Mode

You can bypass the MSAV window and begin the scan immediately by adding either the /N switch or the /P switch. With /P, MSAV displays progress messages on the command prompt screen while it works, as in `Scanning memory for viruses...` and `Scanning files for viruses....` The scanning summary report is displayed at the end.

With /N, MSAV displays the text of the /MSAV.TXT file, if it exists; otherwise, it simply displays `working....` No report is displayed at the end. Instead, exit code 86 is set if any virus was detected. Use /N if you're setting up MSAV in a batch file for an inexperienced user. You can place whatever message you think is pertinent in MSAV.TXT. Store MSAV.TXT in the same directory as MSAV.EXE for a single-user system. For a multiple-user system, if you have set up separate configuration blocks for the users, you can create separate MSAV.TXT files for the different users. In the configuration block, set an environment variable named MSDOSDATA to point to the location of MSAV.TXT. So, for example, Pete's MSAV.TXT could be in PETEDIR and Judi's MSAV.TXT could be in JUDIDIR.

MSDOSDATA also affects MSBACKUP. See Chapter 13 for details.

With both the /P and the /N switches, MSAV displays the names of the files being searched unless you add the /F switch.

The MSAV.INI file controls the options that are in effect, although some of the options, such as Prompt while Detect and Disable Audible Alarm, don't pertain to batch mode. You can edit this file with any ASCII editor, or you can set up the options in interactive mode and save them as you exit the MSAV window. The /R switch creates a disk report regardless of the setting of Create Report.

Suppose you want to run MSAV in batch mode suppressing all messages except those in MSAV.TXT, create a disk report, scan all local drives, clean any viruses found, and suppress the filename display. You would use this command:

```
MSAV /N /R /L /C /F
```

If this appears in a batch file, the next command could be IF ERRORLEVEL 86 to determine whether any viruses were detected.

Some of the other MSAV parameters cause MSAV to run automatically, although not in batch mode. The MSAV window appears, but the scan starts immediately and you have no chance to select options or press buttons. When the scan is done, MSAV terminates before you can to read the on-screen report. The command-line parameters that cause this to happen are: /S, /C, *path*, or any parameter that specifies more than one drive to be scanned.

Dealing with Known Viruses

When MSAV encounters a known virus in interactive mode and Prompt while Detect is in effect, a dialog box like the one shown in Figure 15.4 appears. If the Clean button is available, choose it to remove the virus from the infected file. Choose Continue to ignore the virus and continue the scan. Choose Stop to terminate the scan without handling the virus. Or choose Delete to delete the infected file.

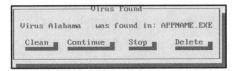

Figure 15.4.
Sample Virus Alert dialog box.

Dealing with Unknown Viruses

When Prompt while Detect is in effect and MSAV is scanning for unknown viruses, any change in a program file produces a dialog box similar to the one in Figure 15.5. Choose Update to update the CHKLIST.MS file with the changed data. Choose Delete to delete the file. If you want to ignore the changed file, choose Continue. Or choose Stop to terminate the scan.

Figure 15.5.
*Verify Error Alert
dialog box.*

Using MWAV

MWAV offers nearly the same interactive features as MSAV. You can't run MWAV in batch mode, of course. There are a few other differences. You can select more than one drive from the drive list, which always appears in the window. MWAV doesn't offer the Create Report option, but it does let you choose to wipe deleted files. Wiping a file overwrites the file's clusters with 0s to totally obliterate them. That eliminates the virus from the available clusters. MWAV's options are saved in MWAV.INI.

Using VSAFE

As you saw earlier, the virus scanners can't detect all unknown viruses. But VSAFE can prevent any virus, known or not, from doing damage to your system. Since VSAFE monitors all system activity and interferes with anything it considers to be suspicious, it can seriously slow your entire system down. Therefore you can choose the activities that VSAFE monitors. The possibilities are:

- Intercept any attempt to perform a low-level format on a hard disk. This is a sure sign of a virus (or a badly corrupted program) if you haven't specifically started a low-level format program.

- Intercept any attempt by a program to establish memory residence. You'll be warned about every TSR you load, which can be irritating (especially during booting), but you'll also be warned about a TSR that you didn't intentionally load.

● Intercept any attempt to write to disk. This is maximum protection and could inhibit your ability to get anything done, but if you're sincerely worried about a virus at work in your system, this will require your permission for every disk write.

● Scan every executable file for known or unknown viruses as it is loaded.

● Scan every disk that is inserted for boot sector viruses.

● Intercept any attempt to write to the boot sector and partition table of a hard disk. Only a formatting program or DOS SETUP should be writing to the hard disk's partition table and boot sector.

● Intercept any attempt to write to the boot sector of a floppy disk. Only a formatting program should be doing this. (This is one of the most common ways that viruses travel from system to system.)

● Intercept any attempt to modify a program file.

You can specify which monitoring options you want as you load the VSAFE TSR, and you can turn them on and off as desired during your work session.

VSAFE must not be installed while running either DOS's or Windows' SETUP program. Unload VSAFE before running either of these programs.

Loading VSAFE

Figure 15.6 shows the format of the VSAFE command, which is used to load the VSAFE TSR. The /n+ and /n- switches turn the various VSAFE options on and off. The numbers correspond to the preceding list of monitoring options. That is, /1+ causes VSAFE to monitor for attempts to perform a low-level format, and /3- tells VSAFE not to monitor for disk writes.

After loading VSAFE, you can see and change the current options by pressing the VSAFE hotkey, which is Alt-V by default. Figure 15.7 shows the dialog box that appears on the screen. To change an option setting, type its number.

Figure 15.6.
VSAFE command reference.

VSAFE

Loads (or unloads) the VSAFE TSR, which continuously monitors your computer for virus-like activity.

Format:

VSAFE [/*option*+ ¦ -] ... [/NE] [/NX] [/A*key* ¦ /C*key*] [/N] [/D] [/U]

Parameters and Switches:

/*option*+ ¦ -	Specifies how VSAFE monitors for viruses; use + or - following an option to turn it on or off.
/NE	Prevents VSAFE from loading into expanded memory.
/NX	Prevents VSAFE from loading into extended memory.
/A*key*	Sets the hotkey that displays the VSAFE options dialog box as Alt-*key*; the default is Alt-V.
/C*key*	Sets the hotkey that displays the VSAFE option dialog box as Ctrl-*key*.
/N	Allows VSAFE to monitor network drives.
/D	Turns off checksumming.
/U	Removes VSAFE from memory; don't use with any other switches.

Figure 15.7.
VSAFE Warning Options dialog box.

Vsafe Warning Options		
	Warning Type	ON
1	HD Low-level format	X
2	Resident	
3	General write protect	
4	Check executable files	X
5	Boot sector viruses	X
6	Protect HD boot sector	X
7	Protect FD boot sector	
8	Protect executable files	

Press 1-8 toggle ON/OFF
Press <ESC> to Exit
Press ALT-U to unload from memory

If you're using VSAFE with Windows, you must load the MWAVTSR.EXE program to permit VSAFE to display its alert boxes in the Windows environment. You can edit WIN.INI and add MWAVTSR.EXE to the load= line in the [Windows] section. Or if you're using Windows 3.1, you can simply add MWAVTSR.EXE to the Startup group.

To view and set the monitoring options in Windows, find the VSAFE Manager window that was opened by MWAVTSR.EXE and press the Options button.

The alert box that appears when VSAFE suspects a virus depends on which option caused the alert. For example, if option 1 (HD low-level format) triggers an alert, your choices are to stop or continue the low-level format. If option 4 (Scan executable files) triggers an alert, you see the same choices as you do when a scanner detects a known or unknown virus.

Upgrading Your Virus Definitions

To keep up with the newest viruses, you should upgrade your virus definitions periodically. There are two ways to do this. You can download a new signature file from the virus bulletin board service. When you install the new signatures, Anti-Virus will be able to detect those viruses, but it won't be able to clean them until you actually upgrade your Anti-Virus software.

Your DOS User's Guide contains an appendix with specific instructions on how to download virus signatures from the BBS. You can also download a README file that tells you how to install the new signatures. There's also a coupon at the back of your User's Guide to purchase your first Anti-Virus upgrade at a special price.

UNDELETE

16

Introduction

DOS 6 has introduced an important new feature to assist in the recovery of deleted files. The Delete Sentry program captures file deletions and moves the deleted files to its own hidden SENTRY directory for a few days. From there, they are easily recovered by the UNDELETE program with near 100-percent accuracy.

If you upgraded from DOS 5, you might be using deletion-tracking, which keeps a record of a deleted file's clusters but does not preserve the file itself. Delete Sentry is a much more effective way of protecting your deleted files. UNDELETE can recover files using the deletion-tracking method also, so if you need to recover some files that were deleted before you installed Delete Sentry, you can do it with the new version of UNDELETE.

If you prefer not to use Delete-Sentry or deletion-tracking, UNDELETE may be able to recover all or part of a recently deleted file simply by locating the deleted directory entry.

DOS 6 includes two versions of UNDELETE, one for DOS and one for Windows. You can install Delete Sentry or deletion-tracking and undelete files by using either version. As you'll see later in this chapter, the Windows version has a few features that the DOS version doesn't.

Files replaced in an operation such as COPY, MOVE, or RESTORE are not considered to be deleted and are not protected by either of the deletion-protection methods. They also cannot be recovered by the DOS method because their directory entries have been replaced. However, their data may still be in the clusters and a third-party recovery utility such as The Norton Utilities's UnErase may be able to locate and recover it.

Using DOS UNDELETE

Figure 16.1 shows the format of the UNDELETE command, which has several functions. You can use it to install Delete Sentry or deletion-tracking, to see what files are available for undeleting by each of the three undelete methods, to undelete files, and to purge files from the SENTRY directory. You can't use UNDELETE to recover a subdirectory or to undelete a file in a directory that has been removed, but you may be able to do that with the Windows version of UNDELETE.

UNDELETE

Enables deletion protection or restores files previously deleted.

Format:

```
UNDELETE /LOAD ¦ /U ¦ /S[drive] ... ¦ /T[drive[-entries]
... ¦ /STATUS
```

Enables or disables deletion protection; reports protection status.

```
UNDELETE [filespec] [/DT ¦ /DOS] [/LIST ¦ /ALL]
[/PURGE[drive]]
```

Recovers deleted files; lists recoverable files; clears a SENTRY directory.

Parameters and Switches:

/LOAD
Loads the UNDELETE TSR with the default protection method.

/U
Unloads the UNDELETE TSR.

/S[drive]
Loads the UNDELETE TSR, setting the current and default methods of deletion protection to Delete Sentry; adds drive to the list of drives protected by Sentry.

/T[drive]
Loads the UNDELETE TSR, setting the current and default method of deletion protection to deletion-tracking; adds drive to the list of drives protected by Tracking.

entries
Specifies the maximum number of entries in the deletion-tracking file for drive; may be 1 to 999. The default depends on the drive size.

/STATUS
Displays the drives protected by the current protection method.

none
Offers to recover all deleted files in the current directory that can be recovered using the highest available method for the current drive.

Figure 16.1.
UNDELETE command summary.

filespec	Identifies the file(s) that you want to recover; the default is all deleted files in the current directory.	
/DT	Recovers only those files listed in the deletion-tracking file, prompting for confirmation on each file.	
/DS	Recovers only those files listed in the SENTRY directory, prompting for confirmation on each file.	

Figure 16.1.
continued

Installing Delete Sentry

To install Delete Sentry, add a command to your AUTOEXEC.BAT file in this format:

```
UNDELETE /Sdrive [...]
```

For example, the following command installs deletion-protection for drives C and D:

```
UNDELETE /SC /SD
```

> If your system is set up to use upper memory blocks, use LH to load the UNDELETE TSR into upper memory or run MEMMAKER after you insert this command in AUTOEXEC.BAT.

Delete Sentry maintains a list of all protected drives, so you really only need to turn it on once for a drive. After that, whenever you load Delete Sentry, every drive in the drive list is protected. But it doesn't hurt to have the /S switches in the UNDELETE command every time you boot, and they serve to remind you which drives are being protected.

After Delete Sentry is installed, you can't add any more drives to the list without uninstalling it. The easiest way to add a new drive to the list is to add the /S switch to the command in AUTOEXEC.BAT and reboot.

To remove a drive from Delete Sentry's list, delete it from the
[sentry.drives] section of the UNDELETE.INI file.

How Delete Sentry Works

When you delete a file, Delete Sentry captures the file into its SENTRY directory.
SENTRY is a hidden directory that is a child of the root directory on each drive that
is protected. Delete Sentry uses several measures to keep your drive from filling up
with deleted files:

● By default, files are purged from SENTRY after seven days. You can alter
the number of days by editing the days= parameter in the [configuration]
section of UNDELETE.INI.

● The oldest files are purged when SENTRY reaches 20 percent of the drive.
You can alter the percentage by editing the percentage= parameter in the
[configuration] section of UNDELETE.INI.

If you are deleting a group of files or a very large file that you don't
particularly want Delete Sentry to capture, disable UNDELETE by using
the UNDELETE /U command so that the deleted files don't push more
important files out of SENTRY. Be sure to reload UNDELETE (you can use
the /LOAD switch to do this) as soon as possible.

● The oldest files are purged from SENTRY whenever DOS needs more room
on the disk to store new data.

If Delete Sentry is not loaded and a SENTRY directory exists, you might
encounter Disk Full errors when DOS tries to save data. Loading Delete
Sentry should solve the problem.

● Temporary files (extensions TMP, VM?, WOA, SWP, SPL, RMG, IMG, THM, and DOV) are not protected. You can edit this list in the [sentry.files] section of UNDELETE.INI. Place a minus sign in front of a filespec for files that you don't want to capture; omit the minus sign for files that you do want to capture. For example, to omit BAK files except for AUTOEXEC.BAK, add these filespecs to the list: -*.BAK AUTOEXEC.BAK.

To use Delete Sentry on a network drive, you must have read, write, create, and delete file access in the drive's root directory.

Recovering Files from Delete Sentry

When you try to recover files from a drive that has a SENTRY directory, UNDELETE automatically uses the Delete Sentry recovery method, even if Delete Sentry is not currently loaded. It will also show you the number of files that are available for recovery by the two other methods.

UNDELETE recovers files from one directory at a time. You can enter a filespec to specify the directory and/or filter the file list. If used, the filespec must precede any switches.

As a first step, it helps to use the /LIST switch to see the full range of files meeting your specifications that are available for undeletion. There might be duplicates in the list, and when you can see the entire list, you'll be able to pick out the version that you want to recover. Suppose that you enter this command:

```
UNDELETE FIG*.TIF /LIST
```

The response might look like this:

```
Directory: C:\WINWORD\ADVDOS
File Specifications: FIG*.TIF
   Searching Delete Sentry control file....
   Delete Sentry control file contains    8 deleted files.

   Deletion-tracking file not found.
```

```
MS-DOS directory contains    0 deleted files.
Of those,    0 files may be recovered.
```

Using the Delete Sentry method.

```
FIG22-2  TIF   112190  3-03-93 12:09p  ...A  Deleted:  3-03-93 12:09p
FIG22-2  TIF   112190  3-03-93 12:09p  ...A  Deleted:  3-03-93 12:10p
FIG18-4  TIF   112190  3-03-93 11:57a  ...A  Deleted:  3-03-93 12:21p
FIG22-1  TIF   112190  3-03-93 11:59a  ...A  Deleted:  3-03-93 12:22p
FIG22-2  TIF   112190  3-03-93 12:10p  ...A  Deleted:  3-03-93 12:23p
FIG22-3  TIF   112190  3-03-93 12:10p  ...A  Deleted:  3-03-93 12:23p
FIG00000 TIF   112190  3-03-93 12:27p  ...A  Deleted:  3-03-93 12:30p
FIG11111 TIF   112190  3-03-93 12:27p  ...A  Deleted:  3-03-93 12:31p
```

You can see that UNDELETE checked all three undeletion methods and then chose Delete Sentry. Suppose that you wanted to recover FIG22-2.TIF. There are three versions available. The most recent version was written at 12:10 p.m. and deleted at 12:23 p.m. This is probably the version you want to recover.

To recover the file, reenter the command without the /LIST switch. UNDELETE presents the available files one at a time, like this:

```
FIG22-2  TIF   112190  3-03-93 12:09p  ...A  Deleted:  3-03-93 12:09p
This file can be 100% undeleted. Undelete (Y/N)?
```

Press N for every file that you don't want to undelete and Y for each file that you do. When you have recovered all the files you want, press Esc to terminate the job.

If a recovered file would duplicate an existing filename in the same directory, UNDELETE asks you for another name for the recovered file.

Purging Files from Delete Sentry

The following command purges all the files from the SENTRY directory on the current drive. You can't select files to be purged with the DOS version of UNDELETE, although you can in the Windows version.

```
UNDELETE /PURGE
```

Working with Deletion-Tracking

If you decide that you want to continue with deletion-tracking instead of upgrading to Delete Sentry, you can install DOS 6's deletion-tracking using /T switches instead of /S in the UNDELETE command. They follow the same rules as the /S switches. You can remove drives from the deletion-tracking drive list by editing the [mirror.drives] section of UNDELETE.INI.

> You can't use both methods of protection. The UNDELETE TSR can be loaded only once, and only one method can be installed throughout all your drives.

When you enter an UNDELETE command to recover one or more files, UNDELETE automatically uses the deletion-tracking method to recover the file if the deletion-tracking file (PCTRACKR.DEL) is present and the SENTRY directory is not.

With deletion-tracking, UNDELETE may not be able to recover all the clusters in a file. When that happens, it offers you the choice of recovering part of the file. Keep these points in mind when considering a partial recovery:

● A partial binary file is useless.

> A partial program file, if executed, could actually do harm to your files.

● A partial word processing, spreadsheet, database, or other application-developed file might be missing header and trailer information that the application needs to open the file. You might have to open the file in an ASCII editor to rescue as much text and data as possible.

● Restoring the file from its backup is a much better choice.

Even when all the clusters are recovered, they might contain the wrong data. If another file reused some of the clusters and was then deleted, UNDELETE would not detect that the clusters had been overwritten. In all cases, restoring files from backups is preferable to recovering them from deletion-tracking.

However, if you really need to recover a file from an old deletion-tracking file that was made before you upgraded to DOS 6, and UNDELETE is now bypassing the deletion-tracking method in favor of the Delete Sentry method, you can force UNDELETE to use the deletion-tracking method by adding the /DT switch to the UNDELETE command.

Using the DOS Directory Method

Every once in a while, you may need to recover a file using the DOS directory method. For example, you might need to use this method to recover a file that was deleted while you had deletion protection turned off; you might need to undelete one of the files that deletion-protection doesn't protect, such as a TMP file; or you might be able to undelete a file that has already been purged from Delete Sentry but is still available as a deleted directory entry.

Add the /DOS switch to the UNDELETE command to force UNDELETE to use the DOS method. The first character of each filename appears as a question mark since DOS deleted that character in the process of deleting the file. If the first cluster of the file is not available, UNDELETE can't recover any part of the file using this method. If the first cluster is available, UNDELETE guesses at the remaining clusters, if any. It might warn you that not all of the file can be recovered.

If you use the /ALL switch with the directory method, UNDELETE assigns the first characters of the filenames for you. It assigns the character # unless that creates a duplicate filename in the directory, in which case it assigns the next character in this list that would create a unique filename:

%&0123456789ABCDEFGHIJKLMNOPQRSTUVWXYZ

Undeleting Files from DOS Shell

DOS Shell includes an Undelete program item in the Disk Utilities directory. Selecting this item opens a dialog box where you can enter the parameters you want to use on the UNDELETE command. The /LIST switch is the only default parameter. If you want to add a filespec, be sure to insert it in front of the /LIST switch. When you press Enter, the DOS command prompt screen appears and the job continues as you have already seen.

Working with Windows Undelete

Figure 16.2 shows the Undelete window, which opens when you Undelete from the Microsoft Tools group. The file list shows all the files available for undeletion by all methods. When the condition is "perfect," the file is protected by Delete Sentry. Lower conditions indicate that the file is protected by deletion-tracking. If the first character of the filename is a question mark, the DOS directory method is being used. The listing occasionally shows files from the directory that can't be undeleted. Their entries are dimmed and their condition is Destroyed.

Figure 16.2.
Microsoft Undelete
window.

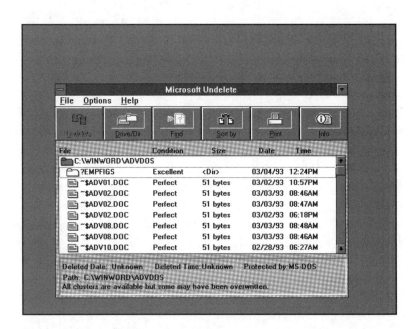

To undelete files, select them in the file list and press the Undelete button. You can change drives and directories by pressing the Drive/Dir button.

Windows Undelete Features

The Find button opens a dialog box in which you can enter a filespec and/or text to search for. The entire current drive is searched. You also can select a group of files to search for, such as the pbrush (Windows Paintbrush) group, which searches for *.PCX and *.BMP files.

The Sort By button lets you choose sort criteria for the file list. The Print button causes the current file list to be printed on the default printer. The Info button opens a dialog box that provides additional information about the currently selected file, such as its first cluster number.

Figure 16.3 shows the File menu. Most of the commands duplicate the buttons you have already seen, but a few of the commands are unique. The Undelete To command lets you select the directory where you want to place the recovered file. The Purge Delete Sentry File purges the selected files from Delete Sentry.

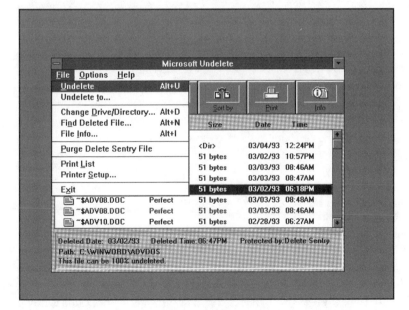

Figure 16.3.
Windows Undelete
File menu.

Figure 16.4 shows the Options menu. Choose Select By Name to enter a filespec to select files to be undeleted or purged. Choose Unselect By Name to enter a filespec that deselects files that have already been selected.

Figure 16.4.
The Options menu.

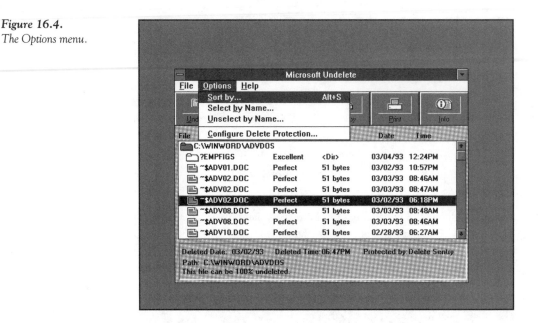

The Configure Deletion Protection option opens a dialog box in which you can select Delete Sentry, Delete Tracker, or Standard (which is the DOS directory entry method). If you choose one of the protection methods, an additional dialog box gives you the opportunity to specify which files you want to protect, how many days files should stay in SENTRY, and similar options. Undelete updates the UNDELETE.INI file based on your choices, but you have to reboot to put them into effect.

Undeleting Directories

You may be able to recover a deleted subdirectory using Windows Undelete. The entry named ?EMPFIGS in Figure 16.2 is a deleted directory, as you can see both by its icon and by the size column. This directory is not being protected by any method, but it can be recovered via the DOS directory method. After it has been recovered, its files can be recovered as well. In fact, they may be protected by Delete Sentry.

A Ton of Cure

17

Introduction

No matter how careful you are or how many preventive measures you take, eventually you're going to lose some data. Whether it's from malfunctioning hardware, a virus, or a simple typo in a command, you have to do your best to recover it.

DOS 6 includes a number of diagnostic and recovery tools that can help you deal with errors in the system areas and directory tree, accidentally deleted files, and accidentally reformatted disks. DOS's tools can handle most of your recovery needs. However, you may need to turn to outside solutions in some cases.

Checking and Fixing Disks (CHKDSK)

The CHKDSK command (see fig. 17.1) identifies file and disk problems by analyzing the file allocation table (FAT) and directory structure. In most cases, CHKDSK can correct problems. You also may use other DOS commands to solve a problem or at least to save as much data as possible. Still other situations can't be easily solved within DOS, and you may need to resort to third-party, data-recovery utilities or a disk repair specialist.

> Some third-party recovery utilities require that they be run before you try CHKDSK with /F. They can't function if CHKDSK has already tried and failed to fix a problem.

When you notice a disk or file access error or a general slowing of disk access, run CHKDSK (without /F) as a first step in determining the problem. Many people run it weekly or daily to head off potential problems. When you run CHKDSK without any parameters or switches, you see a summary report on the current drive similar to the following:

```
Volume FIXED DISK  created 03-27-1993 11:05a
Volume Serial Number is 16E8-7B6A

 33462272 bytes total disk space
   327680 bytes in 11 hidden files
    69632 bytes in 24 directories
 30998528 bytes in 1125 user files
     4096 bytes in bad sectors
  2062336 bytes available on disk
```

```
    2048 bytes in each allocation unit
   16339 total allocation units on disk
    1007 available allocation units on disk

  655360 total bytes memory
  551744 bytes free
```

The report shows information on the drive itself, including the size and number of allocation units (or clusters). This information is followed by a report on conventional memory, a pre-MEM leftover.

The bad sectors shown are not a problem. They were detected when the disk was formatted, and the FORMAT program marked them in the FAT so that no data is stored in them. Any problems identified by CHKDSK would be listed after the first two header lines.

All of CHKDSK's messages, even those indicating problems on the disk, are written as standard output so that they can be redirected to print or to a file for documentation purposes.

The File Allocation Table

DOS locates a file by starting with its directory entry and continuing to its FAT entries. The directory entry tells DOS the size of the file and the first cluster it occupies. The FAT then locates the remaining clusters belonging to the file (if any), in the proper order.

The FAT is a table with one entry for every cluster on the disk. Each entry contains one of the following:

- The number of the next cluster belonging to the same file.

- An end-of-file indicator.

- A 0, indicating that the cluster is available.

- A bad cluster indicator, which prevents DOS from ever using the cluster.

Figure 17.1.
CHKDSK
command reference.

CHKDSK

Reports disk status, reports and fixes problems in the FAT and directory structure, and reports file fragmentation.

Format:

CHKDSK [*drive*] [/F] [/V]

CHKDSK *filespec*.

Parameters and Switches:

none   Checks the current drive.

drive   Checks the specified drive.

/F   Fixes errors in the drive's FAT and directory structure, if possible.

/V   Lists each file while checking the drive.

filespec   Reports on file fragmentation for the indicated files.

Never run CHKDSK on drives on which you have used ASSIGN or SUBST or on network drives.

Do not use CHKDSK /F when files may be open. You must not start CHKDSK /F from another program (such as a word processor) or when Microsoft Windows or DOS Shell is running. You may need to reboot to eliminate TSRs before using CHKDSK /F.

Examining the FAT

There are no clusters 0 and 1, so the FAT starts with an entry for cluster 2. Suppose that these are the first 20 entries (for clusters 2 through 21) in a FAT:

```
            3     4     5    EOF    7     8
16    0     0    BAD   EOF   EOF   15    EOF
17    18    21   EOF    0    EOF
```

Suppose that the drive's root directory indicates that the file named OLDMILL.DOC starts in cluster 2. The FAT entry for cluster 2 contains the value 3, indicating that this cluster starts a chain that continues with cluster 3. The entry for cluster 3 chains to cluster 4, which in turn chains to cluster 5. Cluster 5 contains an end-of-file indicator (EOF), so OLDMILL.DOC ends there; it is completely contained in four clusters. (The file's size, shown in the directory entry, should confirm that the file needs four clusters.)

Suppose that another directory entry indicates that FAMILY.CRD begins in cluster 6. The FAT shows that the file chains to clusters 7 and 8 and then jumps to 16, 17, and 18 and finally to cluster 21, which marks the end of the file. This file uses seven clusters in three fragments.

Entries for clusters 9, 10, and 20 contain 0s; these clusters are available, probably as a result of deleted files.

Cluster 11 was marked as bad by the formatting program (or possibly some other program). A bad cluster will never be used for data.

The EOF marks in clusters 12, 13, and 19 may represent one-cluster files or the last fragments of files begun elsewhere on the disk. You have to check the entire directory tree and FAT to know for sure. Cluster 14 starts (or continues) a file that ends in cluster 15.

Sample FAT Data

DOS itself doesn't let you look at the FAT, but Figure 17.2 shows a section of a FAT in the format displayed by some third-party utility programs. This FAT contains several allocation problems that are explored later in this chapter.

		3	4	4	<EOF>	<EOF>	<EOF>
0	10	11	12	13	14	15	16
17	18	19	<EOF>	21	22	23	24
25	26	18	28	29	30	31	32
33	34	35	36	37	38	39	40
<EOF>	0	0	0	0	<EOF>	47	48
49	1	51					

Figure 17.2.
FAT display.

Notice that each line shows information for eight clusters. As always, clusters 0 and 1 don't exist.

By analyzing the directory structure and the FAT, CHKDSK can tell whether allocation units are in use but not connected to a specific file (lost allocation units), whether an allocation unit is assigned to more than one file chain (cross-linked allocation units), whether a file chains to an invalid allocation unit (such as 1), and whether the number of allocation units assigned to a file matches the recorded file size. It also can determine whether the FAT itself has developed a bad sector and which, if any, files are fragmented.

Detecting and Fixing Errors

When you run CHKDSK without the /F switch, it detects and reports all errors. However, CHKDSK will not make any changes to the disk until you run it with /F. You see a message something like the following:

```
Errors found, F parameter not specified
Corrections will not be written to disk
```

After you know an error was detected and whether or not CHKDSK can fix it, you can decide whether to let CHKDSK fix it or to try something else. To let CHKDSK try, run the command exactly as before (you could use DOSKEY to recall it) with the /F switch added.

The next part of this chapter shows the errors that CHKDSK detects, what causes them, what CHKDSK can do about them, and other solutions you may want to try.

Don't run CHKDSK with /F under another program, such as DOS Shell or Microsoft Windows. If any files are open (which they probably are), CHKDSK will detect and correct false errors.

Lost Allocation Units

CHKDSK's most common error message reports lost allocation units, which are clusters allocated to file data but not linked to a file directory entry. It isn't all that unusual to have several kilobytes involved in lost allocation units.

How Clusters Get Lost

Anything that interrupts DOS before it can finish closing or deleting a file could result in lost allocation units. Some of the more common causes are as follows:

● Shutting down or rebooting without waiting for the drive access light to go out

● Having to reboot when a program hangs up

● Power fluctuations

Lost clusters also can be the result of more serious problems, such as hardware malfunctions, media deterioration, or viruses. However, generally you can assume that lost allocation units are normal unless you detect other symptoms of a malfunctioning system.

Handling Lost Clusters

However they occur, you deal with lost clusters in the same way. Suppose that CHKDSK with no switches produces a report like the following:

```
Errors found, F parameter not specified
Corrections will not be written to disk
    6 lost allocation units found in 2 chains
      12288 bytes would be freed
```

These messages tell you that 12K bytes on the disk are tied up in lost allocation units. Recovering them makes that space useful again. When you use CHKDSK /F, the message appears as follows:

```
6 lost allocation units found in 2 chains
Convert lost chains to files (Y/N)?
```

At this point, you must choose to convert the lost clusters to files or delete them. If you press Y (or Enter), each chain is converted to a file named FILE*nnnn*.CHK. You can examine the resulting files to see what data they contain. If the data is nothing you need to keep (the usual case), all you have to do is delete the files and the space is freed for future use. If you press N, the lost allocation units are zeroed in the FAT, freeing them immediately for future file data. You also can press Ctrl-Break to exit CHKDSK instead of dealing with the lost clusters.

Overfilling the Root Directory

A root directory has a limited number of entries; the maximum depends on the disk size. CHKDSK may recapture hundreds of lost chains at the same time if you have allowed them to build up on your disk or if another error in the FAT or directory structure has caused hundreds of files to be abandoned. Because they are all placed in the root directory, you may see the following message:

```
Insufficient room in root directory
Erase files in root and repeat CHKDSK
```

It's time to examine and deal with all the FILE*nnnn*.CHK files that have been created so far. Delete as many as possible and copy the ones you want to keep to other directories. Then reenter the CHKDSK /F command to recover more lost allocation units.

Cross-Linked Allocation Units

The next most common problem identified by CHKDSK is a cross-linked allocation unit; this allocation unit is assigned to two different files or to two different locations in the same file. The FAT in Figure 17.2 shows several cross-linkages, as shown in the following CHKDSK report:

```
C:\STUDY.CHP
     is cross-linked on allocation unit 4
C:\FOOLS.CAP
     is cross-linked on allocation unit 18
C:\POSTSCRP.WID
     is cross-linked on allocation unit 18
```

If only one file is cross-linked on an allocation unit, such as STUDY.CHP in the preceding report, the cluster is used twice in the file. Notice in Figure 17.2 that the FAT entries for clusters 3 and 4 both contain the value 4, causing the cross-linking problem. The file chain bogs down at that point because there's no indication of what cluster is next. (Cluster 4 is really supposed to chain to cluster 5, but neither DOS nor CHKDSK will make that kind of assumption. It's a good bet that cluster 5 in the example is a lost allocation unit.)

When two or more files are cross-linked on the same allocation unit, both files reference that cluster. In Figure 17.2, both FOOLS.CAP (which starts in cluster 9) and POSTSCPT.WID (which starts in cluster 20) chain to cluster 18. Here again, you can guess that the FOOLS.CAP chain is correct, and POSTSCPT.WID should chain to cluster 27. However, DOS and CHKDSK aren't equipped for guessing. (The chain from cluster 27 to cluster 40 is probably lost.)

How Files Get Cross-Linked

Files become cross-linked in much the same way that allocation units get lost. Cross-linking is less common but more bothersome, because CHKDSK can't even attempt to fix it.

Dealing with Cross-Linked Allocation Units

If you have valid backups of cross-linked files, you have the ideal solution. Just delete the cross-linked files and restore them from the backups. If not, you have to deal with the problem some other way. CHKDSK has no way of knowing which file is correct and which is wrong, nor can it guess at how to fix the wrong one.

As you have seen in the examples, if you could view and edit the FAT, you may be able to guess at the correct way to resolve a cross-link. DOS has no facility for this, but, as usual, you can buy third-party utilities that do. In fact, these utilities enable you to view the contents of the clusters so that you can see whether your guesses are correct.

If you don't have access to such a utility and you want to try resolving the cross-link using DOS, you can try the procedures in the next section. They will be most effective with files containing text. It would be difficult for you to recognize the data in a worksheet, graphic, or program file, for example, by just viewing it.

> Don't try to rescue a cross-linked program file. You could create an invalid program module that, when executed, could damage data on your hard disk. Always restore program files from their original distribution disks or a backup copy.

A Single Cross-Linkage

When a single file is cross-linked, two of its FAT entries chain to the same cluster. A loop is created, and the chain never reaches the end of the file. If you copy the file, DOS follows the chain until the right number of clusters are copied, but the result will not be correct. In all likelihood, the tail end of the file has been orphaned in the FAT. Converting lost allocation units to files will probably recover it for you.

Following these steps could recover all, or most, of the file:

1. Copy the file under a new name. The new file will not be cross-linked, although it probably will not contain the right data.

2. Delete the cross-linked file to get rid of the cross-linkage in the FAT.

3. Recover all lost allocation units into files.

4. Examine the new file under the application that created it, if possible. Eliminate duplicated data and decide what data is missing, if any.

5. Examine the FILE*nnnn*.CHK files to see which ones, if any, contain data belonging to the damaged file.

6. Use the file's original application to insert the desired CHK files into the damaged file, if possible.

7. Deal with the other CHK files, if any, as you do when recovering lost allocation units.

Multiple Cross-Linkage

When two files are cross-linked, a FAT entry for one of them contains a cluster number that really belongs to the other. When DOS tries to trace the FAT chains, both files end with the same cluster(s). One of the files is probably correct. If you don't have valid backups of the files, your problem is to discover which file is correct and recover as much as possible of the other file. The following steps may help for a text file:

1. XCOPY each file to a new name.

2. If the cross-linkage causes one file to be shorter than its directory entry indicates, XCOPY will go into a loop, endlessly repeating the filename on the screen. When this happens, press Ctrl-Break to end it.

3. Delete the original, cross-linked files.

4. If you still don't know which file is damaged, examine each copy under the application that created it, if you can. You should be able to see which one is valid and which is damaged.

5. Delete any invalid data in the file.

6. If any data is missing from the damaged file, recover lost allocation units with CHKDSK.

7. Examine the CHK files and locate any data belonging to the damaged file.

8. Use the application to insert the desired CHK files into the damaged file, if possible.

9. Deal with the other CHK files, if any, as you do when recovering lost allocation units.

Invalid Allocation Units

A value in a file's FAT chain represents an invalid allocation unit if it is 0, 1, or larger than the number of allocation units on the disk. Although 0s are valid for unused clusters, they should not show up in a file chain.

Figure 17.2 shows an invalid allocation unit in the file that starts in cluster 46; cluster 49 contains the value 1, which breaks the chain. In this case, CHKDSK knows the file has more clusters from the size in the directory entry, but it has no way to find the rest of the file's chain. (As always, it can't guess.)

Any other clusters that belonged to the file are orphaned; you may be able to find them among the lost clusters on the disk.

CHKDSK notifies you about invalid allocation units as follows:

```
C:\BOOK1\CHAPTER.CPY
    First allocation unit is invalid, entry truncated
C:\BOOK1\STUDY.STY
    Has invalid allocation unit, file truncated

19 lost allocation units found in 4 chains
    38912 bytes would be freed
```

If the first allocation unit is invalid, no part of the file can be saved directly. At least one chain of lost allocation units probably belongs to this file. The invalid allocation unit in the second example is not the first cluster in the file, so at least part of the file can be found. Unless the invalid entry is at the end of the file, at least one lost chain should have data from this file.

How CHKDSK Fixes Invalid Allocation Units

If you can't restore the file from its backup and you use the /F switch, CHKDSK replaces an invalid entry with an end-of-file marker and adjusts the file size in the directory to match the number of clusters. When asked, press Y to tell CHKDSK to save any lost chains as files. Now you can access the file (if possible) and find out how much data you have lost; then examine the CHK files to recover what you can. As always, don't try to run a program file that has been treated this way.

Allocation Errors

CHKDSK reports a general allocation error when it detects that the size recorded for the file in the directory entry doesn't match the number of allocation units assigned to it. You see a message like the following:

```
A:\NEWSTUDY.DOC
    Allocation error, size adjusted
```

If you haven't used /F, the size in the directory entry isn't really adjusted.

How CHKDSK Fixes an Allocation Error

When /F is specified, CHKDSK fixes an allocation error by adjusting the file's size in the directory entry. The entire last cluster is considered as part of the file, because CHKDSK can't tell where the file ends and slack begins.

If the recorded size really was wrong and the number of allocation units in the FAT was correct, CHKDSK's repair may add slack (garbage) to the end of the file. If the recorded size was correct and the FAT included too few or too many allocation units for the file, the resulting file is incorrect; it is either too long or too short. Either the file now contains garbage at the end or some lost allocation units are on the disk. At any rate, now you can access the file to figure out what to do next.

Dealing with Allocation Errors

When CHKDSK reports an allocation error in a file, and if you can't restore the file from its backup, run CHKDSK again with /F and let it adjust the file's size. Save any lost chains as files. When CHKDSK is finished, examine the damaged file under its original application, if you can. You may have to delete unwanted garbage at the end, or you may have to locate and insert missing data from the CHK files created by CHKDSK.

If CHKDSK detects an allocation error on a program file, delete the file and reinstall the program from its original disks.

Invalid Subdirectory Entry

Subdirectories are stored as files with a special directory attribute. They can be corrupted in many of the same ways that files can. If the .. directory entry shows the wrong cluster number for the parent, for example, DOS can't find the linkage from that subdirectory to its parent. If the parent's link to the child is corrupted, DOS can't locate the subdirectory.

When CHKDSK detects an invalid subdirectory, the message depends on the severity. You may see the following:

```
C:\BOOK1\CHAP03.DOC
    Invalid subdirectory entry
```

In this case, CHKDSK can fix the problem. It may be a corrupted entry for the backlink to the parent directory, for example. CHKDSK can search the tree, find the address of the parent that way, and fix the subdirectory entry. In this case, no files or allocation units are lost.

An invalid subdirectory entry message also may be followed by some lines like the following:

```
324 lost allocation units in 5 chains
   165888 bytes disk space would be freed
  Convert lost directory to file (Y/N)?
```

This message usually indicates that you can't access anything in the subdirectory, and all its files appear to be lost chains, as do all its subdirectories and their files. CHKDSK can't do anything to fix the subdirectory entry.

What CHKDSK Does

If it doesn't ask about converting the subdirectory to a file, CHKDSK with the /F switch can find the information it needs. It quietly fixes the problem without losing any data.

However, if CHKDSK asks and you press Y to convert a lost directory to a file, DOS makes the cluster that formerly contained the subdirectory into a file. Because they are no longer linked to the directory structure, allocation units for all files in the branch headed by that subdirectory are lost. You should respond with a Y when CHKDSK asks whether you want to convert them to files.

Dealing with Invalid Subdirectory Entries

If you are offered the opportunity of converting an invalid subdirectory into a file, you may say yes for safety's sake, although you can do very little with the resulting file. However, it is important to recover lost allocation units into files if you can't restore the branch from backups.

To restore the branch, remake all the subdirectories and then examine all the CHK files and copy them to their former subdirectories with their correct names. As a final step, delete any CHK files you don't need anymore.

Bad FAT Sectors

CHKDSK doesn't check for bad sectors or other surface problems on a disk. However, if the FAT itself has developed problems, you may see one of the following messages:

`Bad sector in FAT`

or

`Probable nonDOS disk`

The `Probable nonDOS disk` message may reflect a bad spot in the boot record, rather than in the FAT. Either message indicates too major a problem for CHKDSK to handle.

If the problem is with a floppy disk and you have a valid backup, you probably will just throw away the damaged one. However, if the problem is on a hard disk, you will want to go further to rescue it. A third-party utility such as Norton Disk Doctor might be able to succeed where CHKDSK can't. Even if you can't repair the disk, you may be able to recover the data from it before repairing it or replacing it.

> The Norton Utilities can do a surface analysis of a disk, giving you more information about bad spots and how to work around them.

Rescuing Accidentally Formatted Disks

If you have never reformatted a floppy disk in error, you may be unique among your fellow computer users. DOS 6 includes an UNFORMAT program to rescue accidentally reformatted disks. As long as the format wasn't done unconditionally, the format wasn't destructive and can be undone. How much of the data on the disk can be recovered depends on several factors:

- Whether the format was unconditional

- Whether the disk contains unformatting information

- Whether any data was added to the disk after formatting

- Whether the disk contained fragmented files if no formatting information was recorded

When you use DOS 6's FORMAT in the safe or quick mode, you see the message `Saving UNFORMAT information` early in the process. A snapshot of the FAT and root directory are stored in an image file. This image file is deleted before the format is done, but UNFORMAT can find and use the saved information.

The UNFORMAT Command

Figure 17.3 shows the UNFORMAT command. The /PARTN switch can be used in conjunction with /L to display your hard disk's partition table, but you can always examine the partition table with FDISK, as explained in Chapter 23. All the other switches are used to prepare for and unformat disks. UNFORMAT looks for an image file unless you specify /L or /P on the command.

The /J switch is used to verify the image information, and /TEST simulates UNFORMAT without image information. Neither switch actually unformats the disk.

Figure 17.3.
UNFORMAT
command reference.

UNFORMAT

Restores a disk reformatted by the FORMAT command; undeletes deleted directories; displays partition table.

Format:

UNFORMAT *drive* [/L] [/TEST] [/P] [/PARTN] [/J]

Parameters and Switches:

drive   Identifies the drive to be unformatted.

/J   Verifies image file.

/L   Lists every file and subdirectory found by UNFORMAT; without this switch, only fragmented files and directories are listed.

/TEST   Shows how UNFORMAT would re-create the information on the disk but does not actually unformat the disk.

/P   Sends output messages to LPT1.

/PARTN   When used with /L, displays partition table.

Notes:

When you unformat a hard disk, the sectors must be 512, 1024, or 2048 bytes.

With /L, /TEST, or /P, UNFORMAT bypasses mirror information and searches the clusters (very slowly) for subdirectories.

When used with /L or /P, UNFORMAT may be able to restore a deleted directory, even if the disk has not been reformatted. This method of re-creating directories, however, is slow and uncertain; sometimes, it creates strange directories, and it truncates fragmented files, even in existing directories.

How Unformatting Works

UNFORMAT searches the clusters on the specified disk to see whether image information is available. It will find deleted image files. If more than one image file is found, you can choose which to use. After you verify that UNFORMAT should use a particular image file, it replaces the system information on the disk with the saved data. The root directory and the FAT are both restored.

If no changes have been made to the FAT or root directory since the image information was saved, the restoration gives you complete and accurate access to all former files and subdirectories. No further restoration is necessary. If you have made a few changes to the disk after saving the image information, you may find discrepancies in some files, which could be preferable to losing all the former data.

When UNFORMAT doesn't use image information, it searches the disk for subdirectories and uses their backlinks (the .. entries) to locate their parents. By this means, it can rebuild the entire directory tree. When a subdirectory is recovered, its files are also recovered as much as possible. However, UNFORMAT can find only the first fragment of any fragmented files.

When image information is not available, the biggest problem lies with the files in the root directory. They can't be recovered because their directory entries were obliterated when the new root directory was installed. First-level subdirectories will be discovered in the data area, and UNFORMAT knows they belong to the root directory because they backlink to cluster 0, but there is no way of discovering their names. UNDELETE restores them to the root directory using generic names in the form SUBDIR.n. You can examine and rename them. You will not be able to recover the files from the root directory, however, unless you use a third-party utility that enables you to examine available clusters and make up files from them.

When it is not using an image file, UNFORMAT lists on-screen the complete path of any subdirectories it finds. It lists fragmented files and asks whether each should be truncated or deleted. (If you include the /L switch, it lists all files, fragmented or otherwise.)

UNFORMAT Using Image Information

If you have reformatted a disk in safe or quick mode, it can be restored. FORMAT saved unformatting information on the disk, so complete recovery is possible as long as you haven't added anything to the disk since the format.

You see the following messages when you enter UNFORMAT A: (with no switches) as the command:

```
Insert disk to rebuild in drive A:
and press ENTER when ready.
```

After you follow these instructions, the messages continue:

```
Restores the system area of your disk by using the
image file created by the MIRROR command.

    WARNING !!          WARNING !!

This command should be used only to recover from the
inadvertent use of the FORMAT command or the RECOVER
command. Any other use of the UNFORMAT command may
cause you to lose data! Files modified since the MIRROR
image file was created may be lost.

Searching disk for MIRROR image.

The last time the MIRROR or FORMAT command was used was
at 15:03 on 08-05-92.

The MIRROR image file has been validated.

Are you sure you want to update the system area of your
drive A (Y/N)?
```

MIRROR and RECOVER are two programs from earlier versions of DOS. They have been dropped from DOS 6, but UNDELETE's messages haven't been updated to reflect the change.

At this point, UNFORMAT has examined the disk and discovered a valid image file; it hasn't yet made any changes to the disk. Examine the date and time of the image file carefully; using out-of-date information can be disastrous. If you decide to rebuild the disk from scratch rather than using the image file, cancel UNFORMAT and start over with the /U switch to do that. After you tell it to continue, UNFORMAT restores the root directory and FAT from the image file. In a few seconds you see the following:

```
The system area of drive A has been rebuilt.
You may need to restart the system.
```

Restarting the system is a good idea to clear any old directory information out of buffers and caches. After the disk is unformatted, the directories and FATs are back as they were when the image file was saved.

Missing Image Information

If UNFORMAT can't find image information in its normal location, you see messages like the following:

```
Unable to find the MIRROR control file. If you want to
search for the MIRROR image file through the entire
hard drive, press Y, or press N to cancel the UNFORMAT command.
```

If you want, the rest of the disk (which is not necessarily the hard drive) will be searched; even on a floppy disk, the search takes a long time. To run UNFORMAT without using the image file, press N here and then run UNFORMAT with /U, /L, or /P so that it will not look for an image file.

UNFORMAT without Image Information

Unformatting a disk without image information may be necessary in the following conditions:

- You reformatted the disk with a third-party format program that did not save image information.

- You used the /U and /Q switches together on the FORMAT command.

- The formatting program was unable to save image information because the disk was too full.

- The image file is corrupted or missing.

When image information is not available, you see the following messages:

```
  CAUTION !!
```

```
This attempts to recover all the files lost after a
format, assuming you've not been using the MIRROR command.
```

```
This method can't guarantee complete recovery of your files.
```

```
The search-phase is safe: nothing is altered on the disk.
You will be prompted again before changes are written to the
disk.
```

```
Using drive A:
```

```
Are you sure you want to do this?
If so, press Y; anything else cancels.
N?
```

At this point, you can back out and nothing happens. If you enter Y, however, UNFORMAT begins searching the available clusters for subdirectories. The display shows you the percentage of the disk that has been searched and the number of subdirectories that have been found. When the search is finished, you see the number of files and subdirectories found in the root directory. It may find subdirectories that were removed long ago that you don't want; you can remove these later. The messages appear as follows:

```
Searching disk...
n% searched.   n subdirectories found.
Files found in the root: n
Subdirectories found in the root: n
```

Next UNFORMAT checks the entire directory tree looking for files. Any first-level subdirectories that have been removed will have lost their names. You see the names UNFORMAT creates in the list:

```
Walking the directory tree to locate all files...
Path=A:\
Path=A:\SUBDIR.1\
Path=A:\SUBDIR.1\CHAPS\
Path=A:\SUBDIR.1\
etc.
```

```
Files found: n

Warning! The next step writes changes to disk.

Are you sure you want to do this?
If so, press Y; anything else cancels.
?
```

This is your last chance to back out. If you choose to go ahead, UNFORMAT begins recovering subdirectories and files. If only the first fragment of a file is available, you see messages like the following:

```
Checking for file fragmentation...
Path=A:\
Path=A:\SUBDIR.1\
Path=A:\SUBDIR.1\CHAPS\
GETTY2.DOC     2560  9-25-92  11:32am  Only   512 bytes
are recoverable. Truncate or Delete this file?
```

You can decide whether UNFORMAT should save what it can (truncate) or just delete the file.

Handling Image Files

The /J switch causes UNFORMAT to compare an image file to the current system area of a disk. The report appears as follows when they don't match:

```
Restores the system area of your disk by using the
image file created by the MIRROR command.

    WARNING !!          WARNING !!
```

```
This command should be used only to recover from the
inadvertent use of the FORMAT command or the RECOVER
command. Any other use of the UNFORMAT command may
cause you to lose data! Files modified since the MIRROR
image file was created may be lost.

Searching disk for MIRROR image.

Just checking this time. No changes written to disk.
```

```
The last time the MIRROR or FORMAT command was used was
at 15:03 on 10-05-92.
```

```
The MIRROR image file has been validated.
```

```
The system area does not agree with the MIRROR image file.
```

If the image file does match the current system area, you see the following message:

```
The system area of drive A has been verified
to agree with the MIRROR image file.
```

This facility can tell you whether running UNFORMAT will make any changes on the disk.

Simulating an UNFORMAT

Sometimes, you just want to know what UNFORMAT would do to a disk. You can't find out exactly what using the image file would do, but you can use the /TEST switch to find out what would happen if you ignore any image files. When you use /TEST, UNFORMAT performs the entire search phase, showing you what would be rebuilt as it lists the subdirectories and fragmented files. You can use this switch with /L to list all files on the disk and with /P to get a hard copy of the information.

When a Disk Develops Bad Spots

Occasionally, when DOS tries to read or write a file, it encounters a read or wait error, indicating that a cluster within the file has developed a bad spot. Under normal circumstances, DOS will not access any part of a file that contains a bad cluster.

Some surface errors are intermittent, so try several times before giving up.

How to recover from such a situation depends on whether the problem is on a floppy or hard disk and on whether you have a valid backup. If you have a backup and the damaged file is on a floppy disk, copy other files to a new disk. Restore the damaged file to the new disk and then get rid of the damaged disk.

If you have a backup and the damaged file is on hard disk, the best solution is to give the bad copy of the file a new name and then restore the desired file from its backup. Don't delete the bad file; if you do, DOS will reuse (or try to reuse) the bad cluster. You can prevent DOS from using that cluster again in several ways:

- Give the defective file a meaningful name (such as BADSPOT) and the system attribute, and then just leave it on the disk.

- Reformat the drive to block out the bad cluster in the FAT so that it will not be used again. Then restore all files from the backup set.

- Use a third-party utility that can block out the bad cluster without reformatting the rest of the drive.

If you don't have a recent backup, your best bet is to use a third-party utility to rescue as much of the file as possible and block out the bad spot. Earlier versions of DOS included a program called RECOVER that was supposed to do this, but RECOVER was capable of trashing the entire directory structure of a drive, and most experts recommended against using it. DOS 6 has dropped the RECOVER utility.

> If you upgraded from DOS 5, RECOVER.EXE may still be in your DOS directory. You should delete it. If you decide to try it out, be sure to include a filename with it, as in RECOVER C:\BADSPOT.DOC. (Bring your backups up-to-date first.) If you omit the filename, RECOVER will turn every directory entry on your drive into a generic filename in the root directory. You then will need a third-party utility like the Norton Utilities to recover from RECOVER.

Sector Not Found Errors

Another sign of a disk in trouble is a `sector not found` error. One such message could be a fluke, but when these messages appear with increasing frequency, the disk's low-level formatting needs to be redone. Low-level formatting lays out the sectors on a disk, storing the sector's address and other information, such as the CRC value, in a few system bytes immediately preceding each sector.

In time, sector information can be damaged. Specific sectors could be damaged by an unparked head landing on the disk surface. A little refrigerator magnet can do untold damage (not just to the sector information). However, even when a disk is treated with respect, the low-level formatting can degrade over a period of time.

When the controller can't find a sector address requested by DOS, it reports back a `sector not found` error. DOS, in turn, refuses to access any part of the file. If this happens with only one file, you may be able to use RECOVER to rescue as much data as possible from the file. However, if it's happening consistently on a disk, it's time to redo the low-level formatting.

Many low-level formatting programs will destroy all data on a disk.

For floppy disks, an unconditional FORMAT redoes the low-level formatting and will make the disk usable again. DOS does not include a low-level formatting program for hard disks. If you did not receive one with your hard disk, you may be able to get one from your dealer or repair technician, or you can buy one at your software store.

Your best bet for reformatting a hard disk is a utility that will redo the low-level formatting without damaging the data in the tracks. If you don't have access to such a utility, you have to do a destructive format, repartition the disk, redo the high-level format for each drive, and reload the data from backups.

Console Control

18

Introduction

The DOS command prompt screen, by default, is about as interesting as yesterday's blackboard: white text on a black background, 24 lines per screen, and no graphics. The keyboard types the characters shown on the keycaps and very little else. But you can do a lot to jazz up both the screen and the keyboard.

You can add color and (somewhat limited) graphics to the screen, flash blinking messages at users, even splash a colorful banner across the top of the screen showing the date, time, and other useful information. You can redefine keys on the keyboard to type international characters such as ¨, graphics characters such as █ , even complete macros such as "Peter Norton's Advanced DOS Guide" or "CD\NORTH\ALASKA." The techniques in this chapter can make your own work, as well as the batch programs you create for others, more exciting and more effective.

DOS and Your Video Monitor

DOS supports several types of video: monochrome display adapter (MDA), color graphics adapter (CGA), extended graphics adapter (EGA), and the video graphics array (VGA). Other types of video adapters are usually compatible with one or more of these. A video adapter or monitor with more features than these basic types (such as more pixels or a two-page display for desktop publishing) is usually accompanied by software to help you take advantage of its features.

The CON Driver

DOS's command-prompt interface uses the built-in CON device driver to interact with whatever video adapter is installed. CON provides simple text-oriented services so that DOS can write messages to the command-prompt screen. CON uses functions built into the video controller to drive the hardware, which keeps DOS independent of the actual video equipment and lets the operating system function regardless of what display adapter is used. Unfortunately, the result is the dull-as-dishwater white on black screen that DOS users love to hate.

The Video Buffer

Every video adapter card has a memory area called the video buffer. Whatever will be displayed on the screen must first be stored in the video buffer. The video is said to be memory-mapped because every byte in its buffer corresponds to a specific location on the screen.

In text mode, the video buffer contains two bytes for each screen character position. The first byte contains the ASCII value of the character to be displayed, and the second byte contains its attributes (color, blinking, and so on). Figure 18.1 shows the beginning of a typical buffer. In this case, it contains the message `Sanity Reigns!` starting in the first character position on the screen. The first byte shows the ASCII value of the letter S. The next byte shows its attributes; 07H represents DOS's usual white-on-black style. The third byte shows the ASCII code for the letter "a"; the fourth byte shows its attributes.

```
 S    a    n    i    t    y         R    e    i    g    n    s    !

 53 07 61 07 6E 07 69 07 74 07 70 07 20 07 52 07 65 07 69 07

 67 07 6E 07 73 07 21 07 20 07 20 07
```

Figure 18.1.
Video buffer in text mode.

On color systems, the attribute byte specifies the foreground and background colors, as well as the foreground intensity and blinking/steady status. On monochrome systems, the attribute can be used to specify intensity, underlining, blinking, and normal or reverse video in text mode. Programs that run in graphics mode handle their attributes differently; they work with smaller screen elements than text mode.

What ANSI.SYS Offers

The CON driver can't use color. It just pokes ASCII codes into even-numbered (character) bytes of the video buffer and doesn't affect any odd-numbered (attribute) bytes, so the current attributes are never changed.

The ANSI.SYS device driver is sort of a super-CON; it gives you many more options to take advantage of your video and keyboard features. ANSI.SYS gives you a way to specify color and the other video attributes. It also lets you control the cursor position and clear the screen. It lets you use 43 or 50 lines if the monitor can handle that, and 40 columns instead of 80. Additional features let you manipulate the meanings of the keyboard keys.

Some programs depend on ANSI.SYS to provide enhanced video and keyboard services. Their documentation will advise you that ANSI.SYS must be loaded. Other programs use the PC's video BIOS, which contains even more efficient screen functions. Even a nonprogramming user, however, can use ANSI.SYS to spice up displays, the command prompt, and batch files. The results affect only the DOS command prompt screen (which includes DEBUG). It doesn't affect the Shell or EDIT screen or any third-party software that doesn't use the command-prompt screen.

The ANSI.SYS Device Driver

You load ANSI.SYS from the CONFIG.SYS file with a DEVICE or DEVICEHIGH command. Figure 18.2 shows the command format. After ANSI.SYS is installed, it scans all standard output looking for its own commands.

Figure 18.2.
ANSI.SYS
DEVICE
command.

ANSI.SYS

Provides functions that control screen colors, cursor position, and key assignments.

Format:

```
DEVICE[HIGH]=[path]ANSI.SYS [/X ¦ /K] [/R]
```

Parameters and Switches:

path   Identifies the location of the ANSI.SYS file. The default is the root directory of the boot drive.

/X   With a 101-key (extended) keyboard, forces DOS to recognize that the extended (gray) cursor control, deletion, and insert/overlay keys have different scan codes than the numeric keypad keys for the same functions.

/K   Causes ANSI.SYS to treat a 101-key keyboard like an 84-key keyboard. Use this if you have a program that does not recognize the extended keys on the 101-key keyboard. If you use the /K switch with the Switches command, use /K with ANSI.SYS also.

/R   Adjusts line scrolling to improve readability when used with screen-reading programs

You may want to use the /X switch if you assign different characters to keys that have duplicates, such as the up-arrow key, Home, and the + (plus) key. If you don't specify the /X switch, two matching keys are mapped the same; for example both + (plus) keys will have the same effect. If you specify /X, you can assign different functions to each one. Key mapping is covered in detail later in this chapter.

Sending Commands to ANSI.SYS

When ANSI.SYS is installed, it remains in memory, taking about 4K. It continuously monitors all standard output, looking for escape sequences, which it recognizes as commands. An escape sequence begins with an Esc character followed by a left square bracket and ends with a specific terminator character. In between are the codes that make up the command. The details of specific commands are covered later, but the following is an example that sets a color screen to display cyan letters on a red background:

```
Esc[31;46m
```

The code 31 means a red background, and 46 means a cyan foreground. The terminator character "m" must be used with all escape sequences that control color; it tells ANSI.SYS what function is desired. To set the colors back to the defaults, send Esc[m (without any color specification) to standard output.

The case of terminator characters is significant. Using M instead of m to affect color won't work.

Typing the Escape Character

You can't just press Esc at the keyboard to start an escape sequence; it cancels the current command and starts another. How you enter Esc depends on how you decide to send the escape sequence to ANSI.SYS. The useful commands that produce standard output are PROMPT, TYPE, and ECHO.

Using PROMPT

In the PROMPT command, you can type normal text as well as special characters that represent untypeable items. Table 18.1 shows the complete set of PROMPT special characters, which can be typed in uppercase or lowercase. The command PROMPT PG establishes the familiar prompt that shows the current drive and path followed by the greater-than symbol.

Table 18.1. PROMPT Command Special Characters

$B	| (bar or piping sign)
$D	Current date
$E	Escape
$G	> (greater-than sign)
$H	Backspace (to delete character)
$L	< (less-than sign)
$N	Current drive
$P	Current drive and path

$Q	= (equal sign)
$T	Current time
$V	DOS version number
$$	$ (dollar sign)
$_	↵ (Enter)

To use PROMPT to send an escape sequence, you use $E to specify the Esc character. A few examples and their effects follow:

PROMPT $E[36;41m	Sets cyan text on a red background. At the same time, it removes the current prompt; you see only the cursor.
PROMPT $E[m	Restores the default white text on black background, with only the cursor as a prompt.
PROMPT $E[36;41m$P$G	Sets cyan text on a red background and displays the standard prompt.
PROMPT $E[36;41m$PGE[m	Sets cyan text on a red background, displays the standard prompt, and then turns the color off so that the default colors are restored for all except the prompt itself.

The disadvantage of using PROMPT to send commands to ANSI.SYS is that it eliminates your previous prompt unless you are careful to reset it. However, PROMPT is often the quickest way to try out escape sequences and see the effect right away.

Follow the PROMPT command with CLS to set the entire screen to the new color scheme.

Use DOSKEY to easily recall your PROMPT commands for editing.

Using a Text File

When you TYPE a file, DOS sends it to standard output. Any escape sequences are diverted by ANSI.SYS. You can create a text file containing one or more escape sequences and then TYPE it to put them all into effect.

You can use any text editor to create a file containing escape sequences as long as you know how to enter the Esc character into it. To TYPE correctly, of course, the file must be saved in ASCII form; DOS's EDIT program saves all files in this form. In EDIT, first press Ctrl-P and then press Esc to type an escape character. You see a left arrow on the screen, but it functions as the Esc character when you TYPE the file.

Pressing Ctrl-P followed by Esc also works in WordStar. In Microsoft Word, enter the ASCII code for Esc: hold down the Alt key and press 2 and then 7 on the numeric keypad. When you release the Alt key, a left arrow appears on the screen. In WordPerfect, press Ctrl-V followed by Esc, which appears on screen as ^[.

The second character in every ANSI.SYS escape sequence must be a left square bracket, [. This is followed by the characters of the command itself, followed by the terminator letter. If you open a new DOS EDIT file named COLORTST, you could type the following commands into it:

```
¨[36;41m
CLS
```

After you save the file, enter the command TYPE COLORTST. The first escape sequence sets cyan text on a red background from the current cursor location; the second spreads the color scheme to fill the screen. To restore the default colors, TYPE a file containing the following commands:

```
¨[m
CLS
```

Using a Batch File

It's often useful to include ANSI.SYS escape sequences in batch programs. The ECHO command, which sends text to standard output, is more convenient than PROMPT because it doesn't reset the prompt. (Unfortunately, you can't use ECHO outside a batch file because it offers no method to type an Esc character.) The following example displays the message Sorting Records in cyan on red and then restores normal colors:

```
ECHO ˝[36;41mSorting Records˝[m
```

Setting Screen Colors

A NUMBER of ANSI escape sequences control various screen features. One set controls the color background and foreground as well as the text attributes. Another set controls cursor position and clears the screen. Still another set lets you control the graphics mode of your display.

The escape sequences for screen colors require the use of numeric codes; the examples so far have been using the codes for red background (41) and cyan foreground (36). Table 18.2 shows the complete set of attribute and color codes. Each color sequence requires the same terminator character: lowercase m.

Table 18.2. Color Display Codes

Attributes:

0	Normal text
1	High-intensity text
2	Low-intensity text
4	Underline on (monochrome only)
5	Blink

continues

Table 18.2. continued

7	Inverse
8	Invisible text (foreground displays same color as background)

Color codes:

Color	Foreground	Background
Black	30	40
Red	31	41
Green	32	42
Yellow	33	43
Blue	34	44
Magenta	35	45
Cyan	36	46
White	37	47

Exactly how a color appears depends on the monitor; for example, normal yellow looks brown on many screens. You can include as many codes as you need in each escape sequence; separate them with semicolons.

The attributes apply only to the foreground color on most systems. The high-intensity attribute produces a brighter foreground color, quite different from the normal color, so 16 foreground colors are available. But in some systems attribute 5 causes a high-intensity background rather than a blink.

On some systems, low intensity produces still another color, but it's the same as high intensity on most systems. If you use attribute 8, the foreground color is stored as usual, but foreground material is displayed using the background color.

If you are preparing a batch file for other users, check out the colors and attributes on their monitors if you can. They might be different from yours.

Suppose that you want to have a blinking foreground of high-intensity yellow on a magenta background. This command, stored in an ASCII file and TYPEd to the screen, produces the following result:

```
˝[1;5;33;45m
```

Suppose that a batch file displays the message Sorting Members . . . while it works. You could use the following line in the batch file to make the message more noticeable:

```
ECHO ˝[5;33;45mSorting Members . . .˝[m
```

Screen and Cursor Control

By default, the cursor goes to the beginning of the next line when a command terminates. You can position it somewhere else through an ANSI command. The escape sequences for cursor position require a variety of special terminator characters as shown in Table 18.3. You might need to include row and/or column information. As always, the case of the terminator character is critical.

Table 18.3. Screen and Cursor Control Sequences

s	Save current cursor position
u	Restore saved cursor position
xxA	Cursor up xx rows
xxB	Cursor down xx rows
xxC	Cursor right xx columns
xxD	Cursor left xx columns
H	Cursor to upper left (0,0)
xx;yyH	Cursor to specified position
xx;yyf	Cursor to specified position
2J	Clear screen, cursor to upper left

continues

Table 18.3. continued

K	Clear from cursor position to end of line
6n	Display cursor position in form ←[xx;yyR

When controlling the cursor position, be careful not to position it in front of or on top of existing text to avoid confusing users. Careful testing of cursor control changes is recommended.

Creating a Banner

You can use many of the cursor-positioning features in a PROMPT command to create a banner across the top of each screen. Figure 18.3 shows a screen with a sample banner. The command that produces this banner is shown on the screen. The banner is regenerated each time the prompt appears, so the time is kept reasonably up-to-date.

This PROMPT command comprises a mixture of ANSI.SYS escape sequences, PROMPT special characters, and straight text. An explanation of each part follows:

$E[s	Saves the current cursor position
$E[H	Moves cursor to upper left corner
$E[37;44m	Sets the banner to cyan on blue
$E[K	Erases the top line from cursor position
Path:	Displays the indicated text
$P	Inserts the current drive and path here
Ruth Ashley	Displays the indicated text
$E[1;52H	Moves the cursor to row 1 column 52
$D	Displays the current date
@	Displays the indicated text (@)
$T	Displays the current time

HHHHHH	Backspaces six times to remove seconds and hundredths from the time
$E[34;47m	Sets rest of screen to blue on cyan
$E[u	Restores the saved cursor position
QG$G	Displays the new prompt (=>>)

To try a banner, be sure to load DOSKEY first if it isn't active; DOSKEY greatly simplifies experimenting with PROMPT commands.

```
Path: C:\     Ruth Ashley                  Wed 03-03-1993 @ 11:44
=>>dir *.sys

Volume in drive C is MICROMATE
Volume Serial Number is 1A4F-4156
Directory of C:\

CONFIG   SYS       268 03-01-93    3:27p
HIMEM    SYS     11304 05-01-90    3:00a
         2 file(s)       11572 bytes
                      12949504 bytes free

=>>banner

=>>prompt $e[s$e[H$e[37;44m$e[KPath: $p      Ruth Ashley      $e[1;52H$d @ $t$h$h$h
$h$h$h$e[34;47m$e[u$q$g$g

=>>
=>>
```

Figure 18.3.
Sample banner screen.

Displaying a Message Box

You can also use ANSI.SYS to create a colored box containing a message. This makes an interesting, attention-getting display. Figure 18.4 shows a text file containing escape sequences to control the display of a red box with black text. This example uses a separate line for each sequence, but you can combine them if you prefer. You can also modify the commands, changing the position, color, size, and text to fit your needs. Use TYPE *filespec* in a batch file to produce the box. Alternatively, you can put the necessary escape sequences in ECHO commands in the batch file.

The box itself is drawn using the IBM extended character set (see Appendix B), which bears some explanation. A single byte, representing one text character on a monitor or printer, can hold a value from 0 to 255 (0FFH). The values from 0 through 127 are standardized as ASCII code, representing letters, digits, punctuation marks, and so on. The values from 128 through 255 have not been standardized so that they can have different effects with different hardware and software setups. For example, DOS interprets these values according to the IBM extended character set, but Windows doesn't. When displaying a message from a DOS batch program using ECHO commands, you can count on the IBM extended character set to work.

Figure 18.4.
Creating a colored
message box.

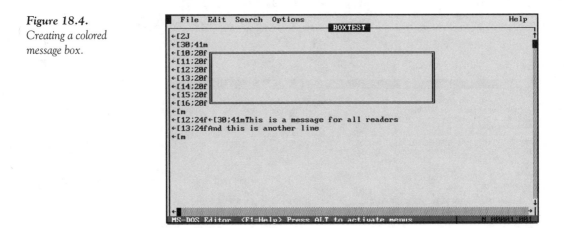

Because a keyboard doesn't have keys for the extended characters, you can type one by holding down the Alt key and typing the byte's value on the numeric keypad. For example, to type the upper left corner of the double-line box, press Alt-201. This method works for any byte value, not just the extended ones.

Explanations of the escape sequences in the file shown in Figure 18.4 follow:

←[2J   Clears the screen with cursor in upper left corner

←[30;41m   Sets the colors to black text on red background

The new colors affect only positions where text or spaces are typed. We limit that to the box itself by positioning the cursor for each line of text. The balance of the screen retains its former colors.

←[10;20f   Positions cursor at row 10 column 20; rest of line draws top of box

←[11;20f   Positions cursor at row 11 column 20; rest of line draws next line of box

The next five commands draw box sides.

←[16;20H	Positions cursor at row 16 column 20; rest of line draws bottom line of box
←[m	Resets default colors
←[12;24f←[30;41m	Positions cursor and sets text color; rest of line displays a message in box
←[13;24f	Positions cursor; rest of line displays another message in box
←[m	Resets the colors

The cursor-positioning sequence using the f terminator is exactly the same as with H. If you omit the row and column values, f has no effect, and H defaults to the home (0;0) position.

Character Wrap

By default, when a command on the screen reaches column 80, characters wrap around to the next line. In earlier versions of DOS, characters were stacked up in column 80, so you could see only the most-recently entered character. Turning off character wrap hides characters at the ends of long lines. Use the following commands to enable and disable the character wrap function:

←[=7h	to enable
←[=7l	to disable

Character wrapping affects not only the commands you type but also the output of commands that display long lines, such as FIND.

Screen Mode (Graphics)

Every video adapter and screen has a default mode. If you do any BASIC programming, you know that the screen mode can be changed to achieve different effects. Another set of escape sequences lets you change the screen mode using ANSI commands. The results might vary on different monitors. Table 18.4 lists the values you can use to specify screen modes; use terminator character h as in

```
¨[=modeh
```

Table 18.4. Screen Modes

Mode	Meaning
0	Monochrome text, 40×25
1	Color text, 40×25
2	Monochrome text, 80×25
3	Color text, 80×25
4	Medium-resolution graphics (4 color), 300×200
5	Same as 4, with color burst disabled
6	High-resolution graphics (2 color), 640×200
13	Color graphics, 320×200
14	Color graphics (16 color), 640×200
15	Monochrome graphics, 640×350
16	Color graphics (16 color), 640×350
17	Color graphics (2 color), 640×480
18	Color graphics (16 color), 640×480
19	Color graphics (256 color), 320×200

If you change the screen mode to one not supported by your system, you may see a strange color pattern or the system may hang up. You may have to reboot to restore normalcy.

ANSI Keyboard Control

ANSI escape sequences also give you control over your keyboard. You can switch the meanings of any two keys, for example. You can set up a key or key combination (such as Ctrl-D) to type an extended character or even a string of characters. Table 18.5 shows how to refer to some keys in ANSI.SYS commands. The ones in parentheses may not be valid on all keyboards. The complete list is included in the online help for the ANSI.SYS driver.

Table 18.5. Selected Key Codes

Key	Normal	⇧Shift	Ctrl	Alt
F1	0;59	0;84	0;94	0;104
F2	0;60	0;85	0;95	0;105
F3	0;61	0;86	0;96	0;106
F4	0;62	0;87	0;97	0;107
Home	0;71	55	0;119	
Up	0;72	56	(0;141)	
PageUp	0;73	57	0;132	
Left	0;75	52	0;115	
PrtSc			0;114	
Pause/Break				0;0
BkSp	8	8	127	(0)
Enter	13		10	(0;28)
Tab	9	0;15	(0;148)	(0:165)
(Grey keys)				
Home	(224;71)	(224;71)	(224;119)	(224;1051)
Up	(224;72)	(224;72)	(224;141)	(224;152)

continues

Table 18.5. continued

Key	Normal	⬆Shift	Ctrl	Alt
PageUp	(224;73)	(224;73)	(224;132)	(224;153)
Left	(224;75)	(224;75)	(224;115)	(224;155)
(Keypad Keys)				
Enter	13		10	(0;166)
/	47	47	(0;142)	(0;74)
*	42	(0;144)	(0;78)	
-	45	45	(0;149)	(0;164)
+	43	43	(0;150)	(0;55)
5	(0;76)	53	(0;143)	
(Typeable characters)				
a	97	65	1	0;30
b	98	66	2	0;48
z	122	90	26	0;44
1	49	33		0;120
0	48	41		0;129
-	45	95	31	0;130
=	61	43		0;131

Assigning a value to a particular key *remaps* that key. Assigning a string of text to a key can be used to set up keyboard macros. The remapping affects only the DOS command prompt interface.

Remapping can be done via a PROMPT command, an ECHO command, or in a TYPEd text file, just as with other ANSI.SYS escape sequences.

Remapping Individual Keys

Many key combinations are unassigned. You can remap them to type extended characters. Or you might want simply to relocate a key. You could change a QWERTY keyboard to the more efficient Dvorak layout, for example.

To remap keys, use an ANSI command in this format:

```
Esc[key;new-valuep
```

The *key* parameter identifies the key or key combination to be remapped; you can identify it by the current character it types, if any, placed in quotes, or by its key code (from Table 18.5). The *new-value* parameter identifies the new value for the key, which you can specify as a character in quotes or as a numeric code from 0 through 255. Appendix B shows the extended characters that result when you use 128 through 255. For example, to set Ctrl-F1 to type the upper left corner of a double-line box, you could use either of the following escape sequences:

```
˝[0;94;"╔"p
```

```
˝[0;94;201p
```

In both commands, 0;94 identifies the Ctrl-F1 key combination. The first command uses quotes surrounding the result of Alt-201, and the second uses the value 201 to specify the desired character.

You might want to assign the value ä (Alt-132) to Alt-A, for example, if you type that character very often, with one of the following escape sequences:

```
˝[0;30;132p
˝[0;30;"ä"p
```

If you want to drive someone crazy, you could swap their "t" and "h" keys:

```
ECHO ˝["t";"h"p
ECHO ˝["h";"t"p
```

An enhanced keyboard includes several keys that duplicate other keys. If you want the duplicates treated the same, don't do anything. If you want to give one of the set a different value, however, use the /X switch in the DEVICE=ANSI.SYS command. For example, the following sequence makes the numeric keypad Home key respond with 7:

```
˝[0;71;"7"p
```

This sequence makes the extra (gray) Home key respond with an asterisk:

```
¨[224;71;"*"p
```

The two commands work only if ANSI.SYS was loaded with /X. On an enhanced, 101-key keyboard, the extra keys—such as gray cursor control keys—are the extended keys. These keys (and a few others) appear in parentheses in the key-code table. If you've disabled them with /K, or if you don't have an enhanced keyboard, then these keys are not available for remapping.

Assigning Strings to Keys

You can assign strings of text to keys. For example, you can assign complete commands, including the Enter key, so you can run a DOS command with a single key or key combination. You could establish a complete set of function key "macros" to run the commands you need most often. These commands aren't the same as DOSKEY macros—for example, you can't use replaceable parameters in them—but you could set them up to run DOSKEY macros for you.

To assign a simple text string, use a sequence in the following format:

```
Esc[key;"string"p
```

The sequence ←[0;84;"Imaginatronics, Inc."p causes the company name to be typed when you press Shift-F1. You can string together quoted values and numeric values, using semicolons to separate them. To cause the CD \ command to be issued when you press F12, use the sequence

```
¨[0;134;"CD \";13p
```

The value 13 sends the carriage return to enter the CD \command, and the terminator character p ends the escape sequence.

If you use DOSKEY, you know that pressing F7 lists the stored command history. There is no comparable function key to list DOSKEY macros. You could set up F10 to list them:

```
¨[0;68;"DOSKEY /M";13p
```

We've looked at some of the most useful ANSI.SYS functions in this chapter. You'll discover even more uses for these functions as you continue to apply them.

Switching the Standard Console Devices

The console device is the device in which you type commands and DOS displays standard output and standard error output. Normally, console device is CON, which represents the keyboard and video monitor. You can change to some other device by using the CTTY command, which has the following format:

```
CTTY device
```

The device can be any standard DOS device name: COM1 through COM4, LPT1 through LPT3, PRN, AUX, PRN, and CON. For example, suppose that you want to control DOS via a remote terminal device connected to COM4. You would enter

```
CTTY COM4
```

As soon as you enter this command, you can no longer enter commands at the keyboard. You must enter them through COM4; messages appear not on the video monitor but on the device attached to COM4. To switch back to the normal console device, enter the following command via the device attached to COM4:

```
CTTY CON
```

If you switch console control away from CON and then find that you can't enter commands from the new device for some reason, you can still reboot from the keyboard. Rebooting restores CON as the console device.

Preserving Your Laptop Batteries

DOS 6's POWER program can help to save battery power in your laptop or notebook computer by reducing power consumption when you're not actually using it. To use POWER, you must load the POWER.EXE device driver via CONFIG.SYS with a command in this format:

```
DEVICE[HIGH]=C:\DOS\POWER.EXE [ADV[:advtype] ¦ STD ¦ OFF] [/LOW]
```

The *advtype* can be MAX for maximum savings, REG to balance power conservation with application and device performance, and MIN for a little power conservation without interfering with system performance. If you load POWER.EXE with no parameters, or if you use ADV without a value, ADV:REG is assumed.

If your computer supports the Advanced Power Management (APM) specification, you can use STD to specify that the hardware's power-management features should be used. But STD turns off power management if your system does not support the APM specification. OFF turns off power management in all cases.

> Your computer will realize more power savings if it supports the APM specification—about 25 percent as compared to about 5 percent.

Use the /LOW switch to load POWER.EXE into conventional memory when upper memory blocks are available.

The POWER Command

When you have loaded the POWER.EXE driver, you can use the POWER command to view and change the current POWER setting. When you enter the command without any parameters, POWER displays the current power setting. To change the setting, enter POWER with the ADV parameter, STD, or OFF. For example, if POWER seems to interfer, with the application you are currently trying to use, try entering

```
POWER ADV:REG
```

If that doesn't work, try

```
POWER ADV:MIN
```

If that doesn't work and your laptop supports the APM specification, try

```
POWER STD
```

If it still doesn't work, turn the power management off with the following command:

```
POWER OFF
```

Controlling the CON (Console) Mode

You can change the number of lines and columns displayed on your monitor with a MODE command; the change affects EDIT and DEBUG, but not the Shell. Figure 18.5 shows the MODE format for modifying the console, which includes the screen and the keyboard.

Adjusting the Display Adapter

The MODE command lets you control a number of characteristics on your video display. You shouldn't have to use these features, but they are present for compatibility with earlier DOS versions.

If your normal text display isn't centered nicely on the monitor, however, you might want to shift it. To shift the display to the left, use the following command:

```
MODE ,L,T
```

To shift it to the right, use this command:

```
MODE ,R,T
```

Specifying Lines and Columns

If you want to use more than the default 25 screen lines, you can use the LINES=n parameter. ANSI.SYS must be loaded before you change the number of lines. A VGA screen can support 43 or 50 lines, while EGA can handle 43.

You can also set up your screen for 40 or 80 columns. The larger characters (40 columns) can be read from farther away, but they can interfere with the layout of formatted output, such as a DIR /W listing.

Figure 18.5.
MODE Command
reference (Console
functions).

MODE

Configures system console devices.

Formats:

```
MODE [display-adapter][,shift][,T]
MOE CON[:] [COLS=c] [LINES=n]
MODE CON[:] RATE=r DELAY=d
```

Parameters:

none	Displays status of all devices.
display-adapter	Specifies an adapter mode, which must be one of the following values:

	40 or 80	Sets number of characters per line
	BW40 or BW80	Selects the color adapter with color disabled and sets the number of characters per line.
	CO40 or CO80	Selects the color adapter with color enabled and sets the number of characters per line.
	MONO	Selects a monochrome adapter with 80 characters per line.

shift	Indicates whether to shift the screen to the left (L) or right (R).
T	Displays a test pattern for use in aligning screen.
COLS=c	Specifies the number of characters per line (40 or 80)
LINES=n	Specifies the number of lines per screen (24, 43, or 50)
RATE=r	Specifies the repeat rate of keyboard characters; range is 1 to 32, which is approximately 2 to 30 characters per second. Default is 20.
DELAY=d	Specifies the elapsed time in quarters of seconds before keyboard repeat starts; values are 1, 2, 3, and 4. Default is 2 (for .5 second).

Controlling Keyboard Response

PC keyboards have a typematic feature that causes keys to repeat when held down. If you hold any key down for more than half a second, the key starts to repeat at about 20 times per second. You may want to alter the typematic rate. The MODE command lets you modify both the DELAY, which sets the start of the repeat, and the RATE, which controls how fast it repeats. The following command causes the repeat to start after 0.25 second and to occur at the approximate rate of 30 per second.

```
MODE RATE=32 DELAY=1
```

The following command causes a delay of one second, with only two repetitions per second. This gives more control to unskilled typists and slow thinkers.

```
MODE RATE=1 DELAY=4
```

Chapter 19 discusses additional ways to adapt the console and printer for use with international character sets.

Another Country Heard From

19

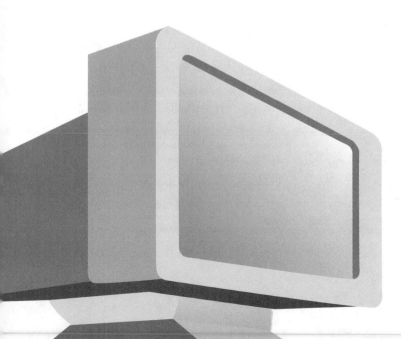

Introduction

DOS-compatible computers are usually set up for the country in which they are manufactured or purchased. If you bought your system in the United States, your keyboard, monitor, and printer probably handle standard American English characters.

Numeric values, dates, and times most likely appear in the traditional American formats. If you bought your system in some other country, its character set, numeric, date, and time formats probably reflect the standard for that country.

However, you may want to use your computer to prepare, read, or produce text for people from other countries who prefer, for example, to see the time and date in a more familiar form. You may have to prepare correspondence or reports for people in other countries or use characters common in other languages not on your keyboard.

This chapter covers various ways you can adapt DOS to deal with the problems of international communication.

Overview

DOS provides a gamut of commands that affect the way it deals with internationality. The KEYB command lets you emulate or interpret a country-specific keyboard. The COUNTRY command causes the system to use numeric formats of another country or region.

Your monitor and printer have code pages built into them. A code page is a table that tells the device what character corresponds to each one-byte code (from 0 through 255). With the standard English code page, code 66 is a "B"; code 123 is a "{"; code 156 is a "ú" and code 168 is a "¿." Changing the code page tells DOS to use a different set of characters for the same codes for the monitor and/or printer.

DOS provides six software code pages, which can be downloaded to devices to replace the hardware (built-in) code pages. The first 128 values (from 0 to 127) are the same in each, because these are the values standardized as ASCII code. The extended characters vary from code page to code page. The appendix in your DOS User's Guide shows the contents of each code page.

You may be able to use a different code page without much preparation with the COUNTRY or KEYB command. If you expect to change code pages often, it's best to set up the system so you can switch easily.

Using Special Characters

A code page includes 256 characters. Many of these can't be typed directly, however. The default code pages built into your monitor and printer have many characters available that don't correspond to keyboard keys or key combinations. You can type any code by holding down the Alt key, typing the code on the numeric keypad (make sure NumLock is on), and releasing Alt. For example, suppose that the standard English code page (437) is current and you have to type the character è. Just hold down the Alt key and type 132 on the numeric keypad. When you release Alt, the character appears on-screen. It will even print on a standard printer.

With font-oriented software, such as word processors or desktop publishing software, the font controls the character set; characters may be different from the installed code page. In fact, the same code might produce different characters depending on which font you're using.

You may want to set up a shortcut for extended characters you must type often using the ANSI.SYS features. The following command assigns the ä character to Ctrl-A so that you can type it easily at the DOS prompt:

```
PROMPT $E[1;"ä"p$P$G
```

In creating the command, use Alt-132 to create the desired character. Chapter 18 covers the use of ANSI.SYS escape sequences in detail.

Remapped keys are effective only on the DOS command-prompt screen; you can't use them in the Shell or in other software.

International Keyboards

If you use many non-English characters in your work, you may want to tell DOS you have a keyboard layout that lets you type those characters directly. You may even want to install different keycaps. The KEYB command enables you to specify a different layout. DOS will then assign different codes to your keypresses, interpreting the characters according to the specified keyboard layout (regardless of what the keycaps say).

Table 19.1 lists the keyboard layouts available with DOS 5, along with the default code page and the alternate code page that can be used with each. The Appendix in the DOS documentation shows the exact layout of each available keyboard.

Table 19.1. Keyboard Codes and Code Pages

Country/Region	Code	Standard	Alternate	ID
Belgium	BE	850	437	
Brazil	BR	850	437	
Canadian-French	CF	863	850	
Czech	CZ	852	850	
Denmark	DK	850	865	
Finland	SU	850	437	
France	FR	850	437	120,189
Germany	GR	850	437	
Hungary	HU	852	850	
Italy	IT	850	437	141,142
Latin America	LA	850	437	
Netherlands	NL	850	437	
Norway	NO	850	865	
Poland	PL	852	850	
Portugal	PO	850	860	
Slovak	SL	852	850	
Spain	SP	850	437	
Sweden	SV	850	437	
Switzerland (French)	SF	850	437	
Switzerland (German)	SG	850	437	

Country/Region	Code	Standard	Alternate	ID
United Kingdom	UK	437	850	166,168
United States	US	437	850	

If you always use a nonstandard layout, put the appropriate KEYB command in your CONFIG.SYS or AUTOEXEC.BAT file so that it becomes the default.

The KEYB Command

Figure 19.1 shows the format of the KEYB command. You can use it at the command prompt or install it from CONFIG.SYS. The two-letter keyboard code identifies which keyboard layout to use. If installed through CONFIG.SYS, KEYB must include the complete path if KEYBOARD.SYS is not in the root directory of the boot drive. When used as a command, you can depend on the established path to locate the KEYB.COM file.

If your system is set up for it, use LH to load KEYB into a UMB. In this case, load KEYB from AUTOEXEC.BAT or the command prompt, not from CONFIG.SYS.

After KEYB has been installed, if you enter KEYB with no parameters, you see a message like the following:

```
Current keyboard code:  LA   code page:  850
```

If a code page hasn't been downloaded, you see the following line as well:

```
Active code page not available from CON device
```

You can still use the keyboard, but it reflects the built-in code page. Later in this chapter, you will see how to load different code pages.

Figure 19.1.
KEYB command
reference.

KEYB

Loads the KEYB TSR, which lets your keyboard emulate keyboard layouts for other languages.

Format:

KEYB [*code* [,[*page*] [,*filespec*]]] [/E] [/ID:*id*]

From CONFIG.SYS:

INSTALL=[*path*]KEYB.COM [*code*[,[*page*],[*filespec*]]][/E] [/ID:*id*]

Parameters and Switches:

none	Displays the current keyboard code and code page and the current console code page.
code	Identifies the country whose keyboard you want to use. See Table 19.1.
page	Identifies the code page you want to use; the default is the current code page.
filespec	Identifies the location and name of the keyboard definition file; the default is KEYBOARD.SYS in the current directory or on the search path.
path	Specifies the path if not in the root directory.
/E	Indicates that you have installed an enhanced keyboard on an 8086 computer.
/ID:*id*	Specifies which keyboard is in use for countries with more than one keyboard layout. See Table 19.1.

Notes:

An alternate code page is made active only if that code page has been installed with MODE. If intervening values are omitted, commas are required. Trailing commas may be omitted. KEYB sets an exit code; see Appendix A.

After a keyboard layout is installed, you can switch between it and the default (US) layout. Ctrl-Alt-F1 activates the built-in keyboard driver, and Ctrl-Alt-F2 goes back to the installed one. For example, suppose that you load the Latin American keyboard with KEYB LA. When you press the semicolon key, you see ñ. If you press Ctrl-Alt-F1 and press the key again, the semicolon produces its usual ; character. Typing KEYB with no parameters at this point produces a message that the current keyboard code is still LA, even though the keyboard is set for the built-in mode. Use KEYB US to restore the default setup.

Some countries have a standard typewriter layout that differs from the keyboard layout; pressing Ctrl-Alt-F7 activates this layout.

Code Pages with Keyboards

When you change keyboard layouts, you may need to change monitor code pages as well so that you can see all the characters you can now type. Each keyboard layout has a standard and alternate code page associated with it (see Table 19.1). For the best results, install the standard code page for the keyboard you want to use (covered later in this chapter). If you want to switch back and forth between keyboard layouts, code page 850 (the multilingual code page) may be your best bet, as it is the standard or alternate code page for every keyboard layout. You can get away with code page 437 (the English code page) for many layouts; it's probably your built-in code page, so you don't have to do anything to use it.

Any code pages other than 437 must be prepared first. If the code page has already been prepared when the KEYB command is entered, KEYB switches to it automatically. For example, suppose that code pages 850 and 852 have been prepared. The following command switches to the Polish keyboard layout and monitor code page 852, the default for the Polish layout:

```
KEYB PL
```

The following command switches to the Polish layout and monitor code page 850:

```
KEYB PL,850
```

International Formats

The date, time, and numeric formats in other countries are frequently different from those in the United States. For example, the year may be first, a different currency symbol may be used, or the use of commas and decimal point characters in numeric values may be reversed. You can tell DOS to use formats specific to another region or country. (These formats affect the output of commands like DATE, TIME, and DIR.)

If a country uses characters like é and ü, they may be placed differently in the sort sequence than they are in a U.S.-oriented code page. If you use these characters very often, you will want them sorted according to their country's standards. (The sort sequence affects commands like SORT and DIR.)

Table 19.2 lists the countries DOS supports, their codes, and the time and date formats they use.

Table 19.2. Countries and Formats

Country	Code	Date	Time
Belgium	032	05/01/1992	17:15:25,00
Brazil	055	05/01/1992	17:15:25,00
Canadian-French	002	1992-01-05	17:15:25,00
Croatia	038	1992-01-05	17:15:25,00
Czech Republic	042	1992-01-05	17:15:25,00
Denmark	045	05-01-1992	17.15.25,00
Finland	358	05.01.1992	17.15.25,00
France	033	05.01.1992	17:15:25,00
Germany	049	05.01.1992	17:15:25,00
Hungary	036	1992-01-05	17:15:25,00
Int'l English	061	05/01/1992	17:15:25.00
Italy	039	05/01/1992	17.15.35,00

Country	Code	Date	Time
Latin America	003	05/01/1992	05:15:25.00p
Netherlands	031	05-01-1992	17:15:25,00
Norway	047	05.01.1992	17:15:25,00
Poland	048	1992-01-05	17:15:25,00
Portugal	351	05-01-1992	17:15:25,00
Serbia/Yugoslavia	038	1992-01-05	17:15:25,00
Slovakia	042	1992-01-05	17:15:25,00
Slovenia	038	1992-01-05	17:15:25,00
Spain	034	05/01/1992	17:15:25,00
Sweden	046	1992-01-05	17.15.25,00
Switzerland	041	05.01.1992	17,15,25.00
United Kingdom	044	05/01/1992	17:15:25.00
United States	001	01/05/1992	05:15:25.00p

Characters sets for Arabic, Israel, Japan, Korea, People's Republic of China, and Taiwan are available with special versions of DOS.

The COUNTRY Configuration Command

If format and sort sequence are the only changes you need, you can use the COUNTRY configuration command by itself to set them. Figure 19.2 shows the format of this command, which belongs in the CONFIG.SYS file.

The COUNTRY command must include the country code (see Table 19.2). The code is often (but not always) the same as the international dialing code for the country. Each country also has a default code page and an alternate one. If it is already available, the default code page for that country will be used automatically. If you want to use the alternate code page, you need the second parameter. Code page preparation is covered in more detail later in this chapter. As with the KEYB command, a different code page is not actually made available unless it has been installed.

Figure 19.2.
COUNTRY
configuration
command reference.

COUNTRY

Specifies the country format for date and time displays, currency symbol, sort order, punctuation, decimal separators, and code pages.

Format:

COUNTRY=*country*[,[*page*] [,*filespec*]]

Parameters:

country   Specifies the code that identifies the country.

page   Specifies a code page.

filespec   Identifies the file containing country information.

DOS must be able to find the COUNTRY.SYS file provided with DOS. If it is stored in the root directory of the boot drive, there is no problem. However, most people store all the DOS files in a \DOS directory, so the command must include a complete file specification.

The following command specifies the use of the Latin American formats:

```
COUNTRY=003,,C:\DOS\COUNTRY.SYS
```

The only way to change which country is specified is to edit the CONFIG.SYS file, change the COUNTRY statement, and restart your computer.

Using Code Pages

By default, your system uses the built-in (hardware) code pages for all text. You can set it up to use a code page arranged for a different language group by downloading a software code page. You can even set up several code pages and switch back and forth.

Several commands must be coordinated in order to use any code pages other than the built-in one. If either KEYB or COUNTRY needs a software code page, the code page must be prepared before it can take effect. The CONFIG.SYS file must install a device driver for the monitor (DISPLAY.SYS) in order to use the code page.

After the environment is established, several commands are needed to handle the code pages. You can put these commands in AUTOEXEC.BAT if you use them every time, or you can enter them individually at the DOS prompt. The NLSFUNC command establishes National Language Support, which makes switching code pages easier. The MODE command installs specific software code pages preparing them for use by DOS. Additional MODE commands can change code pages or display the current status. The CHCP command uses National Language Support to switch code pages.

Monitor Code Pages

Standard monochrome and CGA monitors cannot use monitor code pages. However, all EGA, VGA, LCD, and more advanced types can. Before you can use software code pages on your monitor, you must load the driver DISPLAY.SYS (see Figure 19.3). As with most device drivers, you can use DEVICEHIGH instead to load the driver into upper memory if your system is set up for it. The following command loads DISPLAY.SYS for an LCD monitor:

```
DEVICE=C:\DOS\DISPLAY.SYS CON=(LCD)
```

The following command loads DISPLAY.SYS for an EGA monitor; it specifies the default code page, so the user can switch back to it and allows for two code pages:

```
DEVICEHIGH=C:\DOS\DISPLAY.SYS CON=(EGA,437,2)
```

If you omit the hardware code page in the command, you cannot be able to switch back to it after loading a different one. This doesn't matter if you expect to install a software code page and use it all the time. The number of code pages determines the amount of memory reserved for switching code pages; it defaults to 1. If you want to switch back and forth between the hardware code page (437) and the multilingual code page (850), you need to store only one software code page. However, if you want to switch back and forth between 850, 852, and 860, you need to store three code pages in memory.

Figure 19.3.
DISPLAY.SYS
DEVICE
command.

DISPLAY.SYS

Supports code-page switching for your screen and keyboards.

Format:

```
DEVICE[HIGH]=[path]DISPLAY.SYS CON=([type][,codepage]
[,max ¦ ,(max, sub)])
```

Parameters:

path	Identifies the location of the DISPLAY.SYS file. The default is the root directory of the boot drive.
type	Specifies the display adapter in use. Valid values are EGA and LCD. EGA includes both EGA and VGA adapters. If you don't specify *type*, DISPLAY.SYS checks the hardware to determine the display adapter in use.
codepage	Specifies the code page built into your hardware.
max	Specifies the number of code pages the hardware can support besides the one built into the hardware. Valid values are 0 through 6 for EGA, 0 through 1 for LCD.
sub	Specifies the number of subfonts the hardware supports for each code page.

Notes:

While *type* accepts the values CGA and MONO, DISPLAY.SYS has no effect with these values because CGA and MONO adapters don't support multiple character sets.

Preparing Code Pages

Before any software code page can be used, it must be prepared. This process installs the code page in memory and makes it available to the system, including the COUNTRY and KEYB commands. Figure 19.4 shows how MODE is used to reference code pages. Each command specifies one device followed by the word CODEPAGE followed by the action to be taken. The PREPARE command installs the code page. To install the multilingual code page for the console, you would use the following commands:

```
MODE CON CODEPAGE PREPARE=((850) C:\DOS\EGA.CPI)
```

MODE

Prepares, selects, refreshes, or displays the numbers of the code pages for printers and monitors.

```
MODE device CODEPAGE PREPARE = ((page [...]) filespec)

MODE device CODEPAGE SELECT = page

MODE device CODEPAGE REFRESH

MODE device CODEPAGE [/STATUS]
```

Parameters and Switches:

device	Identifies the device to which the command applies.
CODEPAGE	Identifies this as a code page command; abbreviate as CP.
PREPARE	Prepares *page*(s) for *device*; abbreviate as PREP.
page	Specifies a code page; may be 437 (U.S.), 850 (Multilingual or Latin I), 852 (Slavic or Latin II), 860 (Portuguese), 863 (Canadian-French) or 865 (Nordic).
filespec	Identifies the name and location of the code page information file for *device*.

Figure 19.4.
MODE command reference (for code pages).

Figure 19.4.
continued

SELECT	Loads a code page for use; page must already be prepared with a MODE CP PREP command; abbreviate as SEL.
REFRESH	Reinstates the prepared code pages if they are lost as the result of a hardware or other error; abbreviate as REF.
/STATUS	Displays the numbers of the current code pages prepared or selected for device; abbreviate as /STA.

Notes:

Using this format without PREPARE, SELECT, REFRESH, or /STATUS has the same effect as using /STATUS.

The code page information files provided by DOS are as follows:

EGA.CPI	For EGA or VGA monitor, or IBM PS/2.
LCD.CPI	For IBM PC Convertible liquid crystal display.

You can use a combination of COUNTRY, NLSFUNC, and CHCP to select a code page for both console and printer(s) at the same time.

If you specified the hardware code page in the device driver configuration command, you can switch back and forth between it and an installed code page. If you install several code pages in one or more MODE commands, you can switch among them.

Switching Code Pages

When you switch to a different console code page, the device uses the new code page table to translate one-byte code values into displayed characters. Some characters already on the screen may switch to the new character set.

If you change to a different code page while a program is running, there may be an internal conflict. To avoid this problem, make sure that all programs are terminated before changing code pages.

> If you are using the task swapper, don't switch code pages while any task is active. It causes more problems than it is worth.

DOS provides several ways to switch code pages. The KEYB command can switch to an installed code page. Another method uses a MODE command similar to the one you use to install the code page.

The CODEPAGE SELECT format of the MODE command makes the prepared code page active for the specified device. The following command makes the multilingual code page active for the console:

```
MODE CON CODEPAGE SELECT=850
```

To make the default code page active again, use the following command:

```
MODE CON CODEPAGE SELECT=437
```

If you didn't specify the hardware code page in the device driver command, you can't return to it after you select a different code page.

Complete Code Page Example

Suppose that you need to use the Portuguese keyboard and formatting conventions some of the time, using the alternate Portuguese code page (860). Because you work in English as well and need the built-in code page (437), you want to be able to switch between the two code pages.

Put the following commands in your CONFIG.SYS file:

```
COUNTRY=351,860,C:\DOS\COUNTRY.SYS
DEVICEHIGH=C:\DOS\DISPLAY.SYS CON=(EGA,437)
```

The COUNTRY command establishes the numeric and other formats for country 351, which is Portugal. Its alternate code page is specified. The DEVICEHIGH command reserves memory for one software code page for an EGA (or VGA) monitor. It also defines 437 as the hardware code page so that you can switch back to it as needed.

Because you aren't sure which keyboard or code page to use first, leave those commands for the DOS prompt. The following command goes into AUTOEXEC.BAT:

```
MODE CON CODEPAGE PREPARE=((860)C:\DOS\EGA.CPI)
```

This MODE command installs the software code page for the specified device.

After the AUTOEXEC.BAT file has been executed, you are set up to switch between your keyboards and your code pages. You can type the following commands at the DOS prompt to manage the keyboard and monitor code pages:

`[LH] KEYB PO`	Switches to Portuguese layout; doesn't switch the code page because the default 850 hasn't been prepared
`KEYB US`	Switches to U.S. English layout and code page 437
`MODE CON CODEPAGE SELECT=860`	Switches console to code page 860
`MODE CON CODEPAGE SELECT=437`	Switches console to code page 437

If you use these commands or similar ones, at the keyboard, you may want to set up DOSKEY macros to make them easier to use. The following batch file contains two DOSKEY macro definitions:

```
DOSKEY C8=MODE CON CODEPAGE SELECT=860
DOSKEY C4=MODE CON CODEPAGE SELECT=437
```

You could map the commands to key combinations if you prefer. For example, this command sets up Shift-F1 to switch to monitor code page 860 and restores the usual prompt:

```
PROMPT $E[0;84;"MODE CON CODEPAGE SELECT=860"p$P$G
```

You can switch between keyboards using Ctrl-Alt-F2 to access the memory-resident one (Portugal) and Ctrl-Alt-F1 to return to the built-in one.

National Language Support

DOS's National Language Support feature makes code-page switching easier, both internally and externally, although you still use MODE to install the code pages. To use National Language Support, you must load NLSFUNC as a TSR. Figure 19.5 shows the command format. You don't have to specify the filespec if it's in the COUNTRY command; otherwise it defaults to COUNTRY.SYS in the root directory of the boot drive.

The NLSFUNC program can be loaded at the DOS prompt or through the CONFIG.SYS INSTALL command. Using INSTALL lets you make sure that the TSR is loaded before COMMAND.COM. This can help if the language support functions don't seem to work. If you use the INSTALL method, it must follow the DEVICE command that loads DISPLAY.SYS. (When you use INSTALL, you can't load the TSR into upper memory blocks.)

After National Language Support is installed, you can use the CHCP command (see fig. 19.6) to change code pages for all devices that support code pages. CHCP without a parameter displays the number of the active code page, even if NLSFUNC hasn't been loaded.

NLSFUNC

Starts the program that loads country-specific information for national language support (NLS).

Format:

NLSFUNC [*filespec*]

Parameters and Switches:

none   Uses the default file for country-specific information (see Notes).

filespec   Identifies the file containing country-specific information.

Notes:

There is no error message if the country-specific information file is missing, because NLSFUNC doesn't access the file until DOS requires information from it. The error message shows up later, when CHCP tries to use information from the file.

Figure 19.5.
*NLSFUNC
command reference.*

Figure 19.6.
CHCP command reference.

CHCP

Changes the code page for all devices or displays the number of the current code page.

Format:

CHCP [*page*]

Parameters:

none   Displays the number of the current code page.

page   Changes to the specified code page.

Notes:

A code page is a character set for a keyboard, monitor, or printer. DOS provides six different software code pages so that you can type and display characters for languages other than US English.

Before you can use CHCP to change a code page, you must take the following steps:

● In CONFIG.SYS, load the proper driver so that your monitor can use software code pages.

● Run NLSFUNC to allow changing code pages with CHCP.

● Use MODE to load monitor and/or printer code pages.

CHCP changes code pages for all applicable devices at the same time and can choose between the two pages available for the current country only no matter how many code pages have been loaded. Use MODE to change to other code pages or to change the code page for one device at a time.

Another Code Page Example

Suppose that you want to use National Language Support in the Portuguese example presented earlier. The same commands are needed in your CONFIG.SYS file:

```
COUNTRY=351,860,C:\DOS\COUNTRY.SYS
DEVICE=C:\DOS\DISPLAY.SYS CON=(EGA,437)
```

The same commands to install the code pages can be placed in the AUTOEXEC.BAT file, but you also need the NLSFUNC command:

```
LH NLSFUNC
MODE CON CODEPAGE PREPARE=((860)C:\DOS\EGA.CPI)
```

After the AUTOEXEC.BAT file has been executed, you are all set up to switch between your keyboard layouts and your code pages. You can enter the following commands at the DOS prompt to manage the keyboard and monitor code pages:

KEYB PO	Switches to Portuguese layout; doesn't change the code page
KEYB US	Switches to U.S. layout
CHCP 860	Switches both devices to code page 860
CHCP 437	Switches both devices to code page 437

The CHCP command loads the specified code page to all prepared devices, simplifying the task.

Manipulating Code Pages

Occasionally, DOS may lose track of a code page. This may happen if a monitor is turned off, for example. In that case, use the MODE command to refresh the code page. The following command reinstates the last active code page for the printer:

```
MODE CON CODEPAGE REFRESH
```

If the monitor has locked up, you probably will have to reboot to free it. In that case, the commands in your CONFIG.SYS and AUTOEXEC.BAT files are processed again. Then you can switch code pages at the keyboard with a MODE command or with CHCP (if NLSFUNC was loaded).

Displaying Code Page Information

Several commands give you information on the status of your system; you can use any of these at the DOS prompt or through the Shell as needed.

The KEYB command with no options displays the current keyboard information in this format:

```
Current keyboard code: BE  code page: 850
Current CON code page: 850
```

The messages give you both the keyboard layout and the code page in effect. If KEYB has not been used, you see a message like the following instead:

```
KEYB has not been installed
Active code page not available from CON device
```

The CHCP command with no options displays just the current code page in the following format:

```
Active code page: 850
```

The report is produced even if NLSFUNC isn't in memory.

The MODE command with no parameters displays information on all the attached devices and any current code pages. It provides lots of information. Therefore, use MODE | MORE or redirect the output so that you can see it all.

The /STATUS switch of the MODE command gives you information on a specific device. For example, the command MODE CON CODEPAGE /STATUS gives the following output:

```
Active code page for device CON is 850
Hardware code pages:
  code page 437
Prepared code pages:
  code page 850

MODE status code page function completed
```

In most cases, the /STATUS switch is optional; you get exactly the same information whether or not you use it.

Printing through DOS

20

Introduction

When you print a file from an application, such as a word processing document or a worksheet, the application probably provides its own printer driver. The developers of print-oriented applications put a lot of effort into their printer drivers to make the best use of the popular printer models.

DOS is hardly print-oriented, but it provides some primitive printing services so that you can capture screen prints with the PrintScreen key, print ASCII text files (such as README files), redirect standard output to the printer, and echo the monitor in print. Although DOS assumes that you have a basic printer attached to LPT1, you can get it to use other types of printers in several ways, including a laser printer attached to a serial port.

Printer Types

DOS uses only the most basic printer capabilities. For this reason, it can print on almost any PC-compatible printer. Most modern-day printers can emulate a basic printer of some type. If DOS doesn't seem to communicate with your printer, check its documentation and find out how to emulate an IBM, Hewlett-Packard, Epson, or Diablo printer; DOS handles these types very well.

DOS can't communicate directly with PostScript printers, but most PostScript printers will emulate one of the above printers. You may have to set a switch on the printer itself to make it emulate an Epson (or whatever). Don't forget to return the printer to its normal setting when using it with software that has a PostScript driver.

DOS expects a parallel printer and uses LPT1 as the default printer port; device PRN refers to the same port. When you use echo printing or screen printing, the output is sent to PRN. You can redirect a parallel port to a serial port using a MODE command, as explained later in this chapter.

DOS Print Features

You can print material through DOS in several different ways. Redirecting standard output to the printer is one method. For example, you could use a command like the following to print a directory:

```
DIR > PRN
```

The standard output appears on the printer instead of the monitor. However, any error messages and the next DOS prompt appear on the monitor.

Printer Control Commands

You also can use redirection to control the printer. Printer control commands are often specific to the printer; its documentation should detail the commands to which it responds. The signal generated by pressing Ctrl-L will eject a page on most printers. The following ECHO command sends a Ctrl-L signal to the printer; pressing Ctrl-L displays the ^L in the command. You can enter the following command at the DOS prompt; it doesn't have to be in a batch file:

```
ECHO ^L > PRN
```

The following command creates a DOSKEY macro named PAGE to eject a printer page:

```
DOSKEY PAGE=ECHO ^L $G PRN
```

The following command remaps the F1 key to eject a page:

```
PROMPT $E[0;59;"ECHO ^L > PRN";13p$P$G
```

Details on remapping key assignments appear in Chapter 18.

The macro or the remapped key is particularly useful with laser printers, as they often don't eject a printed page until the page is full. (Some will time-out after a minute or so and eject a partially full page.) However, the page eject command forces the printer to print the page now, even if it has only one or two lines on it.

The following batch program prints the entire hard disk directory, including hidden and system files, ejecting the last page. For a laser printer, this causes the last page to be printed. For a continuous form printer, it rolls the last page up so it's ready to tear off:

```
@ECHO OFF
DIR C:\ /S /A > PRN
ECHO ^L > PRN
```

You could use the same technique to print the results of CHKDSK, TREE, FIND, and other verbose commands.

Echo Printing

Echo printing has a more lasting and inclusive effect than redirection. It copies everything that crosses the screen to the default printer: prompts, commands, error messages, and command output. You may use it to print a series of directory lists or diagnostic reports, for example, or to document a work session. It affects only commands and messages that cross the command-prompt screen. If you start up some other program while echo printing is in effect, echo printing resumes when that program terminates.

To start echo printing, press Ctrl-PrintScreen or Ctrl-P. All DOS commands and messages from that point on are echoed to the printer. If no printer is attached or redirected to LPT1, the system hangs up; make the printer available or reboot to continue. After echo printing is in effect, press Ctrl-PrintScreen or Ctrl-P again to cancel it.

You can't turn echo printing on or off from within a batch program or DOSKEY macro. Ctrl-P or Ctrl-PrintScreen must be pressed at the command prompt.

Text Screen Printing

Echo printing must be turned on before the text you want to capture crosses the screen. If the text is already displayed, you can capture it with a screen print. Just press the PrintScreen key (Shift-PrintScreen on some keyboards) and all the text on the screen is printed on the default printer. Printing graphics screens requires the GRAPHICS command, which is explained later in this chapter.

If you press PrintScreen with no printer available on LPT1, your system may just beep or it may hang up waiting for a printer. If it hangs up, either make the printer available or reboot.

Configuring a Printer

Every printer has a standard vertical spacing measured in lines per inch (lpi), and horizontal spacing, measured in characters per inch (cpi). Most printers use 6 lpi and 10 cpi by default. You can modify the spacing for many printers with a MODE command (see fig. 20.1). For parallel printers, you can set the vertical spacing at 6 or 8 lpi and the horizontal spacing at 80 or 132 cpi. If you use the words to identify the parameters (as in COLS=132), they can be in any order. If you omit the words, the parameters must be entered in the order shown. The following command sets LPT1 to print the maximum amount per page:

```
MODE LPT1 COLS=132 LINES=8
```

The RETRY parameter tells DOS how to react if DOS senses the printer, but the printer isn't ready to receive signals. By default, it simply gives up. The P parameter tells it to continue trying until the printer becomes available. This can cause your system to hang up when you try to print something and the printer is turned off, or is out of paper, off-line, or some other problem exists. To break out of the loop, make the printer available or press Ctrl-C.

After you configure the printer with MODE, it applies to all uses of that printer, including all applications that use DOS's printing services. Some software may over-ride the configuration, but it will be restored when that application terminates.

Using Serial Printers

To use a serial printer for printing directly under DOS, you must first tell DOS the communications characteristics of the device. If the serial printer is your only printer or you want to use it as DOS's default device, you also must redirect LPT1 to it.

Configuring the Serial Port

A serial port, also known as a communications port, may be attached to a printer, a mouse, a modem, or some other device. To use a serial port with DOS, you must define its communications characteristics with a MODE command (see fig. 20.2). This section shows how to use MODE to set up a serial port for a printer. The same parameters are used to set it up for any device.

Figure 20.1.
MODE command
reference (parallel
printer configura-
tion).

MODE

Configures a parallel printer to use specific vertical and horizontal spacing and retry action.

Formats:

```
MODE LPTn [COLS=c] [LINES=l] [RETRY=r]

MODE LPTn [c],[l],[r]
```

Parameters:

LPT*n*   Identifies the parallel port: LPT1 to LPT3. You can use PRN instead of LPT1.

c   Specifies the number of columns per line: 80 or 132.

l   Specifies the number of lines per inch: 6 or 8.

r   Specifies the retry action if a time-out error occurs. Valid values are as follows:

E   Return an error

B   Return "busy"

P   Continue retrying until printer accepts output

R   Return "ready"

N   No retry value (default)

Notes:

If only the values are used, they must be in the order shown. If intervening values are omitted, their commas must be included. (Trailing commas may be omitted.)

384

Figure 20.2.
MODE *command reference (configuring serial ports).*

MODE

Configures a serial (COM) port for use by a device such as a serial printer.

Formats:

```
MODE COMn BAUD = baud [PARITY = parity] [DATA = data]
[STOP = stop] [RETRY = retry]

MODE COMn baud[,parity][,data][,stop][,retry]
```

Parameters:

COMn   Identifies the serial port; *n* may be 1 to 4.

baud   Specifies the transmission rate in bits per second (baud rate). (See Notes for values.)

parity   Specifies how the system uses the parity bit to check for transmission errors. (See Notes for values.)

data   Specifies the number of data bits per character. Values may be 5 through 8; the default value is 7.

stop   Specifies the number of stop bits that identify the end of a character. Values may be 1, 1.5, or 2. If the baud rate is 100, the default is 2; otherwise, the default is 1.

retry   Specifies the action to take if a time-out occurs when Mode attempts to sent output to the port. (See Notes.)

Notes:

If you use the second, abbreviated version of this format, you must use the parameters in the order shown, with the accompanying commas. If you leave out a parameter, be sure to indicate its place by the appropriate comma (trailing commas can be omitted). Values for baud rate are as follows:

11 or 110	110 baud
15 or 150	150 baud
30 or 300	300 baud
60 or 600	600 baud

Figure 20.2.
continued

12 or 1200	1200 baud
24 or 2400	2400 baud
48 or 4800	4800 baud
96 or 9600	9600 baud
19 or 19200	19200 baud

Values for *parity* may be N for no parity, E for even parity, O for odd parity, M for mark, or S for space. E is the default.

Values for retry are as follows:

E	Returns an error if the port is busy.
B	Returns busy if the port is busy.
P	Continues retrying until the port accepts output.
R	Returns ready if the port is busy.
N	Takes no retry action (default value).

Do not use any value for *retry* if you use Mode over a network.

Some values that are valid for MODE are not supported by all computers. These include: BAUD = 19; PARITY = S; PARITY = M; DATA = 5; DATA = 6; and STOP = 1.5.

If you omit any parameter except *baud*, MODE defaults to the most recent value for this port. If no previous MODE command has specified a value, MODE uses the default values. There is no default value for *baud*; you must specify this parameter.

The parameters can be used in any order if the labels are attached (as in BAUD=96). If you omit the labels, the parameter values must be in the order shown in the format, and the commas must be included. The following two examples both configure a serial printer the same way:

```
MODE COM1 BAUD=96 PARITY=N DATA=8 STOP=1 RETRY=P

MODE COM1 96,N,8,1,P
```

The configuration affects all uses of the COM port until another MODE command changes it.

You can't guess at communications characteristics. You must use the correct values for the attached device. In most cases, the device's documentation tells you exactly how to write the MODE command.

Resident Portion of Mode

Some of MODE's functions require a small (0.5K) TSR to be installed. Configuring a serial port is one of these memory-resident functions. Whichever MODE command installs the TSR results in the following message:

```
Resident portion of MODE loaded
```

The TSR needs to be loaded only once, and then all of MODE's memory-resident functions can use it.

> This TSR can't be loaded in upper memory blocks. DOS ignores
> LOADHIGH when applied to a MODE command.

Redirecting a Serial Printer

If you want DOS to use a serial printer as PRN (for screen prints, echo printing, and so on), you must redirect LPT1 to it, using a command like the following:

```
MODE LPTn=COMn
```

For example, MODE LPT1=COM1 tells DOS that any data directed to LPT1 should be sent to COM1 instead. Of course, you can specify any valid serial (COM) and parallel (LPT) ports in the command. But to use the serial printer as the default printer, you must redirect LPT1.

> This MODE command format redirects parallel ports to serial ports only. It can't be used to redirect a serial port, nor can it redirect a parallel port to any other type of port.

Many applications depend on DOS's printing services, so you may need to redirect LPT1 even if you don't plan on screen prints or echo printing. The MODE command that sets the COM port's characteristics must precede the redirection command, or DOS can't use the port.

To undo a redirection, enter MODE LPT*n* (without the =COM*n*). You see a message like the following:

```
LPT1: not rerouted.
```

Viewing Redirection Status

The MODE command with no parameters displays status information for all the devices it controls. In addition, MODE generally displays status information for a device when you enter MODE followed by the device name and no other parameters. The following are some examples:

MODE CON   Displays status information about the console

MODE COM1   Displays status information about the first serial port

However, the following command will not display status information about the indicated parallel printer. Instead, it will undo any redirection applied to the printer:

```
MODE LPT1
```

To see status information for parallel printers, you must include the /STATUS switch (which can be abbreviated /STA), as in the following:

```
C:\>MODE LPT1 /STA
Status for device LPT1:
— — — — — — — — — —
LPT1: rerouted to COM1:
Retry=NONE

Code page operation not supported on this device
```

The /STATUS switch may be used with the other device names, but it is not necessary.

The PRINT Command

When a printer is attached and configured with MODE, if necessary, DOS can print files on it using the PRINT command. PRINT lets you print the contents of ASCII files, one at a time or in a queue. PRINT works in the background, so you can continue with other DOS work in the foreground. The first PRINT command in a session loads a TSR (about 5.5K) and configures background printing for the session. You have to reboot to change its configuration.

Identifying the PRINT Device

Figure 20.3 shows the format of the PRINT command. The first PRINT command after booting results in the following question:

```
Name of list device [PRN]:
```

Whatever you enter here becomes the PRINT device until you reboot. To use the default PRN, just press Enter. To use another device (such as LPT2 or COM1), type the device name and press Enter.

You can avoid the question-and-answer interaction by including the /D switch on the first PRINT command after booting. Many people include a PRINT command with no filespec in AUTOEXEC.BAT to load the TSR and establish the print device, something like the following:

```
PRINT /D:PRN
```

To print from DOS Shell, you must initialize the print device before starting the Shell. Placing the preceding command in AUTOEXEC.BAT (before the DOSSHELL command) does the trick nicely.

Figure 20.3.
PRINT command
reference.

PRINT

Manages background printing.

Format:

```
PRINT [/D:device] [/B:buffer] [/U:ticks1] [/M:ticks2]
[/S:ticks3] [/Q:qsize] [/T] [filespec ...] [/C] [/P]
```

Parameters and Switches:

none	Displays the contents of the print queue or loads the TSR.
/D:*device*	Identifies the printer port on which to print. Valid values are LPT1, LPT2, LPT3, COM1, COM2, COM3, and COM4. LPT1 is identical to PRN. If used, /D must precede *filespec* on the command line.
/B:*buffer*	Sets the size, in bytes, of the buffer used to store data before printing; may be 512 to 16,384; 512 is the default.
/U:*ticks1*	Specifies the maximum number of clock ticks to wait for a printer to be available; may be 1 to 255; the default is 1. If the printer is not available in *ticks1* clock ticks, the job is not printed. (There are about 18 clock ticks per second.)
/M:*ticks2*	Specifies the maximum number of clock ticks to print a character on the printer; may be 1 to 55; the default value is 2. If a character takes longer than *ticks2* clock ticks to print, DOS displays an error message.
/S:*ticks3*	Specifies the number of clock ticks the DOS scheduler allocates for background printing before returning to foreground work; maybe 1 to 255; the default value is 8.
/Q:*qsize*	Specifies the maximum number of files in the print queue; may be 4 through 32. The default value is 10.
/T	Removes all files from the print queue.
filespec	Identifies a text file to place in the print queue; may be up to 64 characters.

| /C | Removes file(s) from the print queue. |
| /P | Adds file(s) to the print queue. |

Notes:

/T empties the queue. If any filespecs precede /T, they are removed from the queue. If any follow /T, they are added or canceled depending on whether /P or /C applies to them.

Configuring PRINT

You may want to configure other PRINT features in the initializing command. You can control such features as print-buffer size, print-queue size, and the balance between background and foreground processing.

PRINT can be configured only by its initializing command. It can't be reconfigured without rebooting.

The /B switch sets the size of the print buffer; a larger buffer speeds up printing but decreases the amount of available conventional memory. (You can't kick PRINT or its buffer into upper memory.)

The rest of the configuration switches control how DOS does time-slicing when PRINT runs in the background. A clock tick is about 1/18 of a second. Normally, DOS will abort the PRINT command if the printer isn't available within one clock tick; if you want more time, increase it with the /U parameter. The /M parameter specifies how many clock ticks are allowed for printing one character. If you have an extremely slow printer and PRINT often aborts with an error message, you might want to specify a higher value here. The /S switch specifies how much background printing is done before DOS checks for a foreground action. If you increase this value from the default 8, print speed is increased but your foreground work may be impeded.

Controlling the Print Queue

Normally, the print queue holds up to 10 files. Each new file is placed at the end of the queue; if the queue is empty, the file is printed immediately. You can include several filespecs separated by spaces or even a global filespec to queue several files at the same time. A message warns you when the queue is full.

The /Q switch, which belongs on the initializing command, sets the size of the print queue; if you often need to queue up more than 10 files, you may want to specify a larger number.

You can see the current queue by entering PRINT with no parameters. The /T switch, with no filenames, terminates the queue immediately, right in the middle of the current file.

> When /T is entered, PRINT stops shipping data to the printer, but the printer will keep printing until its own buffer is empty. A printer with a large buffer may print several pages before stopping. You can stop the printer and empty its buffer immediately by turning it off.

You can cancel files from the queue by issuing another PRINT command with the /C switch before or just after the filename to be removed. All filenames following /C are removed from the queue; if a filename precedes it, that one is removed as well. To add files to the queue in the same command, use /P. Just like /C, it applies to all filenames following it and the one immediately before it. Files named in a PRINT command without either /P or /C are added to the queue. For example, the following command cancels ACT.1, ACT.2, and ACT.3 and prints PART.1, PART.2, and PART.3:

```
PRINT /C ACT.1 ACT.2 ACT.3 PART.1 /P PART.2 PART.3
```

You can't directly change the order of files in the print queue. To force a later file to be printed quickly, you would have to cancel any files preceding it in the queue and then add them to the queue again following that file.

Printing GRAPHICS Screens

DOS normally can't print graphics screens that can be displayed by CGA, EGA, and VGA monitors; it may try to convert them to text characters. You can use several third-party software programs to capture, print, and even modify graphics screens. On occasion, however, you may want to print a graphics screen from a CGA, EGA, or VGA monitor using PrintScreen. The GRAPHICS command may make this possible. DOS can't handle video modes that aren't supported by the BIOS; many SuperVGA graphics can't be handled, for example. Some applications reprogram the VGA display to a different mode; these displays can't be printed under DOS.

How GRAPHICS Works

The GRAPHICS command loads a TSR that lets DOS print supported graphic screens on several types of printers. After GRAPHICS is loaded, the signal generated by the PrintScreen key is intercepted. If the screen is in text mode, the request is passed back to the BIOS for standard text-screen printing. If the screen is in graphics mode, however, GRAPHICS takes over. It scans each pixel on the screen, translates it for the printer, and prints it. Both the number of pixels (screen resolution) and the number of dots per inch (printer resolution) affect the result. Some graphic displays are printed sideways for best effect.

Your DOS directory includes a file called GRAPHICS.PRO that includes printer profiles for the printer types DOS supports, including details on translating different video formats for printing. This is an ASCII file; you can examine it with EDIT or print it with PRINT.

The GRAPHICS Command

Figure 20.4 shows the format of the GRAPHICS command. GRAPHICS with no parameters is equivalent to GRAPHICS HPDEFAULT; DOS prepares to print graphics screens on a printer that recognizes the PCL (page control language) commands used by most Hewlett-Packard printers. Table 20.1 shows a complete list of the available printer-type parameters.

GRAPHICS

Loads the Graphics TSR to enable DOS to print graphics screens.

Format:

GRAPHICS [*type*] [*filespec*] [/R] [/B] [LCD] [/PRINTBOX:*size*]

Parameters and Switches:

none	Loads the Graphics TSR with default values.
type	Identifies the printer type. See notes for possible values. The default is HPDEFAULT.
filespec	Identifies the printer profile file; default is GRAPHICS.PRO.
/R	Specifies that images should be printed as they appear on-screen (a positive image). Default is to print a reverse, or negative, screen image, which sometimes looks better in print.
/B	Prints background in color for printers COLOR4 and COLOR8.
/LCD	Prints image using LCD aspect ratio instead of CGA aspect ratio. The effect of this switch is the same as /PRINTBOX:LCD.
/PRINTBOX:*size*	Specifies the size of the printbox. You can abbreviate /PRINTBOX as /PB. *Size* may be STD or LCD. This must match the first operand of the PRINTBOX statement in your printer profile.

Notes:

You can't print a graphics screen to a PostScript printer via DOS.

After GRAPHICS is loaded, press Shift-PrintScreen or PrintScreen (depending on the keyboard) to print the screen. The number of shades of gray depends on both monitor and printer. If the monitor is 640x200 or better, the screen will be printed sideways.

Table 20.1. GRAPHICS Printer Types

Type	Printers Included
COLOR1	IBM PC Color Printer with black ribbon
COLOR4	IBM PC Color Printer with RGB ribbon
COLOR8	IBM PC Color Printer with CMY ribbon (cyan, magenta, yellow)
DESKJET	Hewlett-Packard DeskJet
HPDEFAULT	Any Hewlett-Packard PCL printer (the default)
GRAPHICS	IBM Personal Graphics Printer, Proprinter, or Quietwriter; also most Epson dot-matrix printers
GRAPHICSWIDE	Any GRAPHICS printer with a wide carriage
LASERJET	Hewlett-Packard LaserJet printer
LASERJETII	Hewlett-Packard LaserJet II printer
PAINTJET	Hewlett-Packard PaintJet printer
QUIETJET	Hewlett-Packard QuietJet printer
QUIETJETPLUS	Hewlett-Packard QuietJet Plus printer
RUGGEDWRITER	Hewlett-Packard RuggedWriter printer
RUGGEDWRITERWIDE	Hewlett-Packard RuggedWriter Wide printer
THERMAL	IBM PC-convertible Thermal printer
THINKJET	Hewlett-Packard ThinkJet printer

To find out how the GRAPHICS command works on your printer, choose the printer option that seems closest to your printer. If it emulates one of the listed types, specify that type. Most dot-matrix printers emulate the Epson; the GRAPHICS option works on most of them. Use GRAPHICSWIDE if your printer has a wide carriage. Many laser printers emulate one of the Hewlett-Packard models. Don't try printing a graphics screen on a PostScript printer, however, unless it emulates a printer DOS can handle. It will just hang up, and you will have to turn off the printer and reboot your system.

If GRAPHICS.PRO isn't in the same directory as GRAPHICS.COM or the current directory, you have to tell DOS where it is by using the filespec parameter.

GRAPHICS Switches

Normally, screens are printed with a white background; this is easy on a printer because the background is ignored. The average screen, however, is displayed on the monitor with a dark background. If you want the screen print prepared with a dark background, use the /R switch; the result will more closely match the displayed screen. (Most printers don't do a very good job of solid black areas, however.)

When you print to a color printer, GRAPHICS also uses white for the background by default. The /B switch tells it to use a color; this is valid only for COLOR4 and COLOR8 printers. If you examine the GRAPHICS.PRO file following these two headings, you see listings of how each displayed color is printed.

Aspect Ratio

The aspect ratio of a screen is different on an LCD monitor than on a standard one. Normally, you can trust GRAPHICS to choose the correct one, as they are specified in GRAPHICS.PRO for each printer as the PRINTBOX value. If you find that the ratio is not quite right on a printed graphics screen (if circles come out as ellipses, for example), check GRAPHICS.PRO to see whether your monitor can handle both LCD and STD; the values follow the word PRINTBOX for each screen resolution. Either /LCD or /PB:LCD specifies the LCD aspect ratio. Use /PB:STD to specify a standard one.

You may have to reboot to replace the GRAPHICS profile. If the new profile takes less space in memory, it can be loaded over the existing one. If not, you see an error message, and you have to reboot and start over.

After you decide on the correct GRAPHICS command for your system, load it through AUTOEXEC.BAT so it is always available. If you can't load it in upper memory and cannot afford the conventional memory space on a regular basis, make a batch program or DOSKEY macro to load GRAPHICS as you need it.

Configuring Disks and Networks

21

Introduction

In every computer's life, a little change must fall. If you change the type of hardware attached to a system, particularly the disk drives, you may have to tell DOS what you did so that it can handle the new drives properly. The DRIVPARM command and the DRIVER.SYS device driver let you redefine your disk drives.

You can even set up extra logical drive names for floppy disk drives to make certain processing is more convenient. You learn when and how to use these configuration commands in this chapter.

Attaching a PC to a network requires both hardware and software changes. The network operating system handles most of the software needs, but you have to consider a few DOS features when running DOS under a network. These features are covered in this chapter.

Configuring Physical Disks

A *block device* is a device that reads and writes more than one character at a time. It may be a floppy disk drive, a hard disk drive, or a tape drive. DOS senses block devices during booting and creates a table of parameters (number of heads, number of tracks, and so on) that tells it how to access the device. This procedure works most of the time, but DOS may be fooled by newer devices. In that case, you have to use DRIVPARM to define the device. If DOS has difficulty accessing a new block device, especially in formatting it, try DRIVPARM to correct the problem.

DRIVPARM

The DRIVPARM configuration command (see fig. 21.1) lets you change internal device parameter tables so that DOS accesses the drive correctly. Include the DRIVPARM command in your CONFIG.SYS file with the correct switches, and DOS will always use valid drive parameters.

Each type of device has its own set of defaults for heads, sectors, and tracks. Table 21.1 shows the defaults for standard disk types. If you are installing a different device type, specify the correct values from the device documentation if you aren't sure what the defaults are. If you specify wrong or inconsistent values, DOS will do erratic or bad formatting on the drive.

DRIVPARM

Specifies new parameters for an existing physical drive.

Format:

```
DRIVPARM /D:drive [switches]
```

Switches:

/D:*drive*   Specifies the physical drive number; 0=A; 1=B; 2=C, etc.; this switch is required.

/F:*type*   Identifies the type of drive. Valid values are as follows:

0	360K or less
1	1.2M
2	720K (default)
3	Eight-inch, single-density
4	Eight-inch, double-density
5	Hard disk
6	Tape drive
7	1.44M
8	Read/write optical disk
9	2.88M

/H:*heads*   Specifies the number of heads (or sides).

/S:*sectors*   Specifies the number of sectors per track.

/T:*tracks*   Specifies the number of tracks.

/C   Indicates that the drive has change-line support.

/N   Indicates a nonremovable drive.

/I   Indicates an electronically compatible 3 1/2-inch drive.

Figure 21.1.
DRIVPARM
configuration
command reference.

Table 21.1. Standard Floppy Disk Parameters

Capacity	Heads	Sectors	Tracks
160K	1	8	40
180K	1	9	40
320K	2	8	40
360K	2	9	40
720K	2	9	80
1.2M	2	15	80
1.44M	2	18	80
2.88M	2	36	80

If you specify your boot drive in the DRIVPARM command and give it the wrong parameters, you may not be able to start up your system, or it may start up as usual and then destroy the root directory when it writes to the disk. Be sure that you have a valid backup and a recovery disk handy before redefining the boot drive.

Suppose that you plug in a 720K drive to replace an old 360K drive on B and DOS has difficulty recognizing the new drive. You would include the following command in CONFIG.SYS:

```
DRIVPARM /D:1 /F:2 /C
```

This command sets the parameters for drive 1 (the B drive) to match type 2 (720K) and says that the drive has change-line support.

Change-Line Support

A *change line* is a mechanism that lets DOS know that a drive door has been opened, signaling that a disk may have been changed. Most 360K and below disk drives do not have this feature. If DOS thinks that there is change-line support, it saves time by referring to a cache of the directory instead of rereading the directory itself.

A malfunctioning change-line mechanism could threaten the integrity of data on your floppy disk. If DOS accesses one floppy disk using another floppy disk's directory, data could be read from or written to the wrong clusters. If you suspect this is happening, repair or replace the drive or use DRIVPARM to tell DOS that the drive does not have change-line support.

Configuring Logical Floppy Disks

The DRIVER.SYS device driver creates a logical floppy disk drive based on a physical one. It assigns a new drive letter, the next one in sequence. Two major uses of DRIVER.SYS are as follows:

● To force DOS to recognize and assign a logical drive name to an external disk drive.

● To assign an alternate logical drive name to a diskette drive.

> To create a logical drive name for a hard disk, use the SUBST command.

Figure 21.2 shows the switches you can use with the DRIVER.SYS device driver. Notice that you can use DEVICE or DEVICEHIGH to load the driver. You can use more than one DRIVER.SYS command to define multiple logical drives. Each loaded driver takes about 240 bytes in memory.

DRIVER.SYS

Creates a new logical drive corresponding to a physical disk drive.

Format:

```
DEVICE[HIGH]=[path]DRIVER.SYS /D:drive[switches]
```

Parameters and Switches:

path	Identifies the location of DRIVER.SYS if it is not in the root directory of the boot drive.
/D:drive	Specifies the number of the physical disk drive: 0 = first, 1 = second, up to 127.
/F:type	Identifies the type of drive.

       0   360K or less

       1   1.2M

       2   720K (default)

       7   1.44M

       9   2.88M

/H:heads	Specifies the number of heads (or sides).
/S:sectors	Specifies the number of sectors per track.
/T:tracks	Specifies the number of tracks.
/C	Indicates that the drive has change-line support.

Notes:

This command applies the next available drive letter to the newly created logical drive.

When you use /F, the default shown in table 21.1 applies. To specify any other parameters, use /H, /S, and /T.

Creating an Alternate Drive Name

Many computers these days have floppy drives of two different types, such as 1.2M and 1.44M. To copy files from one disk to another of the same type, you cannot do it directly, because DOS rejects a command such as the following:

```
XCOPY A:\*.* A:
```

You can use DRIVER.SYS to assign a second logical drive name to a physical drive so that you can copy files from one disk to another in that drive using COPY or XCOPY commands. This command sets up a second drive letter for the second disk drive (with a 360K capacity):

```
DEVICE=C:\DOS\DRIVER.SYS /D:1 /F:0
```

Be sure to notice what drive letter is set up. A message like the following appears when the driver is loaded:

```
Loaded External Driver for Drive D
```

With the logical drive created in this example, you could use the following command to copy files:

```
XCOPY B:\*.* D:
```

You are prompted to insert one disk at a time (starting with the target disk so that DOS can check it out). The messages look something like the following:

```
C:\>XCOPY B:*.* D:
Insert diskette for drive D: and press any key when ready
Insert diskette for drive B: and press any key when ready
Reading source file(s)...
Insert disk for drive D: and press any key when ready

A:CHAP02.CHP

  ...

A:APPP.CHP

Insert diskette for drive B: and press any key when ready
        7 File(s) copied

Insert disk for drive D: and press any key when ready
```

When you are copying more than one file, use XCOPY rather than COPY. You have to do a lot less disk swapping because XCOPY fills memory with files before writing any; whereas COPY handles each file separately.

Setting Up Two Alternate Drive Names

Suppose that your computer has two floppy disk drives, 1.2M and 1.44M, and two hard drives. You can include the following commands in your CONFIG.SYS file:

```
DEVICE=C:\DOS\DRIVER.SYS /D:0 /F:1
```

```
DEVICE=C:\DOS\DRIVER.SYS /D:1 /F:7
```

When the system boots, you see the following messages on the screen:

```
Loaded External Disk Driver for Drive E
```

```
Loaded External Disk Driver for Drive F
```

You can refer to drives E and F as needed during your DOS work; they have exactly the same characteristics as drives A and B. Most importantly, you can copy files from drive A to drive E (which is the same physical drive) and from drive B to drive F.

DOS keeps track of which logical drive name was used last. If drive E is in effect and you enter DIR A:, you see the following message:

```
Insert diskette for drive A: and press any key when ready
```

Adding an External Floppy Disk Drive

If you install a drive that DOS doesn't recognize automatically, either DRIVPARM or DRIVER.SYS can be used to tell DOS that you have added the drive to your PC. For example, the following command specifies a 1.2M external drive as the third disk drive:

```
DEVICE=C:\DOS\DRIVER.SYS /D:2 /F:1 /C
```

If you want to be able to copy files in that drive, you need a second, identical DEVICE command to set up a second logical drive. It will be assigned the next drive letter.

DRIVER.SYS or DRIVPARM

If you use DRIVER.SYS to change the parameters of a physical drive, a new logical drive name is assigned to the drive. It is better to redefine drive characteristics with DRIVPARM, which lets you continue to use the drive's original name. DRIVPARM also takes up less space in conventional memory.

Adding an Unsupported Drive

If you add a floppy disk drive not supported by the BIOS, a driver supplied with it may not work. For example, suppose that you get a 2.88M drive at a swap meet for your drive A and your BIOS doesn't support it (most older ones don't). As a first step, add the following DRIVPARM command to CONFIG.SYS:

```
DRIVPARM /D:0 /F:9 /C
```

If you still have access problems, try using DRIVER.SYS to define it; then two logical drive names will refer to the same floppy disk drive. Use a configuration command like the following:

```
DEVICE=C:\DOS\DRIVER.SYS /D:0 /F:9 /C
```

It's possible that you may need both commands.

Running DOS on a Network

A network is a collection of two or more computers linked to each other via hardware and software; the details differ from network to network. The hardware includes network adapter cards in each computer, cables, and a network drive. The software includes the network operating system and a file server, which manages file access. It may also include other servers to handle printers and communications.

Each computer in a network is often called a workstation or node. The workstations can range from a simple keyboard and monitor to a full-fledged 486 computer; some PC networks can handle Macintosh computers as well. In any network, each node can access at least one network disk (network drive) and peripheral devices on the other nodes. They can transfer files among nodes, access a central database, send messages to each other, and share the same printer.

Special network commands set up the system when it is turned on. Some DOS commands, such as JOIN and SUBST, may be used to set up the required access paths for the network. Although these commands are valid, they should not be used on a network for any purpose other than what is required to establish the network, as they can cause trouble within DOS.

Each workstation can still operate independently of the network, using most DOS commands. Neither the processing nor the commands differ while the programs and data are contained within the operative computer. However, time does become a factor when transferring data across connections, particularly if several users are doing it at the same time.

DOS Command Limitations

Most DOS commands work the same under a network as on an independent computer. However, some DOS commands can't be used over a network connection. Other commands can't be used to refer to network drives. Table 21.2 lists these commands.

Table 21.2. DOS Command Network Restrictions

Do not use the following on network drives:

CHKDSK

DEFRAG

DISKCOMP

FDISK

RECOVER (from earlier DOS versions)

SYS

Do not use the following across network connections:

FASTOPEN

FORMAT

LABEL

UNFORMAT

A command that can't be used on a network drive can be used to refer to local drives on a networked computer, as long as those drives are not specified as network drives. Any DOS command that can't be used across network connections can be used to refer only to drives on an individual computer.

If your system includes a token ring network and if you are having trouble running MEMMAKER, add the IT switch to the MEMMAKER command to disable detection of the token-ring network.

Logical Drives

The network operating system establishes logical names by which people can access data on network drives and drives on other computers. Each node includes the LASTDRIVE command in its CONFIG.SYS file to allow for enough drive names.

Sharing and Locking Files

When working on a network, it is possible that two people may try to access the same file at the same time. They may even try to make simultaneous changes to the file. Large databases accessed by everyone are frequently stored on network drives. Most network file servers prevent this problem. However, you may need the SHARE command to allow only one person at a time to access a file. Figure 21.3 shows the command format.

The SHARE command specifies the amount of space reserved for storing file specifications and a maximum number of files that can be locked at a time. If your network requires SHARE, it was probably placed in your AUTOEXEC.BAT file when the network was installed.

Special Considerations

Some Local Area Networks (LANs) have special features or problems that affect DOS usage. For example, PC LAN has a command named APPEND. If you happen to use the DOS APPEND command, you may get unexpected results. If your computer is connected to a PC LAN network, the DOS APPEND program may have been renamed or removed.

Figure 21.3.
SHARE command reference.

SHARE

Installs file locking and sharing functions on a hard disk, usually used in a network or multitasking environment. After SHARE is installed, it validates all read-and-write requests.

Format:

From the command prompt:

```
SHARE [switches]
```

From CONFIG.SYS:

```
INSTALL=[path]SHARE.EXE[switches]
```

Parameters and Switches:

path   Identifies the location of the SHARE.EXE file if it is not in the root directory of the boot drive.

/F:space   Specifies the space (in bytes) for recording file sharing information; default is 2,048.

/L:locks   Specifies the number of files that can be locked at the same time; default is 20.

Notes:

Each open shared file requires space for the full file specification; the average length is 20 bytes.

SHARE can be loaded high from the command prompt.

Upgrading to QBASIC

22

Introduction

QBASIC is a more advanced language than many earlier forms of BASIC, including GW-BASIC and BASICA, which were supplied with earlier versions of DOS. With QBASIC, you can create structured programs that not only execute more efficiently but also are easier to code and debug.

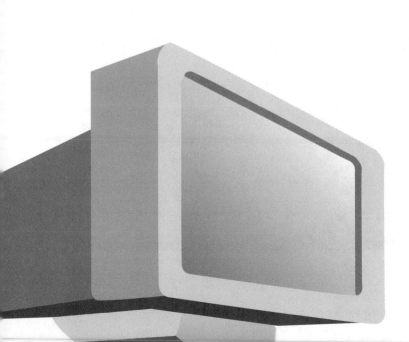

QBASIC is an interpretive version of Microsoft QuickBASIC; unlike the full QuickBASIC, it has no compiler. Any programs you create under QBASIC can be compiled and run under QuickBASIC. QuickBASIC source code will run under QBASIC.

Many differences exist between the earlier supplied forms of BASIC and QBASIC. The major differences concern the user interface, data types, line numbers, and new statements that enable you to create control structures. This chapter is not designed to teach QBASIC programming. Instead, it is intended for BASIC programmers and discusses only the major differences between QBASIC and unstructured versions of BASIC.

QBASIC's Interface

The QBASIC programming environment is provided by the same full-screen ASCII text editor accessed by DOS 6's EDIT command. But EDIT starts up the editor in its document mode; whereas QBASIC normally opens the editor in its programming mode (see fig. 22.1), which is quite a bit different. You can start up QBASIC in document mode by adding the /EDITOR switch to the QBASIC command.

Figure 22.1.
QBASIC Editor
screen.

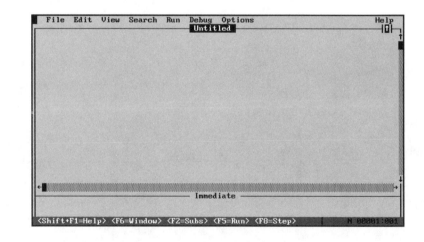

The QBASIC Editor

The QBASIC menus assist you in creating, testing, and debugging QBASIC programs. The File menu lets you open and save files as well as to exit QBASIC. The Edit menu includes commands to cut and copy text and create subprograms and functions. The View menu lets you view and edit any procedure of the current program, split the screen so you can see two parts of the same program, and switch immediately to the output screen. Search menu commands will find and replace text strings. Run menu commands execute all or part of a program. The Debug menu offers several tools, such as tracing and stepping through a program. The Options menu includes commands to modify the display and set the status of Syntax Checking.

The screen includes two windows. The larger window is the standard program-editing area. Its title bar shows Untitled unless the currently loaded program has a name. The smaller window, called the Immediate window, holds one line at a time, which is executed as soon as you press Enter. You can use the Immediate window to test parts of your program as you work.

The status line shows the position of the cursor as well as some of the function keys that you can use. Once the window contains statements, pressing F1 gets context-sensitive help on the QBASIC word containing the cursor. Table 22.1 includes a complete list of the hotkeys when the editor window is active. Different hotkeys are available when you aren't in edit mode.

Table 22.1. Hotkeys in QBASIC Editor

Key	Unshifted Key	Shift-Key	Ctrl-Key
F1	Help	Using Help	
F2	View SUBs	Next Procedure	Previous Procedure
F3	Repeat Find		
F4	Output Screen		
F5	Continue	Run Start	
F6	Next Window	Previous Window	

continues

Table 22.1. continued

Key	Unshifted Key	Shift-Key	Ctrl-Key
F7	Execute to cursor		
F8	Step		
F9	Breakpoint		
F10	Procedure Step		Zoom
Del	Clear	Cut	
Ins	Overtype/Insert	Paste	Copy

Smart Editor Effects

The editor begins to work on your program lines as soon as you type them. Once you press Enter or move the cursor to another line, any QBASIC words are converted to uppercase and spaces are inserted around equal signs and operators. If Options Syntax Checking is turned on, you are informed immediately of any syntax errors. You can press F1 to view the correct format of the current statement. The editor automatically keeps the capitalization pattern of names consistent by converting all to the layout of the latest typed one. If a reference is made to a different procedure, the editor inserts the required DECLARE statement at the beginning of the program. If the main program includes a DEFtype statement, the editor includes it automatically at the beginning of other procedures.

You can copy or cut lines by selecting them and using the Edit menu or the hotkeys. Copied or cut lines are stored in the clipboard until another copy or cut replaces them; you can paste the clipboard contents as often as you need. You can even copy or move lines to another program or procedure, since the clipboard is unaffected by anything except another cut or copy or exiting QBASIC.

Converting a GW-BASIC or BASICA Program

QBASIC stores programs in ASCII format, so if your existing programs are stored in GW-BASIC's or BASICA's default binary format, you'll have to convert them. Start up the other BASIC editor, call up the program, and save it in ASCII format with the BAS extension. To save a GW-BASIC file as OLDPAY.BAS in ASCII form, complete the following steps:

1. Start up GW-BASIC.

2. Load the file.

3. Enter **SAVE "OLDPAY.BAS",A**

4. Type **SYSTEM** to exit GW-BASIC.

Now you can start up QBASIC, use the File Open command to open the program, and run it from within the QBASIC editor.

Running Programs

The easiest way to run a loaded program under QBASIC is to press F5. Alternatively, you can choose Run Start. A program converted from a different form of BASIC should run with no problems unless it uses any of the few features not supported by QBASIC (see Table 22.2). If your program uses any of these features, you have to modify it to run under QBASIC.

Table 22.2. QBASIC Incompatibilities

Statements not supported:

DEF USR
EXTERR(n)
LIST
LLIST
MERGE

continues

Table 22.2. continued

MOTOR
USR

Major features not supported:

CALL (offvar,var1...)
CHAIN (ALL, MERGE, DELETE, linenumber)
CLEAR (,n)
DRAW (*var=;*)
PLAY (*var=;*)
VARPTR (*#filename*)

Other possible problems:

QBASIC has additional reserved words
PEEK and POKE in Data Segment may have different effects

A message prompts you to press F1 for help if a syntax error occurs.

Line Numbers

In QBASIC, line numbers are not required, but they are permitted. If you use GOTO to transfer control, you can reference a line number if you like; just number the target line as in other BASICs. If you prefer, you can use a label, which is a QBASIC word followed by a colon. For example, the statement GOTO ERRORLINE transfers control to a line beginning with ERRORLINE: and continues from there. Any string of up to 40 letters and digits that is not a QBASIC reserved word and is not used for another purpose in the program can be used as a label. The trailing colon tells QBASIC that the string is a label.

New Constant and Variable Types

You have more choices for constants and variables in QBASIC than in GW-BASIC or BASICA. The names can have up to 40 characters, in any combination of uppercase and lowercase letters, digits, and the period. If the same string of characters is used, however, QBASIC assumes it is the same name even if the capitalization is different. The editor helps you be consistent by converting all strings of the same characters to the same capitalization format. If you use FIRSTNAME$, then later type Firstname$, all other occurrences of FIRSTNAME$ are converted to the last typed configuration.

As in the earlier forms of BASIC, you can use the DEFtype statement to specify names as string (DEFSTR), integer (DEFINT), single-precision (DEFSNG), or double-precision (DEFDBL) numbers. Any DEFtype statements you use in the main program are automatically copied to any procedures you create later. If you add a DEFtype statement to the main program after creating procedures, the procedures aren't updated, however. Data type suffixes on names override the DEFtype statements.

Constants

You can create named constants with a CONST statement, which looks much like an assignment statement:

```
CONST ConstantName=value
```

The ConstantName and the value must be of the same type. You can use CONST Logo$ = "IBM" or CONST TotalLines% = 400, for example. The value can't include a variable name or function, but it can include expressions and other constant names if necessary.

QBASIC won't let you change the value assigned to a constant. If you define CONST Rate=.0935, you cannot specify Rate=Rate+.01 later in the program. Of course, you can use literal constants of any type just as in other forms of the BASIC language.

Numeric Variables

In addition to the standard numeric variable types, QBASIC provides the long integer, which can handle values between _2,147,483,648 and 2,147,483,647. (Standard integers must be between _32,768 and 32,767.) The long integer is stored in four bytes of memory, while the standard integer takes only two bytes. Even though the long integer takes as much space as a single-precision value, it is stored in two's complement form and allows for more efficient execution of the program.

You can use the DEFLNG statement to reserve initial letters for a long integer or use the type character & at the end of the name. Once declared by its appearance in a statement, a long integer is used just like other integers.

String Variables

String variables can be declared and used much as in earlier forms of BASIC. In QBASIC, you also can define fixed-length string variables using a form of the DIM statement:

```
*DIM StringName AS STRING * n
```

The following statement defines a 30-character variable named Fullname:

```
DIM Fullname AS STRING * 30
```

It overrides any DEFSTR statement; in addition, you cannot use the $ type character on the name. Fixed-length strings are useful in many file and database applications. If you want an array of fixed-length strings, include the array dimension following the StringName. The following statement defines an array of 50 string variables, each 30 characters long:

```
DIM Fullname(50) AS STRING * 30
```
When data is placed in a fixed-length string variable, it is left-justified and padded with blanks on the right. If a value is too long for the variable, it is truncated on the right with no warning.

Additional String Functions

QBASIC supports the standard string functions, as well as several new ones. The UCASE$ and LCASE$ functions change the string's letters to all uppercase or all lowercase. The following statement converts the value in Fullname (a string variable) to all uppercase and assigns it to the variable Fixname$ (a variable-length string).

```
Fixname$=UCASE$(Fullname)
```

In this case, the resulting value in Fixname$ is as long as the fixed-length string variable.

The LTRIM$ and RTRIM$ functions let you remove leading or trailing spaces and/or tabs from a string. The following statement removes any number of trailing spaces from the string Fullname and assigns the result to Fixname$:

```
Fixname$=RTRIM$(Fullname)
```

The resulting value in Fixname$ has no trailing spaces, so it may be shorter than the fixed-length string that provided the value.

Array Variables

Arrays can be defined and used just as they are in unstructured BASICs. Alternatively, you can specify the subscript range in a TO clause. The following statement sets up a 12-element array with the specified subscripts:

```
DIM MONTH(1 TO 12)
```

The following statement sets up a 61-element array with subscripts ranging from 1940 to 2000:

```
DIM YEAR(1940 TO 2000)
```

You can define arrays that contain several different data types in one element by using the user-defined or record data type, described in the following sections.

Record Data Type

QBASIC supports a user-defined data type called a record data type, which is defined with the TYPE block and creates a record. It can contain any combination of existing data types, so that the result can contain several values. The record data type is especially useful in defining an array that contains several data types in each element or in defining a record of mixed data for use in files:

```
TYPE usertype
    element1 AS typename1
    element2 AS typename2
    ...<CE>END TYPE
```

The *usertype* is a standard QBASIC name that is not used for any other purpose in the procedure. Each element is a data item within the record; each can be accessed individually by the program. The typename specifies the type (and hence the length) of the individual element; it can be INTEGER, LONG, SINGLE, DOUBLE, STRING * n, or another already defined usertype. For example, the following block defines user data type GPA to contain three different elements:

```
TYPE GPA
    StudentNumber AS STRING * 6
    StudentHours AS INTEGER
    StudentPoints AS SINGLE
END TYPE
```

The *usertype* defines a data type, not a variable name, so it can't be used directly in statements. It can be used only as a *typename* in its own definition or as an element in another TYPE block. To use data in the defined format, declare a variable as that data type. For example, after defining the data type above, you could use the following statement to define Student as a 12-byte variable; six bytes for the string, two bytes for the integer, and four bytes for the single-precision value:

```
DIM Student AS GPA
```

To reference a part of the record, join the variable name with the element name, connecting them with a period as in the following example:

```
Student.StudentHours = Student.StudentHours + NewHours
```

Records in Arrays

A variable of a user-defined data type can be used in an array. The following statement sets up an array of 180 elements, each 12 bytes long.

```
DIM Student (180) AS GPA
```

Student(25).StudentNumber refers to the six-character string in the twenty-fifth occurrence of the array.

The following example defines datatype Employee and uses it for the array variable Worker:

```
TYPE Employee
    EmpNumber AS STRING * 9
    EmpSalary AS SINGLE
```

```
      EmpDependents AS INTEGER
END TYPE
DIM Worker(240) AS Employee
```

The program refers to elements of the record by connecting them to the variable name with a period. For example, Worker(Next%).EmpSalary refers to the EmpSalary element of the array component indicated by the value of Next%.

Records in Files

Record data types can be used instead of FIELD variables in QBASIC programs, which lets you create and modify file data much more easily, without all the restrictions on FIELD variables. For compatibility, QBASIC supports the FIELD statement, of course.

New Flow of Control Facilities

In earlier forms of BASIC, a program had an essentially linear form with branching. The single-line IF statement handled decision making, and GOTO statements and line numbers let you create a morass of decision-based loops. The WHILE...WEND statement allowed some looping control. QBASIC provides more techniques and statements to handle flow of control in your program in a structured, efficient manner.

Expanded IF Statement

QBASIC can handle all the earlier formats of IF, including the one-line IF...THEN and IF...THEN...ELSE statements. It's often hard to read these IF statements, much less debug them. So QBASIC includes an expanded, multiline IF block that conforms to structured programming principles. Here's the format:

```
IF condition THEN
    statements to be executed if condition is true
```

```
[ELSE
     statements to be executed if condition is false]
END IF
```

The line beginning with IF starts the block; it must include the conditional expression and the word THEN. When the condition is true, statements on all lines down to ELSE are executed; if there is no ELSE statement, statements on all lines down to END IF are executed. When the conditional expression is false, statements on all lines between ELSE and END IF are executed; if there is no ELSE statement, control passes to the statement following END IF. The following example executes several commands if the condition is true:

```
IF TotalBill! >= CreditLimit! THEN
     PRINT OverLimitMessage$
     OverFlag$ = "Y"
     CALL warningflash
END IF
```

The following example executes only one set of statements, depending on the condition's value:

```
IF ApplicantAge% < 21 THEN
     PRINT MinorMessage$
     AgeProblem$ = "Y"
ELSE
     PRINT NoProblemMessage$
     AgeProblem$ = "N"
END IF
```

Another QBASIC option makes it easier to code complex nested IFs. You can include the ELSEIF element, as follows:

```
IF condition THEN
     statements to be executed if condition is true
[ELSEIF condition-n THEN
     statements to be executed if condition-n is true]...
[ELSE
     statements to be executed if all conditions are false]
END IF
```

The following example uses ELSEIF to include a second condition and allow execution of one of three possible sets of statements:

```
IF ApplicantAge! < 21 THEN
```

```
      PRINT MinorMessage$
      AgeProblem$ = "Y"
ELSEIF ApplicantAge% > 65
      PRINT SeniorMessage$
      AgeProblem$ = "Y"
ELSE
      PRINT NoProblemMessage$
      AgeProblem$ = "N"
END IF
```

You can use as many ELSEIF elements as needed to fully create the desired branches.

> You can optimize processing time by arranging the IF and ELSE conditions from the most likely to least likely to occur.

Using a Case Structure

You may be familiar with using ON...GOTO or ON...GOSUB to handle multiple branching situations. While such situations can often be handled with a nested IF or ELSEIF, QBASIC provides a special statement block that is designed for just such situations. The SELECT CASE statement lets you name a variable, then execute specific blocks of statements based on its value; the entire block sets up a case structure. The simplest format is as follows:

```
SELECT CASE variable
    [CASE valuelist
        statements to execute if variable = any value in valuelist]...
    CASE ELSE
        statements to execute if variable <> any value in valuelist
END SELECT
```

When the SELECT CASE block is executed, the CASE variable has a single value. One CASE block or CASE ELSE block is processed, then control jumps to the END SELECT statement and continues from there. You can include as many values as you like (separated by commas) in each valuelist, and as many CASE blocks as you need. The CASE ELSE block specifies statements to be executed if the value of the CASE variable is not equal to any of the specified values in any of the CASE statements.

For example, suppose that you have a menu or multiple-choice question to display. The input value is a single character, supposed to be A through D. A different subprogram is executed for each situation. You could handle it in a CASE block as follows:

```
SELECT CASE MenuChoice$
     CASE "A", "a"
          CALL DoSubA
     CASE "B", "b"
          CALL DoSubB
     CASE "C", "c"
          CALL DoSubC
     CASE "D", "d"
          CALL DoSubD
     CASE ELSE
          CALL DoBadChoice
END SELECT
```

This example lets you enter uppercase or lowercase letters. If a character that is not in the desired range is typed, subprogram DoBadChoice asks you to try again. If you prefer, you can include a set of statements, as many as needed, following each CASE statement.

Actually, SELECT CASE doesn't limit you to a single variable and valuelist for each case. The complete format follows:

```
SELECT CASE variable
     [CASE expressionlist
        statements to execute if any expression is true]...
     CASE ELSE
        statements to execute if no expressions are true
END SELECT
```

The *expressionlist* lets you use more than a single value or list of values to determine which block is executed. To include a condition, assume the variable name and type the word IS followed by the rest of the relational operation. You might use CASE IS > 65 or CASE IS <= 20, for example. To specify a range, use the TO keyword, as in

CASE 1 TO 5 or CASE "X" TO "Z." You can even combine expressions, as in CASE 0, 18 TO 20, IS > 65. Just make sure each individual value or expression is valid, and separate them with commas.

Loop Structures

In earlier forms of BASIC, loops are created with FOR...NEXT, with GOTO statements, and with WHILE...WEND statements. While these forms are still available for consistency, QBASIC's DO blocks allow easier structuring and clearer code than WHILE...WEND. A DO block begins with a DO statement and ends with a LOOP statement. All statements in between are executed during the loop. The block includes either a WHILE or an UNTIL element, added to either the DO or the LOOP statement. A DO WHILE...LOOP block is equivalent to a WHILE...WEND block.

The WHILE or UNTIL element includes a conditional expression. The expression is tested at the beginning of the loop if it is included on the DO statement, at the end if it is included on the LOOP statement. The loop is executed repeatedly as long as the condition is true when WHILE is used or until the condition becomes true when UNTIL is used. Use the following DO format if you want the condition to be tested before the block is executed the first time:

```
DO [WHILE|UNTIL] condition
     statements to be executed
LOOP
```

Use the following format if you want the block to be executed at least once, regardless of the truth of the condition:

```
DO
     statements to be executed
LOOP [WHILE|UNTIL] condition
```

Contents of Loop

Any statements can be used within a DO...LOOP block. You can use IFs, FOR...NEXT, WHILE...WEND, nested DOs, even subprogram references. Nested DO loops can be of any type; inner loops don't have to match the outer loop's structure. The only rule is that an inner loop of any kind (even FOR...NEXT) must end before its outer loop does.

If you must terminate a loop before the condition causes it to end, use an EXIT DO statement. When EXIT DO is executed, control passes immediately to the statement following the LOOP statement that marks the end of the current DO block.

Modular Programming

Earlier versions of BASIC are essentially linear; statements are executed in sequence unless a branch directs execution to another location in the program.

QBASIC enables you to work with modules. Execution of a program always starts and ends in the main module. The program can include as many procedure modules as you need, either subprograms or functions. Each procedure is a separate, named entity, called by the main module.

When a subprogram is created, you give it a name. Using that name as a statement or including it in a CALL statement starts its execution. After the statements in the subprogram are executed, control returns to the statement following the one that called it, much like a GOSUB procedure.

A user-defined function also is given a name. You then use it just like you use the built-in functions. Defining a QBASIC function has much the same effect as the DEF FN statement, but it allows more than one program line.

For compatibility with other versions, GOSUB and DEF FN both work in QBASIC. You can reference a label in a GOSUB statement instead of a line number.

A subprogram or function is a separate procedure, so variables in the main module (or any other procedure) have no effect in other procedures unless you make them global (COMMON SHARED). You can pass specific values to either a subprogram or a function in an argument list. (Global variables and passing values are covered later in this chapter.)

Examining a Structured Program

A structured program has a main module, along with several functions and subprograms. When you open the program file, you can examine the main module in the editing window. If you press F2 or choose View SUBs, you can select another procedure to view and edit in the window. You can use Shift+F2 to see the next procedure directly or Ctrl+F2 to see the previous one without going through the SUBs dialog box again.

Creating a Procedure

To create a subprogram or function, choose Edit New SUB or Edit New Function. If the cursor rests on text, you'll see the current word in the dialog box like the one in Figure 22.2. You can accept that as the procedure name or type in a name and choose OK. The resulting window is an editing window for the procedure. QBASIC puts in the first line (SUB or FUNCTION) with the name you provided followed by an empty set of parentheses and the last line (END SUB or END FUNCTION). You can add whatever you need between these two lines. If you used any DEFtype statements in the main program, they are copied to the beginning of each procedure when you start creating it.

```
    File  Edit  View  Search  Run  Debug  Options                  Help
                            REMLINE.BAS                               |8|
 ' Start of module-level program code

    Seps$ = " ,:=<>()" + CHR$(9)
    InitKeyTable
    GetFileNames
    ON ERROR GOTO FileErr1
    OPEN InputFile$ F              New SUB
    ON ERROR GOTO 0
    COLOR 7: PRINT "W   Name:                              OLOR 7: PRINT
    BuildTable
    CLOSE #1
    OPEN InputFile$ F
    ON ERROR GOTO Fil    < OK >    < Cancel >    < Help >
    OPEN OutputFile$
    ON ERROR GOTO 0
    GenOutFile
    CLOSE #1, #2
    IF OutputFile$ <> "CON" THEN CLS
 ┌─────────────────────────── Immediate ───────────────────────────┐

 F1=Help   Enter=Execute   Esc=Cancel   Tab=Next Field   Arrow=Next Item
```

Figure 22.2.
New Procedure Specification dialog box.

Type SUB *ProcedureName* in a program and press Enter. You'll get to the editing window for the new procedure immediately.

After a procedure has a name and has been saved, you can view or edit it by choosing View SUBs or by pressing F2. The resulting dialog box, like the one shown in Figure 22.3, lets you choose from all the procedures for the current program. You can even delete them if necessary. When the program is saved, a DECLARE statement for each new procedure is generated and added to the beginning of the main module.

Figure 22.3.
View SUBs
dialog box.

```
   File   Edit  View  Search  Run  Debug  Options                    Help
                          REMLINE.BAS
                              SUBs
  Choose program item to edit

    REMLINE.BAS
       BuildTable
       GenOutFile
       GetFileNames
       GetToken
       InitKeyTable
       IsDigit
       StrBrk
       StrSpn

  REMLINE.BAS is the Main Module

     < Edit in Active >     < Delete >     < Cancel >     < Help >

                            Immediate

 F1=Help   Enter=Execute   Esc=Cancel   Tab=Next Field   Arrow=Next Item
```

Global Variables

By default, all variables used in a procedure are local variables; they apply only to the procedure in which they appear. A variable named TaxRate in the main program has no effect on a variable named TaxRate in a subprogram or function unless you make special arrangements. You can tell QBASIC up front to make certain variables available to all procedures; these are called global variables.

Global variables must be declared in the main program in a COMMON SHARED statement, with the following format:

```
COMMON SHARED VariableList
```

You can include as many variables as needed, separating them with commas. Multiple COMMON SHARED statements may be used.

> Use one COMMON SHARED statement for all variables used together for easier program maintenance.

Suppose that your main program includes the following statement:

```
COMMON SHARED PrimeRate!, CreditLimit!
```

If the value of PrimeRate! is set in one procedure, it is the same in every procedure used by the program. If the variable were local, the value would apply only in the procedure in which it was set.

Subprograms

A subprogram is a block of code between SUB and END SUB statements. When you choose Edit New SUB, these lines are included automatically. If you type a SUB statement as part of the main module, the smart editor assumes you want to create a new subprogram and puts you in a new editor window to create it; the effect is the same as choosing Edit New SUB. Once defined, subprograms can be called by the main module or by other subprograms. When execution reaches the END SUB statement, it returns to the statement following the one that started the subprogram.

The general format for a subprogram is as follows:

```
SUB subprogramname [(parameters)]
    [local variable or constant declarations]
    statements to be executed
END SUB
```

Subprograms can be used to handle many complex operations. You might use a subprogram to print headers on each page of a printed report. Another subprogram might print footers.

The following is an example of a subprogram that plays "Happy Birthday":

```
SUB birthday
' Play a tune
```

```
PLAY "L4 C8C8DCFE2 C8C8DCGF2"
PLAY "C8C8>C<AFED2 B-8B-8AFGF2"
END SUB
```

A subprogram is invoked by naming it in a CALL statement or by using its name as a statement in the main program or another procedure. If the subprogram has no parameters, you can use CALL or omit it. The subprogram above could be run by either of the following statements:

```
CALL birthday
birthday
```

Each time a subprogram is invoked, any local variables in it are reset to their default values. Any global variables maintain their current values. If you want the subprogram to hold its local values between executions, add the word STATIC to the first line. The following statement causes local variables in taxwithholding to keep their values when the subprogram ends and use them again the next time it is executed:

```
SUB taxwithholding STATIC
```

The main program finds out about subprograms through DECLARE statements, which must precede any executable statements in the program. When you create a subprogram, QBASIC generates an initial DECLARE statement for the program using information currently available in the SUB statement:

```
DECLARE SUB subprogramname (parameters)
```

If there are no parameters, an empty set of parentheses is used. If you change the content of the parameter list later, be sure to change it in the DECLARE statement as well.

Passing Values

Sometimes, a subprogram has to use specific values passed from the calling program. If you use the CALL statement, the values to be passed must be enclosed in a single set of parentheses. If you omit the word CALL, you also omit the parentheses around the value list.

You can pass constants in the form of named constants, quoted strings, numeric values, or expressions. You can also pass local variables or expressions by including them as arguments. Every passed local variable can be changed in the subprogram, and the changed value will be available back in the calling procedure. If you want to prevent a passed variable from being changed, create an expression by enclosing it in an individual set of parentheses in the calling statement.

In the following example, changes to Taxrate do not affect the calling program when control returns:

```
CALL taxwithholding (Gross, Dependents, (Taxrate))
```

Any changes to variables used only in passed expressions are not carried back to the calling procedure.

The arguments are received by the subprogram into a parameter list; every parameter is represented by a variable name. Arguments are passed to parameters by position, not by name. That is, the first argument is passed to the first parameter, the second argument to the second parameter, and so on. Because of the positional relationship, any that are skipped must be represented by a comma. The matched items must be of the same data type. That is, a string argument must be paired with a string parameter, an integer argument must be paired with an integer parameter, and so forth. The following are some examples of valid sets.

Calling statement:

```
MakeMailingLabel Nam e$, Address1$, City$, State$, Zip$
```

Subprogram:

```
SUB MakeMailingLabel (Line1$, Line2$, City$, State$, Zip$)
```

Calling statement:

```
CALL FigureTax (Total#, TaxRate!, TypeTax$)
```

Subprogram:

```
SUB FigureTax (BaseAmount#, CurrentRate!, TaxType$)
```

FigureTax can refer to BaseAmount#, CurrentRate!, and TaxType$ but not to Total#, TaxRate!, or TypeTax$. When control returns to the main module, however, Total#, TaxRate!, and TypeTax$ contain the values the corresponding variables held when control exits the FigureTax subprogram.

Functions

Functions calculate and return a single value, much like the DEF FN statement of GW-BASIC and BASICA. The difference is that a function name need not begin with FN and the FUNCTION procedure can use as many statements as it needs.

Like the subprogram, each function must be defined by a DECLARE statement. When you begin a new function through QBASIC, the appropriate DECLARE statement is generated and positioned in the main program automatically. You have to keep the parameter list up-to-date yourself if you change it later.

Creating a Function

To create a function, choose Edit New FUNCTION or type a FUNCTION statement and press Enter. After QBASIC has a name for the function, you are placed in an editor window for defining the function.

The format of a function is as follows:

```
FUNCTION functionname [(parameters)]
    [local variable or constant declarations]
    statements to be executed
    functionname = expression
END FUNCTION
```

The following is an example of a function that calculates a random integer between 1 and the value of the integer argument:

```
FUNCTION RANDINT%(N%)
    RANDOMIZE TIMER
    RANDINT% = INT(RND*N%)+1
<CE>END FUNCTION
```

This function could be invoked by a statement such as the following:

```
CurrentValue = RANDINT%(GUESS%)
```

Debugging Innovations

QBASIC offers several features that help in debugging files. When a program terminates with an error, you see the critical program line highlighted in the editor document window. You can see the line in context; it may even give you information you need to fix the problem. More likely, you will have to do more in the way of debugging.

The Immediate Window

The Immediate editor window not only lets you check statements during program entry, but it also permits variable checking when a program ends with an error. You can enter PRINT statements in the Immediate window to find the current values of crucial variables.

Tracing a Program

The Debug menu includes three commands that control tracing. Trace On is a toggle that turns it on or off; a dot next to the command indicates trace is on. When tracing is in effect, the program runs in slow motion; the statement being executed is highlighted. By watching the screen, you can see if the statements are processed in the order you expect. You can use Ctrl-Break to interrupt the trace and pause the program. The Immediate window is available to check values, and you can press F4 to see the any screen output. Pressing F5 resumes the trace.

Debug Step sets up a process whereby execution pauses after each statement is executed. Choosing Debug Step or pressing F8 executes the next statement. If the statement produces screen output, you can press F4 to see the result on the output screen; any key returns you to the program window. At any time, you can use Run Start to start over.

The Debug Procedure Step command (F10) is similar, but it executes each function or subprogram as a single instruction. This will speed the stepping process when all your functions and subprograms have already been debugged.

Breakpoints

A breakpoint is a spot where you want execution to pause. You can insert breakpoints in a program at points where you want to check to see how the program is progressing. For example, you might insert a special PRINT command, then flag it as a breakpoint. When you run the program, the output will be generated and the program will pause.

To set a breakpoint, position the cursor in the line, then press F9 or choose Debug Toggle Breakpoint. The line will appear in red or inverse video, depending on your monitor. You can set as many breakpoints as you wish. To remove a breakpoint, place the cursor on the line again, and press F9 or choose Debug Toggle Breakpoint. To clear all breakpoints when debugging is complete, choose Debug Clear All Breakpoints.

FDISK

23

Introduction

Every hard disk must be partitioned after physical formatting and before logical formatting. A hard disk must be partitioned even if it will have only one partition. FDISK is DOS's partitioning program.

Before DOS 4, hard disk drives were limited to 32M, so it was common to partition a large hard disk into several logical drives. Nowadays, most DOS users don't bother. Nonetheless, FDISK still has the facility to create multiple partitions and multiple logical drives per partition. FDISK also lets you view partition information for your hard drives.

FDISK can be used to set up a non-DOS partition. For example, suppose you want to be able to use UNIX as well as DOS. After physically formatting the hard disk, you can use FDISK to create a DOS partition and a non-DOS partition; then you install UNIX in the non-DOS partition. When you boot from the DOS partition, DOS is installed. When you boot from the UNIX partition, UNIX is installed. You'll see how to set this up later in this chapter.

Do not attempt to change your hard disk's partition structure if the disk contains data. You could lose the ability to access your data. Once you have formatted and started using your disk, use FDISK only to view partition information.

Starting FDISK

To start FDISK, enter the command FDISK with no parameters. If your only hard disk has not yet been partitioned, you must do this from a floppy disk that contains the FDISK.EXE program. Figure 23.1 shows the first FDISK screen that appears, which acts as a main menu for the four FDISK functions.

If your system has two or more hard disks, a fifth option lets you select the disk you want to work with.

Creating a DOS Partition

Choose option 1 to create a partition on the hard disk. The next screen lets you choose to create a *primary* DOS partition or an *extended* partition (see fig. 23.2). There can only be one of each per hard disk. The primary DOS partition can contain only one logical drive, which will be your drive C. The extended partition can have multiple logical drives. You must create the primary DOS partition before you create an extended one. And you must create the extended partition before you can create logical drives on it.

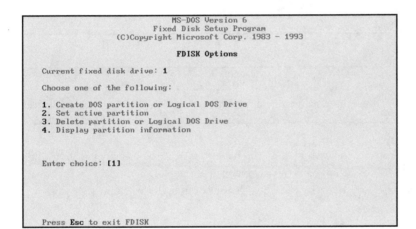

Figure 23.1.
FDISK Options
screen.

Creating the Primary Partition

When you choose to create the primary DOS partition, FDISK asks if you want to include the entire hard disk in the partition and make it the boot drive. If you say yes, you're done partitioning the hard disk. Drive C is established and you can exit FDISK and format it.

If you want to set up more than one logical drive on your hard disk, or if you want to set aside some space for a non-DOS partition, you must say No to the quick-and-easy setup. Then FDISK lets you specify how much space you want to include in the primary partition. Since this partition can have only one logical drive, FDISK creates the drive automatically when you create the partition.

Figure 23.2.
Create DOS
Partition or Logical
DOS Drive screen.

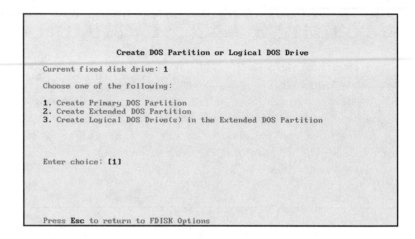

```
                   Create DOS Partition or Logical DOS Drive

      Current fixed disk drive: 1

      Choose one of the following:

      1. Create Primary DOS Partition
      2. Create Extended DOS Partition
      3. Create Logical DOS Drive(s) in the Extended DOS Partition



      Enter choice: [1]




      Press Esc to return to FDISK Options
```

If you reserved space on the hard disk for another operating system, such as UNIX, you must now set up that partition using the other operating system.

When you're done with FDISK, you have to format the primary partition using FORMAT (or a third-party alternative such as the Norton Utilities' Safe Format) with the /S switch so that you'll be able to boot from this partition.

Creating the Extended Partition

If you reserved space for an extended partition, choose option 1 on the main menu again. This time, choose to create the extended partition. Again, FDISK will offer to use the rest of the space for the extended partition. You can have only one extended partition, so say Yes unless you want to reserve space for a non-DOS operating system.

After creating the extended partition, you establish one or more logical drives on it. You can designate how much space to allot to each logical drive. Each logical drive receives a drive name (D, E, and so on). When you're done with FDISK, you must format each logical drive separately with the FORMAT command (or a third-party alternative). There's no need to use the /S switch when formatting logical drives in the extended partition.

Setting the Active Partition

If you created a non-DOS partition for an alternative operating system, you need to designate which partition to boot from. On FDISK's main menu, choose the second option, Set Active Partition. FDISK displays the partitions that are eligible as boot drives and lets you choose the one you want to boot from.

Suppose you set up the DOS partition as the active partition. How can you access the operating system in the other partition? As far as DOS is concerned, that partition doesn't exist. It cannot access any part of it. When you want to boot the other operating system, start FDISK, choose Set Active Partition, and select the non-DOS partition. When you reboot, the other operating system takes over and your DOS partition will be inaccessible.

To return to DOS, you must use the other operating system's partitioning program to set the active partition back to the DOS partition.

Deleting a Partition

If you want to rework the partitioning of your hard disk, you must delete the current partitions to make room for new ones. Deleting a partition does not delete the data in it; FDISK simply deletes the entry from the partition table. If you create the exact same partition again, you'll be able to access the old data (as long as you don't format the restored partition).

However, if you create a new partition that uses some or all of the old partition's space but doesn't exactly coincide with the old partition, you'll lose access to the old partition's data when you format the new partition. Data stored in the new partition will wipe out the old partition's data in the tracks.

On FDISK's main menu, choose the third option, Delete Partition or Logical Disk Drive to delete a partition (see fig. 23.3). You must delete all the logical drives on the extended partition before you can delete the partition itself. If you delete the primary partition, you also delete the DOS boot drive and you won't be able to boot DOS from the hard disk any more. You could still boot from the non-DOS partition if it is set up as the active partition.

Figure 23.3.
Delete DOS Partition or Logical DOS Drive screen.

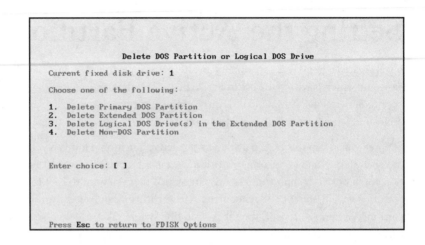

```
               Delete DOS Partition or Logical DOS Drive

    Current fixed disk drive: 1

    Choose one of the following:

    1.  Delete Primary DOS Partition
    2.  Delete Extended DOS Partition
    3.  Delete Logical DOS Drive(s) in the Extended DOS Partition
    4.  Delete Non-DOS Partition


    Enter choice: [ ]




    Press Esc to return to FDISK Options
```

Notice that you can delete a non-DOS partition from this menu. If you want to eliminate a partition belonging to another operating system, you can do it with FDISK. You can add that space to one of your DOS partitions, but you'll have to delete the partition and create a new, larger one, which will make you lose contact with all the data currently in that partition.

If you're careful, you can bury data on your hard disk by placing it in a logical drive in the extended partition, then deleting that drive. When you re-create a drive in the same spot, so that the boot sector, root directory, and FATs are in the same locations, the data magically reappears. But don't count on this technique to hide data from an experienced DOS user. Any data on a hard disk, whether or not it's in a current partition, can be easily found using a program such as the Norton Utilities' Diskedit.

Viewing Partition Information

To see how your partitions are laid out, choose the fourth option on FDISK's main menu, Display Partition Information. In the example in Figure 23.4, the hard disk contains a primary partition and extended partition. The primary partition is drive C. The drives on the extended partition aren't shown on this screen.

The status column shows which partition is active. In this case, drive C is the boot drive. The usage column shows the percentage of the drive that contains data. The System column shows how the drive is formatted. FAT16 means that the drive was formatted by DOS and its FAT entries are 16 bits long. Smaller drives formatted by DOS show up as FAT12 because they have smaller FAT entries; since they have fewer clusters, the maximum value in a FAT entry fits in 12 bits. Drives larger than 32M and drives partitioned and/or formatted by third-party systems might show other values in the System column.

```
                     Display Partition Information

Current fixed disk drive: 1

Partition  Status   Type    Volume Label  Mbytes   System   Usage
  C: 1       A     PRI DOS                   50     FAT16     45%
     2             EXT DOS                   62               55%


Total disk space is  112 Mbytes (1 Mbyte = 1048576 bytes)

The Extended DOS Partition contains Logical DOS Drives.
Do you want to display the logical drive information (Y/N)......?[Y]




Press Esc to return to FDISK Options
```

Figure 23.4.
Display Partition Information screen.

If the disk has an extended partition, FDISK asks if you want to see its logical drive information. If you answer Y, a screen similar to Figure 23.5 appears. You can see the size, system, and usage information for each logical drive in the extended partition.

Exiting FDISK

Whenever you change the partition table, you need to reboot when you exit FDISK so that the new partition table takes effect. After rebooting, you have to format any new drives. Then you're ready to put into practice the techniques you have learned in this book. Have fun!

Figure 23.5.
Display Logical
DOS Drive
Information screen.

```
                    Display Logical DOS Drive Information

Drv Volume Label  Mbytes  System  Usage
D:                    20   FAT12    32%
E:                    42   FAT16    68%







      Total Extended DOS Partition size is   62 Mbytes (1 MByte = 1048576 bytes)




      Press Esc to continue
```

444

Exit Codes

Introduction

Many DOS commands set an exit code when they terminate. You can access these codes only if the command was run as part of a batch program. In most cases, an exit code of 0 means that the command functioned correctly and that the operation was successfully completed. Any other exit code means the operation was not completed correctly.

The IF ERRORLEVEL command enables you to test the code and take action depending on what it is.

Command	Exit Code	Meaning
DEFRAG	0	The defragmentation was successful.
	1	Internal error.
	2	No free clusters (DEFRAG requires one free cluster).
	3	User pressed Ctrl-C to stop.
	4	General Error.
	5	Error-reading cluster.
	6	Error-writing cluster.
	7	Allocation error (use CHKDSK /F).
	8	Memory error.
	9	Insufficient memory.
DISKCOMP	0	Disks are the same; normal exit.
	1	Disks are not the same.
	2	User pressed Ctrl-C to stop command.
	3	Critical error.
	4	Initialization error.
DISKCOPY	0	Disk copied successfully; normal exit.
	1	Not a success; nonfatal read/write error during copy.
	2	User pressed Ctrl-C to stop command.
	3	Fatal hardware error.
	4	Initialization error.
FIND	0	Successful search; at least one match found.

Command	Exit Code	Meaning
	1	Successful completion but no match found.
	2	Not completed successfully; FIND cannot report whether matches were found.
FORMAT	0	Disk formatted successfully; normal exit.
	3	User pressed Ctrl-C to stop command.
	4	Error; program stopped.
	5	User pressed N in response to `Proceed with Format (Y/N)`.
KEYB	0	Keyboard file loaded; normal exit.
	1	Bad keyboard code, code page value, or syntax.
	2	Bad or missing keyboard definition file.
	4	CON device error.
	5	Requested code page not prepared.
MSAV	86	Virus detected when not using the graphical interface.
REPLACE	0	Specified files replaced or added; normal exit.
	1	DOS version incompatible with Replace.
	2	No files affected; source files not found.
	3	No files affected; source or target path not found.

Command	Exit Code	Meaning
	5	Read/write access denied; at least one file not replaced; use ATTRIB to change access.
	8	Not done; not enough memory to run command.
	11	Not done; bad parameter or invalid format.
RESTORE	0	Files restored; normal exit.
	1	No files found to restore.
	3	User pressed Ctrl+C to stop the command.
	4	Error occurred; command interrupted.
SETVER	0	Mission accomplished; normal exit.
	1	Not done; invalid switch.
	2	Not done; invalid filename.
	3	Not done; not enough memory.
	4	Not done; wrong version-number format.
	5	Not done; entry not found in version table.
	6	Not done; SETVER.EXE not found.
	7	Not done; invalid drive.
	8	Not done; too many parameters.
	9	Not done; missing parameter.
	10	Not done; error reading SETVER.EXE file.
	11	Not done; version table in SETVER.EXE is corrupt.

Command	Exit Code	Meaning
	12	Not done; SETVER.EXE doesn't support version tables.
	13	Not done; no space left in version table.
	14	Not done; error writing to version table.
XCOPY	0	Specified files copied; normal exit.
	1	No file found to copy.
	2	User pressed Ctrl-C to stop command.
	4	Not enough memory or disk space, syntax error, or initialization error.
	5	Write-protected disk or other write error.

IBM Extended
Character Set

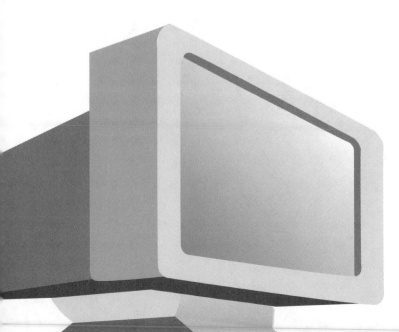

Extended Character Set

128	Ç	150	û	172	¼
129	ü	151	ù	173	¡
130	é	152	ÿ	174	«
131	â	153	Ö	175	»
132	ä	154	Ü	176	▒
133	à	155	¢	177	▓
134	å	156	£	178	█
135	ç	157	¥	179	│
136	ê	158	℞	180	┤
137	ë	159	ƒ	181	╡
138	è	160	á	182	╢
139	ï	161	í	183	╖
140	î	162	ó	184	╕
141	ì	163	ú	185	╣
142	Ä	164	ñ	186	║
143	Å	165	Ñ	187	╗
144	É	166	ª	188	╝
145	æ	167	º	189	╜
146	Æ	168	¿	190	╛
147	ô	169	⌐	191	┐
148	ö	170	¬	192	└
149	ò	171	½	193	┴

Extended Character Set

194 ┬	217 ┘	240 ≡
195 ├	218 ┌	241 ±
196 –	219 █	242 ≥
197 ┼	220 ▄	243 ≤
198 ╞	221 ▌	244 ⌠
199 ╟	222 ▐	245 ⌡
200 ╚	223 ▀	246 ÷
201 ╔	224 α	247 ≈
202 ╩	225 β	248 °
203 ╦	226 Γ	249 ·
204 ╠	227 π	250 ·
205 =	228 Σ	251 √
206 ╬	229 σ	252 η
207 ╧	230 μ	253 ²
208 ╨	231 τ	254 ■
209 ╤	232 Φ	255
210 ╥	233 Θ	
211 ╙	234 Ω	
212 ╘	235 δ	
213 ╒	236 ω	
214 ╓	237 φ	
215 ╫	238 ∈	
216 ╪	239 ∩	

Index

U

V